A HISTO

OF

BERKELEY VALE

BY

ROYCE DENNING

THORNHILL PRESS
Publishers

FIRST PUBLISHED BY THORNHILL PRESS (1994)
PARKEND, GLOUCESTERSHIRE.

ISBN 0 946328 53 6

TYPESET BY THE TELECOTTAGE, CINDERFORD, GLOUCESTERSHIRE.
PRINTED IN GREAT BRITAIN BY THE CROMWELL PRESS LTD.
BROUGHTON GIFFORD, MELKSHAM, WILTSHIRE.

CONTENTS

ACKNOWLEDGMENTS

The author wishes to express his thanks for the help he has received from many quarters in the writing of this book.

To Flora, my wife, for having so much patience over the last twenty years.

To the late Mr. Les Bridges for his help in the early days of this book. Without his hard work and enthusiasm not one word would have been written.

Grateful thanks to the Reverend J E Gethyn-Jones and to Mr. Doug Sidders of Berkeley for identifying many pieces of pottery and sites.

To Major John Berkeley for allowing me access to the Castle and grounds.

My thanks to Mr. John Evans (Jack) for his help on the chapters on the River Severn and Sharpness Docks.

Many thanks to Mrs. D Greatrix late of Wanswell and to the late Mr. Albert Lane for their vast knowledge of events at the beginning of this century.

PREFACE

I gathered information by browsing in old books, church records, parish records, visiting the records office at Gloucester and visits to libraries. People lending me diaries of their parents or grandparents, checking old deeds, talking to people interested in the past. Browsing in old buildings, looking in a freshly dug trench on a site or road side. Walking the Severn shore, brook and stream. Visiting old church yards - one can be pleasantly surprised at the information to be found on tombstones. Following the plough as it turns over the soil in a virgin field. Talking to older people - for example the late Mr. Albert Lane, one of the old time river pilots, who told me many interesting things and of many places of interest. I talked with other very interesting old gentlemen, the late Mr. Jobert Miles of the garage in Newtown who could remember the 'Oldminster Arms' - the old inn in Newtown; Mr. Jack Evans of Berkeley with his knowledge of ships - names and tonnage of hundreds of ships he had worked on in Sharpness Docks; and to Mrs. D Greatrix of Wanswell a grand old lady well into her 80's with a wealth of knowledge and information, who was born on the dock, lived on the dock, and spent many years doing community work in the locality.

I checked A.R.P. communication forms on the bombing in the Vale, actually handling the forms signed by Air Raid Wardens, Home Guards and Police Officers, now a part of our history. The knowledge I have acquired over so many years and from so many people had to be recorded - hence this book.

INTRODUCTION

THOSE WHO DO NOT TREASURE THE MEMORY OF OUR ANCESTORS DO NOT DESERVE TO BE REMEMBERED BY POSTERITY

PALAEOLITHIC AGE (ENDS 10,000 B.C.)
MESOLITHIC AGE (10,000 B.C. TO
3,500 B.C.)
NEOLITHIC AGE (3,500 TO 2,000 B.C.)

The prehistoric world is no longer available in any form except in flint tools and these are very rare in the Vale of Berkeley.

The dense forests which prevailed after the final retreat of the ice caps attracted few inhabitants. Only occasional specimens appear between Gloucester and Berkeley.

The first recorded find of Palaeoliths in Gloucester was made in 1917 at Barnwood, near Gloucester (Burkitt 1921). This implement was a flaked hand axe. At Eastington near Stroud there was a find of an elongated blade in a gravel pit, possibly Upper Palaeolithic (Gardiner 1932). Isolated tools of the Mesolithic period were found at Frocester, Coaley and Atkerton (Gracie H S 1938).

By far the largest collection came from Leonard Stanley, 69 flint tools in all (Gracie H S).

All this evidence gives rise to a theory that early man travelled down the Frome Valley to reach the Berkeley Vale and the Severn.

Cam near Dursley is the only known late Neolithic settlement in the Vale. Excavated in 1961, two circular pits were uncovered both containing pottery and bones of both domestic and wild animals. Here man was not only a hunter, but a farmer (Smith 1968).

At the Soldiers Grave at Frocester, between 28 and 44 individuals were interred in a boat-shaped cist (Clifford 1938).

The Roman invaders reached Gloucestershire in 47 AD and rebuilt the Dobuni towns Glevum (Gloucester) and Corinium (Cirencester). There were no other settlements which could be called towns or cities, but there were a number of rural settlements; the largest one near to the Berkeley vale was Kingscote, a settlement covering 75 acres (1975 and 1980 excavations). Uley, West Hill (Ellison 1980) was a small settlement containing a temple accommodation and possibly shops.

Berkeley was another small settlement; remains are found from time to time, in the shape of coins, tiles and pottery. In 1865 while restoration work was made to the church the base of two columns were found under the floor, also found was a tile with a stamp inscription which reads 3.C.L.VI which no one seems able to translate. The church was built on a building of considerable size. At Newport (Hogsdown) by the Glevum - Abona road a Roman burial ground has been discovered; many coins and pottery have also been found there (Ryder T A 1951).

A Roman villa was found at Stinchcombe Park in the 19th century, pottery and coins being taken to the British Museum.

Of Tortworth, a camp in Neolithic times, Rudder 1779 wrote "It is probable that the old road from Bath to Trejectus at Oldbury and to other Roman stations led through this parish, a tessellated pavement was some time since discovered there by about 18 feet and 15 feet composed of small cubical bricks or stones of various colours and set together with a strong cement in a very curious way".

The Berkeley Vale

THE ANGLO SAXON PERIOD

The withdrawal of Roman protection from Britain in 410 AD left Britain vulnerable to attacks by the Saxons, however it was some considerable time before they reached Gloucestershire - The battle of Deorham (Dyrham) in the year 577 gave the Saxons entrance to the Severn Vale thus ending the Romano - British sub-culture.

The Roman temple at Uley presented a remarkable site, being an Iron Age enclosure before becoming a Roman temple and later possibly a Christian church of the fifth century (Ellison 1980).

Penda - King of Mercia (Midlands) - gave permission for monks from Northumbria to enter his domain, and by the year 670 some of these missionaries had reached the Severn Valley, founding religious houses at Tetbury, Malmesbury and Gloucester.

By the year 770 a religious house had been established at Berkeley - a place called Hinetune (Hinton) 2 miles north of Berkeley, a mixed community of monks and nuns (Moore 1982, Ryder T A 1951). This vast estate reached from Frampton-on-Severn to King Stanley, Nymsfield, Ozleworth, Yate, Filton and Lawrence Weston taking in the whole of Mid-Gloucestershire (Old Boundaries). So highly was this Minster thought of in church circles that its Abbot Tilhere was made Bishop of Worcester in 778. He was succeeded by a nun - Abbess Ceolburgh (The Anglo Saxon Chronicle); she is said to have built a nunnery at Berkeley, giving the nuns independence; Ceolburgh died in the year of 805.

Aethelhum, Abbot of Hinetune Minster, also became Bishop of Worcester in 915.

(We know whereabouts this Minster was, now called Oldminster, in the parish of Hinton at Newtown, Sharpness; John Smyth in the Berkeley Manuscripts (1066 - 1618) gave the first clue - mentioning Oldminster Tyth Barn. An old map dated 1810 was lent to me by a Mr. Rennie Smallwood, showing just three houses at what is known today as Sharpness Dock. One House was the Hunting Lodge at Sharpness Point (Sharpness Cottage). The second house was Parkend Farm (Luggs Farm) and the third was Oldminster Farm; this farm lost its land to the development of the new dock. Having lost its livelihood as a farm the buildings were turned into a public house to satisfy the needs of thirsty labourers digging out the new dock, and was known as the Oldminster Arms.

A Census return of 1881 mentions Mr. Ashby, landlord of Oldmister Arms. The final clue was supplied by an old gentleman - Mr. Joebert Miles, of the garage in Newtown, a man in his ninety second year in 1970, who showed me where the Oldminster Arms was with its outbuildings including a large barn at the back; two plane trees stood each side of the pub, now only one is left, the one to the north of the site having disappeared. Later still the site was turned into a railway siding and coal yard know as Oldminster Halt.)

The Monastery at Oldminster seems to have disappeared at about the time Aethelhum was made Bishop of Worcester in 915.

The Danes were raiding the Bristol Channel and the Severn after the death of Alfred the Great in 901 and one such raid could have been the death knell for Oldminster.

One raid was on 5 August 903 landing on the foreshore at Sanigar, led by three chiefs - Helden, Eawyls and Igwor; they were unable to take the minster and turned their attentions inland and moved through Wanswell to Gossington and on to Frocester and elsewhere. On returning to the Longships they were spotted by a lonely scout who reported their movement as they came over Cantbridge wooden bridge (Cambridge). The Danes were set upon by the Saxons at a place known as Wanswell Green and were annihilated; of the 500 Danes only Igwor and eleven others escaped to reach the ships and safety. Whether the minster was abandoned after one of these raids it is not known, but administration of this estate moved to the Nunnery at Berkeley (Hayward E 1970, Taylor C S 1892, Monumenta Britannica.)

EARL GODWIN, ROGER DE BERKELEY and THE DOMESDAY BOOK

A short history of the Kings of England is necessary in order to put the picture of local history into focus.

The Danes under Canute fought the Saxons under Edmund (son of Ethelred) for the throne of England. After a bloody battle at Gloucester both sides, weary of fighting, agreed to divide England between them. This plan did not work for long for after being King for only 7 months Edmund was murdered (1016) and Canute became King over all England. He was popular with his new subjects and many fought for him. When he died (1035) he left 3 sons, Harthacanute, Sweyn and Harold. Sweyn became King of Norway, Harthacanute became King of Denmark but a row developed between Harthacanute and Harold for the kingdom of England.

One of the great Earls Leofric of Mercia supported Harold, while another powerful Earl, Earl Godwin, supported Harthacanute.

It was agreed to divide England between the two kings but this arrangement only lasted two years and in the year 1037 Harold became sole King. On his death Harthacanute succeeded him as King (1040). He was violent, unjust and tyrannical and killed himself through excessive drinking two years later.

The English had had enough of the Danish Kings and asked Edward the second son of Aethelred to take the throne (1042). He became known as Edward the Confessor. Earl Godwin, who at this time was the most powerful Earl in England, sought to increase his power still further by giving his daughter Edith in marriage to the King.

Edward having lived in Normandy for many years brought his Norman friends to court to share his good fortune. The English nobles soon found that power had passed from the Danes only to fall into the hands of the Normans. Open quarrels broke out between the Normans and the Saxon lords led by Earl Godwin and supported by his three sons - Sweyn, Harold and Tostic.

At first, fortune favoured the King and he succeeded in driving Godwin and his sons out of the country but it was not long before the Earl returned stronger than ever.

Earl Godwin, from his castle at Beverstone (near Tetbury) had long set his eyes on the riches of the Berkeley Vale but could not find the means to acquire this vast and rich land. About the year 1044 Godwin is said to have sent his nephew to Berkeley. Feigning illness he was taken into care by the nuns. After some considerable time in convalescence at the nunnery he reported back to Earl Godwin saying that he had got many of the nuns pregnant including the Abbess. Godwin told his daughter Queen Edith who promptly reported to the King that the nunnery at Berkeley was a house of ill repute. The King suppressed the nunnery and granted its confiscated estates to Earl Godwin.

The ill gotten wealth however brought its new owner neither happiness nor prosperity. Godwin's wife Lady Gueda, appalled by the destruction of the nunnery, refused to live in the castle that Godwin had built on the nunnery site. She also refused to eat anything that was produced there in the Berkeley Hundred. Godwin therefore purchased Woodchester and settled it for her residence and support.

The Berkeley Vale

The castle that Godwin built at Berkeley on the site of the nunnery, using much of its material, was typical of that day and age. It was rather primitive, consisting of a round keep (or centre tower) surrounded by a wall some 20ft high; it was square with round towers in each of its four corners and the wall was some 20 yards from the keep with just one entrance to the courtyard from Salter Street. The keep had a doorway halfway up its 25ft wall with access by a ladder which could be withdrawn into the keep at the first sign of danger. It had an earthern floor and the fire in the centre sent smoke curling its way up through the rafters toward a hole in the roof. The glassless apertures served as windows and were covered with hides in inclement weather.

Lady Gueda insisted that the remaining nuns should be given shelter and be allowed to administer to the sick and the poor, so a building was erected very near where the hospital stands today.

After Godwin was banished from the country his possessions were forfeited and retained by the King. The Berkeley Hundreds were no longer his. Godwin returned to England in order to some extent to gain the King's favour but he died soon afterwards (1052).

The Royal Manor of Berkeley as it was now called, became the tenancy of one Roger, a Saxon of ancient family said to be allied in blood to the King. He became known as Roger de Berkeley and paid to the King a large annual fee in rent. Berkeley at this time in history was one of the foremost towns in the Kingdom. It has a royal mint and minted the coins of the realm for Edward the Confessor. (Only three coins of this period are said to be in existence, valued at £5,000 each in the 1960's; each coin depicts the head of Edward wearing what can be best described as a night cap. One coin is in the Museum of New York, one in Sweden and the other is in the British Museum. (The mint was in the street now known as the High Street).

Edward died in 1066 and Harold son of Godwin became King. He was not the true heir - Edgar Atheling, Edward's grandson was the heir, but Harold was on the spot and being all-powerful claimed the throne. William of Normandy also laid claim to the throne but his claim was in truth a slight one - his Aunt, Emma of Normandy, had married King Aethelred and therefore Edward the Confessor was his cousin, which was at least a better claim than Harold's. He also claimed that Edward had made him his heir and successor. William sought for allies in England and found them without difficulty. Tostic, Harold's brother, promised aid to the Normans and among others Roger de Berkeley pledged his support. On the 14th day of October in the year of 1066 on the battlefield north of Hastings, Harold was killed and William became King of England.

After William conquered the southern half of England, only six of the Saxon landlords were allowed to retain their land, one of these being Roger de Berkeley. In the year 1070 the castle built by Godwin was improved by King William I who held court there in the year 1080 seven years before his death. In the year 1086 William completed a record of all the estates - called "The Domesday Book".

Berkeley was written Berchelai, and in Saxon times it was Beorkenlau which derived from two Saxon words - Berk meaning birch and Lea meaning water. A great many old clumps of birch trees grew around the town at that time and of course water surrounded the town.

The Hundred of Berkeley contained 95..5 hides (a hide is 160 acres)

Hill	4 Hides -	640	acres
Alkinton	4 Hides -	640	acres
Cam1	7 Hides -	2,720	acres
Hinton	4 Hides -	640	acres
Gossington	4 Hides -	640	acres
Cowley	4 Hides -	640	acres
Uley	2 Hides -	320	acres

Nympsfield	3 Hides	-	480	acres
Kingscote	4.5 Hides	-	720	acres
Simonds Hall	0.5 Hides	-	80	acres
Beverstone	10 Hides	-	1,600	acres
Ozleworth	0.5 Hides	-	80	acres
Almondbury	2 Hides	-	320	acres
Horfield	8 Hides	-	1,280	acres
Weston (Kings)	7 Hides	- a Virgate -	1,160	acres
Elberton	5 Hides	-	800	acres
Cromhall	2 Hides	-	320	acres
Arlingham	9 Hides	-	1,440	acres
Asheworth	3 Hides	-	480	acres

In all 111.5 Hides or 17,900 acres.

The following is a translation of an account of Berkeley in The Domesday Book:

'In Berchalai King Edward (1042AD) had 5 Hides and in the demesne five ploughs and 20 Villaines five Bordors with 11 ploughs and 9 Bondmen. 2 Mills of 12 shillings rent. There are 10 Radcherstres having 7 Hides and 7 ploughs. There is a Market Place (Forum) in what 17 Vassals dwell and they pay tax according to the rent. Thus, at this period King Edward held 1,440 acres, 84 tenants, 2 mills for his own use, 10 Freemen held 1,400 acres and 17 Freemen resided in the town '.

Radcherstres - or tenants - held their land by service to the Lord of the Manor.

Villaines - Tenant Farmers.

Bordors - Cottagers.

Servi - Slaves or Serfs.

Hide - sufficient land to support one free family.

Tillage - about 120 acres, the work of one plough team.

There were 127 Serfs, 15 female Serfs - depending entirely upon the Lord of the Manor.

There was a mill at Berchelai called Sexton Mill (Salthouse, Jumpers Lane).

The castle at Berkeley was held for the King by the Berkeley family. Castles were also in existence at Sharpness, Gloucester and Chepstow. King Henry I held court at Berkeley Castle in 1121AD, Henry II became King in 1154AD.

History books state (Rudder in 1770) that William, nephew of Roger, was barbarously and violently ejected out of his castle at Berkeley. Smyth, the Historian of Berkeley in 1630AD, wrote that it was his opinion that there was not a castle at Berkeley but at Dursley. Fisher - 1800AD - wrote that in in his opinion Berkeley not only had a castle at Dursley but also one at Berkeley and that this was demolished by Henry II when he deprived William Berkeley of his Baronetcy and Manor and gave them to his friend Robert Fitzs Harding.

In any event, the original portion of the present day castle was founded in 1154AD by Henry II who came to Berkeley to supervise its construction.

The Ruins of Godwins Castle

Ancient records state: Saxon-very anciently, was fortified "The prints where in places not yet digged down and washed out."

DURSLEY CASTLE

The aforesaid hide of land was the habitation of the ancient family of Berkeley who built a castle at Dursley before William the Conqueror and held it in the time of Edward the Confessor and in the time of Stephen. "The ruins where of are fruitful with Barley and Oate there growinge" - Smyth 1639. Rudder 1779 said "The ruins not yet grown over" (situated in the recreation ground behind the Tabernacle). Looking down on the town of Dursley "a fortified Manor" would be a better term than "castle". Its four round turreted towers along the west wall guarded the entrance which opened out into a courtyard. Alongside the high walls were living quarters built partly into the wall.

Roger de Berkeley possess a manor at Dursley when the Domesday Book was compiled and seemed to have escaped spoliation from the hands of Earl Godwin as well as confiscation at the Conquest. The Domesday Book records that he not only had his old inheritance there - one hide on which his castle was built and three hides (480 acres) held on lease of the crown - but also the whole of the Berkeley Hundred and Berkeley Hernesse in fee form at the yearly rent of £500-17s-2d (a mighty sum in those days).

The Berkeleys held this manor of Dursley in regular succession until 1382 when the last male died without issue. Upon his death the manor passed to his sister Maud who was married to Roger de Cantelupe and from her by several generations of daughters it descended to a representative of the old Berkeley family who was married to Thomas Wyke and then for about a hundred years it passed by male heirs to Robert Wyke who sold it in 1567. The material was removed to Dodington for the purpose of building the manor house there.

Rudder, the Gloucestershire historian, said "That in his time (1779) the ruins of the foundations were still visible in a garden which formed part of a castle field about a quarter of a mile North West of the church."

NORMANS

Again we must revert back in history to the Kings of England.

William the Conqueror had ten children; of these we name Robert the oldest, William who became King of England and was known as William Rufus (Red) and Henry I who also became King and a daughter Adela whose son Stephen also became King of England.

On William I's death William II (third son) became King and on his death (1100) Henry I (fourth son) became King. He married an English princess, a descendant of Edmund Ironside, Edward the Confessor's half brother; her name was Matilda. The Normans rose in revolt against King Henry, led by Robert the eldest son. Robert was taken prisoner and died in Cardiff Castle twenty-eight years later.

Henry I died (1135) at the age of sixty-seven leaving a daughter Matilda - named after her mother. His son William was drowned at sea in the "White Ship". The law at that time would not allow a queen to rule, so Matilda was overlooked for Stephen, nephew of Henry I. Stephen reigned for nineteen years. During nearly the whole of his reign there was a fierce war between him and Matilda. Barons built great castles or improved small ones and from these castles they sailed forth to rob and plunder. Great cruelties were carried out by these Barons. At last the great quarrel came to and end and a treaty was signed that Stephen should be King and after his death Matilda's son Henry II should take the throne. Stephen died in 1154.

The Berkeleys had supported Stephen against Henry in his fight for the throne and so paid the penalty. On becoming King, Henry deprived William Berkeley of his barony and he was forcefully ejected from his castle and the castle was demolished. William Berkeley, after the loss of his castle, took to the woods and led a kind of Robin Hood life, fighting Henry's men whenever the opportunity arose. The countryside around Berkeley was very heavily wooded and Berkeley knew his way through the forest paths and even where there were none he made new ones.

In Mychaelwood Chase (Michaelwood) there was a castle or at least the remains of one. It was built by King Offa about 750AD as part of the defence of his kingdom against Wessex. It had laid hidden in deep undergrowth over the centuries. William made it his home and headquarters.

"In Mychaelwood Chase it is said, there is an ancient castle and camp deeply entrenched, but I know not of it". Thus wrote Smyth the custodian of Berkeley Estates who knew nothing of a castle in Michaelwood for he kept records of all past and present events. He knew every oak tree, every bridge, road, and hamlet, how many cattle or sheep each farmer owned, the name of every villager, his age and whether he was fit for the militia, the pedigree of the Berkeley family and of the battles fought. He wrote more than 20 books on the history of Berkeley; unfortunately for us, all but three were destroyed by Fairfax's men in the civil war 1642-1649, and yet he knew nothing of a castle taking in about three acres of land deeply entrenched and with two rows of ramparts situated on a rock 40ft high overlooking the little Avon at Damery.

We know that Michaelwood was four or five times larger than it is now but a castle lost for nine centuries seems incredible or was it such an embarrassment to Henry II and the Fitz Hardings that the castle was never recognized. After a truce between Henry and William Berkeley the castle was raised to the ground to stop its use by future rebels and all records of it were destroyed. (The ramparts can still be seen to this day on the hill opposite the road turning down to Huntingford).

Henry II needed a strong castle midway between Gloucester and Bristol, a castle that would be loyal to him. At Bristol he had a castle guarding the only landward approach to the town. Gloucester had a castle near the banks of the Severn and the small castle at Sharpness was inadequate. There were several places at hand, one favoured was at Sharpness Point with a commanding view over the river, another site was Oldminster but the plans were modified for a site nearer the centre of the Vale where the major road between Bristol and Gloucester was within easy reach and where it would have access to the River Severn. On a red sandstone rock rising fifty feet above the marshes Henry decided to build his castle at Berkeley.

In the time of Edward the Confessor there lived one called Eadroth the staller who was an ancient Saxon Thane. Master of horse to Edward and later to William the Conqueror he gave his allegiance whole-heartedly to the Norman Conquest, and was one of the few Saxons to hold a military command. He fell in battle against the sons of Harold in 1068 leaving a son called Harding. Harding appeared in the Domesday Book as Lord of the Manor at Meriet in Somerset. He played a part in public business and was more accustomed to sharpen his tongue than his sword. His son Nicholas inherited his father's estates at Meriet. His younger brother, known as Robert son of Harding at the time of his first appearance in history, was a prosperous merchant in Bristol. From 1142 to 1144 the young Prince Henry lived in Bristol. Robert became his friend and laid foundations for his profitable dealings by providing financial aid to Henry. In return Henry executed a charter conveying to Robert Fitz (son of) Harding a hundred pounds worth of land at Berkeley. On becoming King and needing a loyal friend to man the castle he was planning, he granted the whole of the manor at Berkeley to Robert. With the valuable rights of a market and a mint this large territory consisted of nine estates on the Western edge of the Cotswolds and five others scattered down the Berkeley Vale. This grant brought Harding into conflict with William Berkeley, a descendant of Roger, who held Berkeley in fee form. Berkeley held his inheritance by force of arms as has already been stated. Henry needed peace in the Vale; his policy was to conciliate so he gave William the Manor of Dursley in fee on condition that he surrendered all claims to Berkeley, and at the same time a double marriage was arranged between the two families. Robert's eldest son Maurice was to marry Alice the daughter of William while William's son Roger was to marry Helena one of the daughters of Robert. Peace was restores and Fitz Harding took the title of Berkeley.

900 years before, on the same site as the new castle, stood a beautiful Roman villa in peaceful

setting with landscaped gardens that gave great pleasure with its flowers and trees. People moved about freely, living in harmony with one another. Peace had reigned for over 300 years and now hundreds of years later man built for his own protection a sinister ugly forbidding building that was to dominate the lives of men for generations. Where was man's progress ? He had not made any in a thousand years. Where he once had glass windows he now has apertures in a wall where he could fire arrows at his fellowman. Where he once had underfloor heating he now had a dirt floor with a fire that curled its smoke out through a hole in the roof and the only time he came into contact with water was when it rained or he fell from his horse into a stream or brook !

The castle Henry built at Berkeley for Robert was at first a simple affair. It had a keep with towers around it, surrounded by a moat and had a doorway 7 feet 9 inches wide that would allow two horsemen to enter at once. Secured by a drawbridge across the moat it was worked by men in such a way that when raised it closed the doorway. Built on hard marl the four towers were much higher than they are now. The southern half of the keep was roofed over and the walls in places were 13 feet thick. There were projecting structures which unmistakably were a means of pouring molten lead or boiling oil on any attacker attempting to force an entry. The keep moat ran

alongside the keep wall and was still in existence up until 1650.

Contrary to modern belief Robert Fitz Harding did live in his castle at Berkeley until he retired to the Bristol religious community in about 1165; then Maurice his son took over and continued to build and improve the castle.

Besides building a castle at Berkeley Henry II also built a park at Sharpness, then called Shepnafh Parke. It was a park in Richard I's time (1189) and retained the name until Queen Elizabeth departed it in the year 1572. The park took in its boundaries Sanigar Pill, up the River Din to the Saltings below Purton, incorporating the whole of the peninsula of Sharpness Point and the marshes. The entrance to the park was at Luggs Farm (then called Parkend Farm) on the coach-road from Brookend. The road crossed the Din and the marshes to the high ground at Sharpness Point where a royal lodge was built for the use of Henry and his friends and later other kings followed. Game was plentiful and geese and ducks were in abundance. Long before the Newgrounds were formed the migration of geese every winter to the Severn estuary and particularly to the rich marshes gave pleasure to the bowmen. The River Severn was teaming with fish, as also was the fresh water River Din.

PLACE NAMES AND NAMES OF INHABITANTS

Names of villages, hamlets and towns from the time of Domesday to Smyth's account in the 1600's and beyond.

U nfortunately some twenty of Smyth's books were destroyed by Cromwell's soldiers on their raid on Berkeley castle as were the church records by Henry VIII in the protestant reform. We are indebted to Smyth for the information he gave on the history of the Vale and also the names of people living at that time, many names having survived to this day. (Maybe they are your forefathers!). Also, church and parish records give us a look into the past.

ALKINGTON

In the Domesday Book this was written as Alminture and in the time of Henry III (1216) Alcrinton. It held four hides of land. In Alkington half of the Park is called "The Wordly" and in the other half of this manor are Oakeley Park and Mychaelwood Chase. In the Chase was an ancient castle and camp deeply entrenched - but when and where was not known in the middle centuries.

Between the hamlets of Wike and Nuport is a little mead called Rians-Meade, where on the Sunday after Whitsunday, the youth of both sexes from many villages spent the afternoon dancing, leaping, running and wrestling. In a field nearby, in the gravel pits, men's bones and skulls were dug and ploughed up. They were found in urns of earthenware or pitchers, some of the urns being covered with massive broad stones (Roman burial ground at Hogsdown).

"In the hamlet of Wick standeth one of the eight tythe barns of the Berkeleys (the bottom of Haycroft Lane) granted by Thomas II Lord Berkeley to Richard de Wick the Chase of Michaelwood in 1281. In Nuport in 1327 the little hamlet of this tithing of Alkington was seated in the mid-lands and highway between Gloucester and Bristol. It was beautiful with three or four Innes for wary travellers. Nuport had two chanters in 1337 licensed by King Edward III with two chaplains who should live chastely and honestly and not come to market or ale houses, neither frequent play or unlawful games."

" On the second of December King Edward III (1339) granted to Thomas Berkeley II two fairs yearly in the towne of Nuport in July and September. Marle pits were dug anciently for manuring both arable and pasture lands. Coal was looked for in most villages between Nibley and Berkeley. Coventry borers were employed at different depths; oily earth was uncovered but no coal. Mukewood remained a vast wood of 1,000 acres, a solitary uninhabited and uncultivated place up to the time of Richard I (1189)."

Men fit for war between the ages of 18 - 70 in 1600 AD.

John Millard (Husbandman) 40 years Pioneer
Maurice Nelmes (Weaver) 40 years Horseman
Thomas Peglar (Weaver) 20 years Horseman
John Lane (Fuller) about 20 years Horseman
Thomas Walkin (Innkeeper) 60 years Musketeer
Robert Browning 20 years Horseman
John Mason 20 years Trained Soldier
Thomas Bayly (Clothmarker) 60 years Horseman
Thomas Moore (Fuller) 20 years Horseman
William Curnocke (Weaver) 60 years Horseman
Robert Sherman (Paperman) 40 years Musketeer
John Kitchly (Paperman) 20 years Musketeer
Richard Crome (Weaver) 60 years Horseman

William Sherman (Labourer)
40 years Musketeer
James Cole (Labourer) 20 years Horseman
John Curnocke (Husbandman) 40 years Pioneer
Richard Rogers 40 years Trained Musketeer
Edmond Aston (Paperman) 20 years Musketeer

One can tell from the register the occupations of the district of Alkington. Many were weavers or fullers so clothmaking along the little Avon was one of the main industries and also papermaking at Woodford.

ARLINGHAM

In the Domesday Book Arlingham was named Erlingehame. It is a parish of rich ground on the banks of the Severn. From Holden to Berkeley town twice every year all males above 12 years old made their appearance before the Lord of the Manor granted by Henry II to Robert Fitz Harding. Men fit for war between the ages of 20-60 numbered 96, of these 4 were trained soldiers and 12 trained in the use of Muskets (1600).

BERKELEY

In the Domesday Book Berkeley was spelt Berchalai and in Saxon times Beorkenlau. A market was granted to Robert Fitz Harding by Henry II in the year 1154, to be held each Tuesday. A market was held there according to the Domesday Book from the time of Edward the Confessor (1016). Fairs were not held at Berkeley until the reign of Richard II (1377) on "Holy Rod Day". The Lords of this town with held permission until this date because they would not allow a large crowd to congregate under the castle walls for fear of an attack.

Lockfast or Locksast bridge was built by the Saxons over the water and marshes south of the town leading into Hame. Built of wood on wooden piles, it stretched for 400 yards. There was a water mill by the side of the bridge at the town end called Sexton Mill belonging to the Lord of the Manor.

Longbridge was situated at the eastern approaches to the town; also built of wood on timber piles it was later pitched with stone and made into a causeway. At the town end of this bridge was a chapel and priory in Longbridge Street, while at the other end of the bridge over the marshes was Longbridge Hospital called St. Trinity and founded by Maurice Berkeley in 1177. Flowing under Longbridge was the brook that rose as a spring at Wanswell Court. It supplied two parts of Berkeley with its waters before falling into the Pill where it turned salty. The streets in this town were High Street, Salter Street, Marybroke Street, Redcum Street, Longbridge Street (later called Splurryer Street and later still Canonbury Street), St. Michael Lane and Stocke Lane.

The town itself was demolished in the year 1422 and again in 1455 by Richard Beauchamp, Earl of Warwick. Much of old Berkeley never recovered from the burning down of her streets, and some disappeared forever. St. Michael Lane disappeared as did the Rentalls - a courtyard with narrow alleyways lined with dwellings packed close together, their upper windows nearly touching across the alleyway. Built mostly of timber they burnt with ease when the torches of Warwick's men were put to them. The Rentalls led off the market place to come out again into Marybroke Street (Bird in Hand). Redcum Street was a turning off Salter Street and ran behind the market place to turn out into High Street. Being only a cart track in width with its small houses consisting of timber and wattle with thatched roofs, fire quickly spread through this street in 1422.

The Little Avon, rising in the Cotwolds at Kingscote, contributed many springs, streams and brooks and as it flowed down to Berkeley and on to the Severn its waters powered 30 mills of different kinds (1600). At Berkeley it met Doverly Brook from Waterly Bottom and so completed the defence of Berkeley. Berkeley had two mills, one for the town on the Little Avon below Ham in Hamfields, the other already mentioned - Sexton Mill.

The town's wharf, a safe haven for barges of 40 tons where they could safely ride out the spring tides, was situated at the bottom of Stock Lane (the name of Jumpers Lane came at a later date) and was extended on down the Pill (farther than today). It derived its name from the way barges came up the Pill - jumping, moving farther up towards Berkeley as each tide became higher until they reached the wharf taking maybe three or four tides.

Great wealth was obtained by the Berkeleys for wharfage and toll, chartered in the reign of Henry III (1216-1272) - two pence for wheelage taken by the Manor for every load of coal, wine, oil, salt and the like unloaded there and taken through the town. Ancient freeholder Robert Avery, who lived in the time of Edward II (1307), son and heir of Richard Avery, was the last of that surname owning this haven and place of landing and unloading of merchandise; not only did the name of Averye's stick to this place which is now known as Stock Lane, but also nearby was Averye's Place or Averye's Mansion House - now known as "The Mariners Arms". The landing and storing of wares took place on a parcel of waste ground below the Mansion. Later this property came to the Thorpe family of Wanswell. Six ale houses brewing their own beer paid the rate of 4d and 6d (2p and 3p) for their brewage.

The parish church had eight tythe barns
Canonbury site - Old Police Station
Ham   site - Berkeley estate yard
Stone   site - On the South side of the
                Green
Wick   site - Lower Wick, Haycroft Lane
Blisbury site - Bevington at Blisbury Farm
Hill   site - Hill Court
Oldminster site - Newton opposite Pier View
                Hotel
Breadstone site - South of Marlpool in
                Twyditch Lane.

Men were paid three pence in money for the tythe hay of every acre mowed. If a farmer had only six calves or under in one year he paid nothing in tax. The breed of cattle bred in the vale was known as "Rothers" (Long Horns).

In 1635 there stood an ancient Inn and Wine Tavern called "The Ivy Bush" that was a great favourite with the middle classes of that time. The Landlord's name was Charles Jaye (the Inn and Tavern were situated near the kitchens of the Berkeley Arms Hotel).

Able men in the parish fit for war in 1600, between the ages of 20-60, were 482. 2,064 able men were fit for martial service in the whole of the Berkeley Hundred in the year 1609. Men were tied to the Berkeley Lords by deed, land, house or just labour.

Pikemen were tall in stature and while middle-stature men of thick build were musketeers, small men were used as Pioneers to fetch and carry and be general labourers. Horsemen were not necessarily cavalry but grooms and stable hands.

Here are a few names of the men at war (names that are still among us to this day).

John Neale age 20 years Musketeer
John Dymocke Surgeon
William Gryffin age 40 years Musketeer
William Fryer (Cobbler) age 20 years Musketeer
James Atwood (Yeoman) about 40 years
                Musketeer
John Denninge (Weaver) age 20 years Pioneer
John Webb (Taylor) age 20 years Musketeer
John Skidmore(Weaver) age 60 years Horseman
John Nelmes (Labourer) about 40 years Horseman
John Price about 40 years Horseman
John Plamer (Inn Keeper) age 40 years
                Musketeer
Richard Jones about 20 years Horseman

In the book "Nornince Villarum" written in 1316 it stated that "in the Hundred of Berkeley there were two burrow townes - Berkeley where Thomas de Berkeley was Lord and Dursley where John, son of William Berkeley was Lord. In the town of Berkeley are sundry men, Orchard and Garden called "The Hall", the land of Robert Points" (opposite the main castle entrance in High Street). Thomas Atwood of Hinton had an appartment called "Brewarne House" in High Street (the old White Hart Hotel site).

The priory and chapel at Longbridge were sold to Richard Denys in 1562 and were still standing in 1573. The remains of this priory were removed to build the arched stone bridge leading into the first gate at Berkeley Castle by Henry Lord Berkeley in the year 1588 and it had held monks, friars and nuns.

Before the present Church of St. Mary was built, a church stood on the site of the Church Tower called "The Church of Our Savior and his Saints". It was demolished in the twelfth century.

Berkeley claimed 12 Parks and 2 Chases:

Wordly or Castle Park
Whitecliffe
New Park
Oakeley Park - all at Berkeley
Shepath Park, Sharpness
Beverston Park
Hill Park
Owpelworth Park
Almondbury Park
Camhall Park
Ewly Park, Uley
Michaelwood Chase
Redwood Chase, Halmore.
Hawe Park, Wotton

Names of Villages and Townships within the Hundred of Berkeley up to the year 1600 :

Berkeley, Hame, Clapton, Bevington, Pedington, Stone, Swonhanger (Sanigar), Wanswell, Egeton, Alkington, Nuport, Woodford, Swanley, Wike, Winton, Rockhampton, Came, Hurft, Kingefton, Gofenton, Slinteframbe, Stonecombe, Combe, Wortly, Bradley, Nybley, Binefeley - Dentyinge.

The Townships of Beverston, Afheworth, Durfeley, Vleg, Kingfcote, Owlpen, Newenton, Owlfelworth, Huntingford and Erlingham were all within the Hundred and yet none of them claimed to have free warren.

BEVINGTON

This place was called Bampton and was framed by John Hurne, who took his surname from the thicket of thorns called a 'hurne'. It was also farmed by Richard Hicks and Maurice Mallet. It had 19 men at arms.

William Summers about 20 years Horseman
Nychalas Webb (Labourer)age 20 years
Musketeer
Richard Hicks(Yeoman) about 40 years Pikeman
Richard Nychalas(Husbandman) age 20 years
Horseman

BLISBURY

Farmhouse within the hamlet of Bevington, inheritance of William Baffet containing 100 acres held of the crown by Knight service, it also held a tythe barn.

BREADSTONE

Anciently written as Bradston, Bradefton, Brailefton, Brethefton and Brodestone it is now called Breadstone. The name came from a great number of broadstones found covering the ground at the manor house which were found in no other part of the Hundred.

"It held a manor in the year 1180 the inheritamce of Bernardus de Bratheston at the site of Manor Bengaugh Covert." Thomas de Bradston died in 1361 of wounds when he fought in France at Poitier and Crecy. Among many gifts he received from King Edward III was 500 marks a year, and for his heirs a Baron and Peer of the realm. Tenants of Bradston were Trotman, Burchier and Nelmes in the year 1600. It too held a tythe barn.

CAME

In the Domesday Book it was called Camma, now it's Cam. "A long and good parish divided by a pretty sweet river running through the middle." It consisted of Upper Came or Upthorpe, and Lower Came, or Neythir Town.

"It furnished well in timber for fire and building, with arable meadows and pasture grounds for the feed and breed of all cattles. All kinds of graine, plenty of fruit for Perry and Cyder, well being of its own without supplies from any neighbours." It was granted by King Henry II to Robert Fitz Harding and his heirs.
"Water Mill called Mabson was held by John Trotman, Knight service, yearly rent 13 shillings and four pence."

Also on the River Came was a grist mill and two fulling mills (a grist mill was a corn mill and a fulling mill was a wool mill) where someone back in the past (Romans) discovered that a wet clay found in the Cotswolds, a sticky mess called 'fuller's earth' when mixed with water would dissolve the natural oils in sheep wool.

CAMEBRIDGE

Called Cantbridge in Saxon times. Cambridge was a small village within the manor and parish of Slimbridge, "holden by George Lord Berkeley by Knight services through which lyeth the great roadway leadeing between the cities of Gloucester and Bristol."
In this village, on St. Katherine's day - 25th of November, there was a fair. It also had a chapel in the time of Henry V (1418).

COALEY

Cowley - Through this town and parish run two streams arising from the foothills of the Cotswolds. "One holding its race through the heart of the town close to the churchyard where women folk made much use of this water." The other streams watered most of the old and new pastures in which was found certain stones resembling cockles, winkles and oysters (fossils).

Some of the freeholders in 1600:
Thomas Atwood, George Davis, Thomas Trotman, Richard Partridge, John Browning, John Cowly, Elizabeth Cowly, Thomas Bayard, William Docket and Henry Bicke.

GOSSINGTON

At Gossington, Gofintune in the Domesday Book, William the Conqueror had four hides, apart of the manor before Edward the Confessor and before in the time of the Berkeley Monks at Hintune. This manor of Slimbridge was held by the family of Berkeley of Dursley.

Freeholders were John de Gosinton, Roger Ander ,Thomas Jame and John Bridgeman. Gossinton Hall was tenanted to Laurence Bridges in the year 1639.

DURSLEY

Derfilege and before Duneslega in the Domes day book, from the Dubunni word Dour meaning water and the Saxon word Lega also meaning water.
William I held three hides by the Roger de Berkeley family. Berkeley held a castle at Dursley built in 983 and rebuilt in 1030, built of local stone quarried in the Ferney Hill district, called Dursley rock - a strange stone of great strength called a "puffa" or "pussa" or as some would call it a tough stone or tuft. To quote ancient writing:- "Noe chinke cracke choppe or sinfne at all". It was made of incredible durance as the wall and doorway at Berkeley Castle attest for themselves. Vaults, houses, cellars and watercourses were all made of this stone. Market day was each Thursday and two fairs were held on the 25th of April called St. Mark's Day and 23rd of November called St. Clement's Day.

The Berkeley Vale

This small town nestled in a Cotswold bottom which formed the end of a valley, surrounded on three sides by the Cotswold slopes which were well wooded with beech. In 1471 Dursley was made a market town and about the same time the church was enlarged and made independent of the Monks of Gloucester.

Dursley was now undergoing some changes which raised the population and made it a place of some importance - the newly created cloth trade. Webb's name appeared in the church register of 1566 at the time when Queen Elizabeth "privileged him to farm for 31 years the taxes of all woollen cloth that was sold at Gloucester and Bristol." The founder of this family was a Flemish cloth maker, invited over to England by Edward III about 1335, and dubbed by the King with the English name appropriate to his calling.

Others were moving into Dursley with crafts in the cloth trade, with names such as Weaver, Clothier, Shearman, Millman, Boardweaver and Drawer. It is to be feared that there is also another trace of the old Dursley Clothmen in a certain proverb of wide acceptance - "You are a man of Dursley" meaning a person who breaks his word and fails his promise (in modern day terms - Twister).

In 1756 De Foe writes in his tour of Britain - "Dursley is a good clothing and market town governed by a bailiff and four Constables and has been noted for sharp over-reaching people. These Dursley men tacked and folded together their lengths of cloth in such a manner that they looked sound enough on the outside but were bad in colour and narrow in width and shoddy within the roll. The cloth was over strained to make more length and starched or chalked to give weight and whiteness."

Another hard reflection on the character of Dursley folk took the form of a rhyme:-
"Dursley Baboon - who yet (ate) their their pap th'out any spoon." "Pap" was the 'harty pudding' which formed the evening meal in most households in the Vale and Cotswolds throughout the middle ages. It consisted of a concoction of wheatflour, barley meal and butter milk. The family sat around a large table in the centre of which was placed a large bowl of Pap, and each with his wooden spoon would take his dip. No doubt the people of Dursley did the same but malicious slanders were put about by some rival clothiers.

Dursley became a Christian town about the same time as most other places did. Theocum, the monk from Tewkesbury was undoubtedly one among many who preached in Dursley. There was a hermitage on the high land overlooking that town called "Hermitage Wood" to this day. The ancient church of Dursley was not originally as large as it is at present. It consisted only of a nave with a much lower roof, a channel which was smaller than it is today and a western tower surmounted by a spire both of which were destroyed in 1699.

I give now some accounts from church records to show the conditions people lived in and their wages. This applied to most towns and villages in the Vale in the middle ages. Poor Relief - there were frequent entries made in the church records of Dursley in the 1500's - 1600's of money being given by the church wardens for the relief of the poor. The poor, the travellers, the wounded soldiers and sailors and especially the many Irish people travelling across the country all received help.

To a poor man - two shillings and sixpence (1592).

A Captain maimed in Ireland - two shillings and sixpence (1621).

To a man and his wife travelling out of Ireland into York - sixpence (2).

To a poor woman whose husband was taken prisoner by the Turks - sixpence.

Maimed soldiers and sailors in their distress received as much as £7.6s.10d. (Chelsea Hospital was not built until 1690).

The county authorities found it necessary then to bring down the hand of the law upon travellers in 1678 to stop rogues, vagabonds and beggars annoying the inhabitants. Constables were sent to search every suspect place for beggars and vagabonds who were then stripped naked from middle upwards and openly whipped until their "bodies be bloody". This order did not interfere with such domestic charities as paying Doctor Berks for setting Edward Curtaise's child's bone - one shilling, or paying Mary May for poultising Gilles Davis's leg - one shilling. Nor did the church wardens exercise partial sternness to prevent the paying of the bellringers two pounds ten shillings for beer.

In the parish of Cam vigorous efforts were made by the church wardens to exterminate their fellow parishioners - the sparrows; those of Dursley waged war chiefly against the fox, pole cat and hedgehogs. For the heads of three crows one penny was paid and one penny was paid for the heads of six young crows or unbroken eggs. One penny for twelve starlings heads and one penny for the head of a hawk, buzzard or kite. For the head of every jay, kyle or wood owl one penny. For bullfinch or kingfisher one penny. For the fox or gray one shilling. For falcon, pole cat, weasel or badger one penny. For otter or hedgehog two pennies and for moles a halfpenny. These accounts were for the year 1679 (there could hardly have been any wild life left at all - or were the creatures too crafty to be caught ?).

On March 4th 1722 at a public meeting in the parish, it was stated that no churchwarden for the time to come should be allowed to pay for foxes. (Fox hunting had now reached Dursley). Church Wardens regularly received a small sum yearly towards the expense of the church under the name of 'hoggling money'. In the fifteenth and sixteenth centuries New Year's Day was March 25th, right in the middle of the lambing season. The name hog meant a lamb or young sheep, and hoggling money was a tax on lambs. In the year 1597 the tax was five shillings. Fines for swearing

on a Sunday were not infrequent. Selling beer on the Sabbath Day and drunkenness created fines for the offenders:-

John Morgan for swearing - fined 6 shillings.
Tho Clift for selling beer - fined 6 shillings.
Edward Jobling for selling beer - fined 10 shillings (50p).
Dan Wyman for drinking the beer - fined 10 shillings.
The Archard for swearing - fined 1 shilling.
Edward Jobling for swearing - fined 1 shilling (5p).
John Dallimore for swearing - fined 1 shilling.
Tho Heath for swearing - fined 1 shilling.
Robert Hancock for swearing - fined 1 shilling.
This money was distributed among 27 persons and on the list that appeared were the names of several of the above offenders.

Edward Jobling, apprentice, received five shillings, Dan Wyman four shillings for his children. Tho Heath received one shilling. Thomas Roe was fined three times in one year for swearing, first on the 10th of June he was fined 12 shillings and on 18th of June, one week later, he was fined two pounds and on the 8th of August he was fined one pound ten shillings. He also received back from the church wardens fifteen shillings because he had no money left! There was a long list of poor people waiting for the fine money to be paid out - 120 people in all.

The Dursley boys of the 1600's were not so well behaved at church service so the church wardens paid John Stockwell six shillings for whipping the boys and to Walter Jerkins two shillings and sixpence for beating the boys in the year 1694. Wages were very low in the year 1566. A joiner was paid 10 pence a day (4p), Sawyers - 9.5 pence, Carvers - 10 pence and Tilers 10 pence, and on a six day week the sum of five shillings if they worked a full week. There was a frequent payment of a penny a sack for dried ferns - for strewing on the floor of the church instead of rushes. Ferns abound near Dursley but rushes were scarce.

In the year 1688 there seems to have been some apprehension that the tower of the Church was unsafe for there is an item in the accounts as follows:- "Paid Edward Wick for his advice about the tower - two shillings and sixpence". The result of the advice seems to have been some trumpery contrivance for propping up the tower from the inside. "Paid Jonathon Danfold for a piece of timber and drawing it up into the tower loft - £1.11.10". This temporarily gave a sense of security and in the year 1694:- "Paid Richard Lathern for pointing the tower and steeple - £10.10s". In 1699 some extensive repairs were carried out, old lead weighing 46cwt was sold at a penny a pound bringing in £21.0.0.and new lead was bought from James Brown, plumber, weighing 52cwt and costing £37.17.0.

However, the same year, the tower fell down while the bells were ringing; apparently the extra 6cwt of lead was "the straw that broke the camel's back".

Richard Clarke (Labourer)
age 40 years Musketeer
Thomas Sheppard (Labourer)
age 40 years Pioneer
Thomas Nelmes (Weaver)
age 60 years Horseman
Jef Webb (Yeoman) about 60 years Horseman

Penington had 16 men under arms:-
Thomas Nelmes (Yeoman)
over 60 years Pikeman
John Howell - servant of Thomas Nelmes,
age 40 years Pikeman
John Carter about 20 years Pikeman
Chapton had 17 men under arms:-
John Baker (Yeoman)
about 40 years Musketeer
Anthony Hooper (Yeoman)about
20 years Horseman
Mathewe Hall (Husbandman)
age 20 years Pioneer

HAME

Hame had no name in the Domesday Book and was the homestead of the Manor of Berkeley before the building of the Norman castle. Here stood an ancient house called "The Grange" (near the Public House "The Salutation"). Divided into two parts, one called Ham and the other called Hamfallow, it had within its boundary two parks, Whitecliffe and Newparke, and it also had three tythe barns in its parish, Ham, Stone and Blisbury.

Freeholders living in the parish in 1600 were :- William Tyndall, William Thorpe, George Clutterbooke, William Atwood and William Hurne.

In the year 1600 men fit for war between the ages of 20 and 60 were 186. Here are some of the names of a few men at war:-

Richard Hall (Taylor)about 40 years Horseman
John William age 20 years Horseman
John Denninge (Yeoman)age 20 years Horseman

HALMORE

Hamer, Halmere, Hathemere, Eketon also called Egeton, it had 23 dwellings. John de Eketon was heir, Herts - grove - two acres gave to William Hert in the year 1357.

Freeholders in 1600 were:- William Donell, Sir William Usher, William Gaffe, Richard Hatheway, John Oldland, Thomas Butler and John Hicks. On July 6th 1494 a court case arose in Berkeley between William Reme of Halmer and Richard Thorpe of Wanswell whereby the contravened tenement in High Street, Berkeley was awarded to Thorpe.

Men at war were 40:-

Robert Palmer (Labourer)
about 40 years Horseman
John King (Husbandman)
about 40 years Musketeer
John Clutterbooke(Weaver)
age 40 years Horseman

William Fryer (Labourer)
age 40 years Horseman
William Smith age 20 years Pioneer
Water Merye (Weaver)age 40 years Horseman

HILL

In the Domesday Book called Hull. King Edward the Confessor had four hides here. This village, through the low situation and bad weather was said to be "evil in the winter and grievous in summer and never good for the habitation." The most remarkable places were Brighamton, Bibury, Woodend, Redland, Wickstone, Shepwarden and Shepardine. Sherpardine had a passage over the Severn and also a chapel built in 1352.

Freeholders were:- Thomas Mallet, Thomas Veal, William Holford, Richard Moore and Dimery and Nicholas Baker.

HINTON

Called Hinteton in the Domesday Book. Hinteton means settlement of monks. William the Conqueror held four hides here as did Edward the Confessor before him. The Manor of Hinton consisted of small hamlets named as follows:- Midleton, Ffishringe, Ridlesford, Hinamfield, Oldminster, Kinghill, Ffrogpit, Shobenaffe, Metreden and Pockhamton.

Midleton, Oldminster and Kinghill we know, as they are commonplace names in that parish to this day. Ridlesford as Riddlestreet, Pockhamton is Pockington. Hinamfield we now call Hinton. Shobenaffe is Sharpness. Ffrogpit is Brookend. Metrefden is a small hamlet of six dwellings near Sunnybrook (the home of fishermen). Ffisheringe (Fishrine) is Sanigar (near the railway arch). Barry Court was the manor House of the parish held by Richard Walsh in the year 1605 (known today as "The Elms" (The Malthouse). Severn Hanger was the wooded cliffs overlooking the River Din and the Severn.

Trained soldiers living in the parish were 19, 8 of which were swordsmen and 11 were musketeers (1603). Able men fit for war were 46 some of whom were:-

Thomas Lewis (Husbandman)
age 20 years Musketeer
William Clutterbooke (Husbandman)
age 20years Musketeer
John Everet (Husbandman)
age 20 years Pioneer
Gyles Aldrudge (Cooper)
age 20 years Musketeer
William Fryer (Taylor)age 20 years Horseman
William Sanigar (Weaver)
age 40 years Horseman

Freeholders were:- John Hurne - Pockhampton. John Fryer - Hinamfield (1573 rent - 3 shillings a year). Pockhampton belonged to Alexander de pockhampton in the year 1043. Midleton belonged to William Dancey and Nathaniell Mallet, George Lewis and John Swonhunge were also freeholders.

HUNTINGFORD

Not mentioned in the Domesday Book it was given by King Henry II to Robert Harding. The whole hamlet in 1157 consisted if five dwellings besides the farmhouse - in all 27 people.
Freeholders were:- William Hicks, Robert Veal, Jerome Vizor and Thomas Morgan.

HURST

A manor lying within the parish of Slimbridge it consisted of the small hamlets of Gosington, Kingston, Morend and Woodward Green.
Hurst or Hirst, called after the manor house, was a farm seated upon the rise of a small hill. In Saxon times Redwood, Brandwood and Priors wood were a parcel to this manor. Priorswood belonged to the Priory and Chapel at Longbridge, Berkeley before 1590.

Freeholders were:- William Saham, Alured Kington, John Archer, Richard Haris, Thomas Cook, Richard Tindall and Simon Large. The inhabitants had two commons, "one called Eyland reputed as part of Slimbridge which would cure rotton sheep or at least make them fat, the other called Woodward Green would rot a sheep."

Men at war between the ages of 20 and 60 :-

John Organ (Labourer)
Trained Soldier Horseman
Walter Munday Trained Soldier Horseman
Edward Organ (Labourer)
age about 40 Horseman
George Vaughan (Gent) age 40 Musketeer

KING WESTON

"Being one of the nookes and corners thereof near to the outer bounds of the Hundred it was not far from the passage over the River Hungrode (Bristol Avon) called Croch and leading into Somerset."

LORNENGE or LORWINCH

Is a "farmhouse near Berkeley Heath, now the inheritance of Thomas Hodge." By the death of Robert Harding in 1177 it decended to Maurice his son who converted it into a priory and hospital called "The Master and Brethren of Lorwinch". By the time of Elizabeth I the farm was tenanted to Sir James Stumpe; now called Lorridge Farm.

NIBLEY

North Nibley or Nybley - "here was sited a chapel as it was the healthiest place in the whole vale." People came here to take the air and to repair their health by the sweet air and clear spring waters. Anciently written as Nublelei, it was a large village with 162 dwellings and within lived 1,000 souls. It was held by the Hinton Monks.

In 1563 Lord Maurice Berkeley "leased to George Denninge of Nibley the chapel and tyths for 60 years, and the other lease to Bedle rectory of Wotton." The Green, called Nibley Green, was a common or parcel of waste ground containing 100 acres. It was famous for the encounter between Thomas Talbot, Viscount Lisley, and William Lord Berkeley. In the eastern part of this village arose springs of excellent sweet water which united into a stream making a pretty river "whereon are seated seven tuck" and grist mills most of them being double mills now known as Doverte Brook. The village is divided into parcels of land called Fourdend, Nyland, Horend, Forthay, Southend, Churchend, Woodend, Swyney, Srytend, Birchley and the Green.

Freeholders at Pitcourt:- Anthony Hungesford, William Purnell, Sam Trotman, Thomas May, William Cornocke and James Gribbs.

At Burrows Court:- William Hungesford and William Cornocke.

At Warren Court:- Anciently inhabited by Sir Peterson of Warren Knight.

Smalcombe Court:- Thomas de la Church de Nubbeley changed his surname to Smalcombe.

Bassetts Court - Manor House belonging to James Gribbs.

Hunts Court - Ancient, with 58 acres, land of Robert le Venor, land at Michall Venator in 1316.

Bellamias Place - Land of Robert de Stone.

Drayside - 76 acres held by Thomas Denninge, son of Richard descended of Thomas Dreysey and of Maud 1327, ancient owners of Woodmancote.

Chantry Schaies - Tenure of George Denninge it was the charity house where lived the Charity Priest. Thomas Trotman, Richard Nelme, David Roges, Patrick Denninge - mason of Bourstream who held a quarry near by - were the freeholders in 1600.

PIRTON and the Severn

Or Piriton Passage called Puitua in Roman times, now called Purton, was a ford before Roman times - a passage way across the River Severn from Purton (Dean) and Gatecombe, noted for the passage of drovers and their cattle. "In this place the tide flows 3 hours and ebbs 9, twice in 24 hours (writes Smyth in 1630) where between Berkeley and Slimbridge 53 sorts of fish were taken."

Sturgen, Porpoise, Thornpole, Jubertas (young whale), Herringe, Hogge, Seal, Swordfish, Wheattrout, Turbut, Lamperne - Lamprey, Shad, Tweat, Wray, Dogfish, Sole - Flouder, Sand - slooks (resembling a sloe), Barne, Cod, Card, Eel - pout, Mackarnell, Sunfish, Hake, Haddock, Roucote, Sea Tad, Plaice, Millet, Lynge, Dab - yearling, Horn - cake, Lumpfish, Gurnard (both red and grey), Cuttle - fish, Whiting, Crab, Conger (male), Quaver (female), Dorny, Huswife, Herring - sprat, Pitchard, Prawns, Shrimps, Eels, Faiyon (great fat eel), Elvers, Bass, Sea - Bream, Halibut and Salmon could all be found in the Severn. A young whale 22 ft in length was taken from the Severn on the 18th of June 1620, it took 35 yoke of oxen to draw it up the Pill to Berkeley. When it reached Stocklane it was cut into strips and rendered down into oils, much of which was used for medicinal purposes for aches and pains. A sole was called a Severn Capon and prawns and shrimps were plentifully caught and were an excellent food for master and servant alike. Oysters were out of favour with local people in the Vale at this time as were mussels.

Lampreys were taken in the first five months of the year. On the 12th of March 1230 King Henry III commanded that 24 Lampreys be sent to him in London. On the 4th of March 1237 he asked that all the Lampreys caught in the Severn be cooked and sent to him in Canterbury. In 1242, 188 Lampreys and 56 Herrings were sent to the King who died in 1272 in his 66th year of Lamprey poisoning!

"The Salmon growes by these degrees, first a Pink, then a Botcher third a Salmon -pink, fourth a Gilling and fifth a Salmon Perfect and full of age", thus wrote Smyth in 1630. (In 1900 the average salmon catch from the net in the Severn was 24,140. In 1920 it dropped to 18,000, in 1937 it was down to 15,000 and at the beginning of the war in 1939 it was down to 4,294 and is now getting steadily worse every year).

John Tayte's house reached out into the Severn at its farthest point and it housed the Head Baliff (Berkeley Arms Inn - Purton). On Tuesday January 27th 1606 the sea overflowed the banks and sea walls and many people and cattle were drowned. All along the Severn side from Bristol to Gloucester this flood is said to have risen nearly as high as Frampton Tower, at least 60ft above the present level of the Severn. There is an account written in the 'Gentleman Magazine' of London in the year 1762 of that event:

"At about 9am, the sun fair and brightly spread, when a huge and mighty hill of water was seen in the elements, tumbling one over another in such sort as if the greatest mountains in the world had overwhelmed the low vallies. In the inexpressible astonishment and terror of the spectators, who at first mistaking it for a great mist or fog, did not on the sudden prepare to make their escape from it, but on its nearer approach, which came on with such swiftness as it was verily thought the fowls of the air could not fly so fast as to escape. The huge waves were so violent and swift that in less than five hours space most parts of the countryside on the Severn banks were laid under water and many hundreds of men, women and children perished in the flood. From the hill might be seen herds of cattle and flocks of sheep, with husbandmen labouring in the fields, all swept away together and swallowed up in one dreadful inundation. Houses, barns, ricks of corn and hay were all involved in common ruin. Many, who were rich in the morning, were beggars before noon".

The Severn flooded to a distance of six miles inland and most bridges and adjacent buildings were destroyed. Glamorgan, Monmouthshire, Carmarthenshire, Newport, Cardiff, Swansea and Bristol and Avon all suffered great losses. Many travellers on the roads were swept away, while others climbed to hill tops or the roofs of houses to escape, but later perished from cold and hunger. One five year old boy was saved by holding onto the wool of a dead sheep as it swept by him. There was little left to see but huge water like the main ocean. The tops of church steeples looked like the top of rocks in the sea. Bodies of men could be seen lying in the branches of trees, and everywhere bodies of beasts and men floated by. 500 souls perished in the vale between 9 am and 11 pm on that January morning.

Once a week in the Severn was a tide called the 'Lord's tide', when the Lord of Manor took all the fish caught in certain pools and places. The tide after that was called 'Parson's tide' with the church taking all fish caught on that tide - called tythfish. The Lord's day was Thursday and the Parson's day was Friday.

At certain places and certain seasons of the year any stranger could "fish with a becknet or ladnet, but not with a longnet, and take any fish, except royal fish - Sturgeons, Seal, Thornpole or Porpoise, and they were their own except the fish taken be Salmon - Gillings, Shad or Lamprey." The custom was that the fishermen set the price, the Lord of the Manor chose whether he would take the fish and pay half price or refuse the fish and take half the price the fisherman sold it for. This was called "Gale", the Lord's servants were called "Galors" (baliffs) and the fish was called "Galeable Fish". Many a fisherman escaped the Lord's payment by gaffing a fish and dragging it up onto the grass above the high water mark, where it became his own and very often there was a race to see who reach the grass first - the fish of the bailiff! If a Sturgeon was taken, the Lord paid the fisherman half a mark, a longbow and two arrows.

In the year 1607 a suit in the Court of Chancery arose between Henry, Lord Berkeley (Plaintiff) and William Denninge and others, where Henry claimed the whole River Severn as his own and that all fishing rights were his. Another question was who set the price of galeable fish - the fishermen who caught the fish or the galor. The suit was settled in favour of the defendant William Denninge. The Lord's land reached to the centre of the main channel regardless of the change in the course of the River. After the loss of the Court case, Henry Berkeley threw William Denninge off his land, and William moved across the River to fish from the other side. In later years, many fights broke out between the Berkeley fishermen and the fishermen from the Dean - resulting in a few crushed heads from the cudgels they both carried. When chasing after a fish it was easy to over step an imaginary boundary line!

SLIMBRIDGE

Or Slimebridge. There, the Severn washed the shore of the Berkeley Hundred for about 18 miles from Shepardine Passage to the outermost part of Slimbridge parish. Slimbridge concorded the hamlets of Cambridge, Slimbridge, Churchend, Slimebridge Warth, Roules Court, Southridge fields and the Manor of Hurst. It was a parish that was great and rich in the soil yet few of the inhabitants were wealthy, most were very poor.

"The Warth and waste grounds of this parish if inclosed would yeald plenty. That the more waste ground there are the poorer are the inhabitants". (Smyth 1639). In the newgrounds, called New Warth and old ground called Saul Warth, a dispute arose between the people of Frampton and Slimbridge over the use of the Common of Old Warth. After much dispute, the inhabitants of Frampton were permitted to graze their animals on the Common.

In 1620, 300 acres at least of sand earth and mud were heaped together at the lower and of the Newgrounds and by the year 1635 it began to bear weeds and grass and later became fruitful pasture. The change in the course of the River brought newlands from the other side of the Severn at Aure. A writ was awarded to the Sheriff of

Gloucester to give Lord Berkeley the ownership of the newlands. No man could put beast or sheep on the warth unless he lived within the township of Slimbridge or Frampton.

Able men fit for war in 1600 were 116.

Only flat bottomed barges on the highest tide could pass Frampton, and the river was passable and fordable only in the summertime without danger - the water reaching the mid-thighs of a man. Oxen also forded the River at the point - Saulwarth to Hayward at Awre.

Freeholders in 1600:- William Richford, William Taylor, Richard Framelode, John Coxe and William Sheppard.

WANSWELL

Very ancient before Roman times. It was anciently written as Waynewell, Wodenwell, or Wodenfield taken form the Goddess Woden, the idol of our Saxon ancestors from where we take the third day of the week. It was one of the oldest settlements in the Vale. From the well that existed throughout the ages it became a shrine. Many strange curses and miracles were wrought here, one was the cure for eye complaints, so ancient deeds tell.

This was a meeting place of all ages and both sexes with dancing and playing of all kinds of games by the young, in fact it was a place to come and take the waters and spend an enjoyable day. A saying went "That all the maids of Wanswell could dance on an egg" - this could mean either of two things, that the maidens were good dancers and light of foot, or that there were no virgins in the village of Wanswell! Smyth in 1603 took umbrage at this statement saying that it was an insult to his relations who lived there.

"This fair spring in its course watered the meadow ground and three parts of Berkeley Town and Castle, and that done, falls into Berkeley Haven (Pill) where its freshness turns salty" (Smyth). It is now known as Holywells at Haynes Pitbrook.

Wanswell Court in early days was a farm house. Later in the time of Henry III, 1216, it was rebuilt and fortified. It was the inheritance of Henry de Wanswell who sold it to Robert de Stanes for one hundred marks. Henry de Wanswell had a windmill built in a field known afterwards as Windmill Field (near Haynes). In 1256 William, Abbot of St. Augustine Monastery at Bristol, granted to Phillip de Lescester, then husband of Isabel de Wanswell widow of Henry de Wanswell, the Manor house of Wanswell. Also in Wanswell in the year 1364 were lands and tenements called Butlers containing 80 acres of land, meadow pasture and two groves of woods of five acres, which were later granted to Walter Oldland.

Also in Wanswell were two ancient messuages with diverse land, one belonging to John Richard, and the other farm belonging to John Richard (1207). To distinguish between the two Johns - one was called Richard the Bay, for he had a baytree growing at his door which was down the end of a a lane we now call Bay Lane. The fields were called Baylands and the hill named Bayhill. Now a housing estate, it all stems from a man who grew a bay tree at his front door nearly 700 years age. John the Bay's house was near to where the farm called "Buckettshill" now stands. The other farmer, John Richard, became known as Richard the Vine, for he had a vine growing at his front door. There is a farm at Wanswell to this day called "The Vines", and a row of houses called "Vinecroft". The yearly rent for his farm in the year 1207 was four shillings (20p).

Freeholders in the year 1639 were as follows:- Thomas Smyth, John Richard, John Clutterbooke, Giles Hiett, George Lewis, George Clutterbooke, John Winston, John Griffith and William Thorpe. William Thorpe held Wanswell Court as Captain of the guards for Berkeley Castle.

He had over 150 trained soldiers under his command.

The Berkeley Vale

George Lewis (Husbandman)
about 20 years Horseman
George Clutterbooke (Husbandman)
about 20 years Horseman
John Richard (Husbandman)
about 20 years Horseman
John Taylor (Husbandman)
about 20 years Horseman
Thomas Denninge (Husbandman)
about 40 years Musketeer
William Wood about 20 years Horseman
Edward Hayward (Miller
age 40 years Musketeer

In the time of Henry VIII 1509-1547 Wanswell consisted of 28 dwellings on the outer edge of the Common. Cottages were half stone, half timber with thatched roofs and were mostly the homes of fishermen, farm labourers and basket makers. The Severn fishermen hauled their catch of fish by donkey from Ffifhringe (Sanigar Basin) up the pathway by the side of Wanswell Brook to the common inn called "The Lodginge" (now the site of The Salmon Inn). This inn was noted for its local brew - a drink called Perry, the fruit juice of the pear that grew in abundance on the common. This fermented liquor was known in later years as "Choke Dog". Many a traveller on route to the Forest of Dean fortified himself with this beverage before attempting the perilous crossing of the River Severn.

The fishermen of Wanswell and of course Sanigar were of tough stock, they had to be to survive the arduousness of the Severn. As if fighting the primitive forces of nature was not enough, they had to contend with the Galors (already mentioned), rushing to hide their fish at the approach of the bailiffs. There were many battles of wits with the crafty fishermen hiding their fish in the most unlikely places, for as already stated Lord Berkeley took either the fish and paid for half or took half the price of the fish, either way the poor fisherman was a loser. All the fish had to be sold in the market at Salter Street, Berkeley,

under the supervision of the dreaded Galors.

Ways and means were found to avoid this tax and a black-market developed. The very word spoke for itself - "business after the hours of darkness". "The Lodginge" became the centre of this illegal trade. Under cover of darkness merchants would move to Wanswell to buy stocks of fish. They bought it cheaper because they paid no toll tax and the fisherman made a profit because he paid no Gale money. When the Merchant had bought his fish he then had the problem of getting it out of the Vale because the Berkeleys had tolls on all the roads.

(The one remaining toll house to this day is the "Pike House" on the Mobley road out of Berkeley - the others have long gone from our roads. One toll gate was in Ham, at the junction with Hamfields, while others were at Wickselm on the road to Wanswell. Butlers Gate at Breadstone Farm covered the drovers route from Purton and the road from Wanswell, and if the merchants were clever enough to miss the roads and cross by way of the fields, there was a Gate at Billows Farm on Twyditch Lane towards Tumpy Green and Gossington. Toll gates were also sited on Berkeley Road (demolished in the 1940's when the A38 road improvements were made). At Wisloe crossroads, Slimbridge it was called "Wisloe Gate" then "Field Gate" at Field Farm, Cam and "Dursley Gate" (Turn Pike Cafe near the recreation ground). The fishermen of Hill and Sheppardine did not escape either for there were tolls at Rockhampton, Stone and Horse Pool, Falfield.

The Berkeleys of the middle ages had the vale and its people under tight control, with a tax imposed. The 'tyth tax' imposed by the Church meant that the common man was kept in poverty. There was no free movement and people could not emigrate to another village let alone to another part of the county. The inhabitants of Wanswell and Sanigar were luckier in some respects than other Vale dwellers. They did not altogether depend on the produce of the land for survival. The willow and hazel bushes gave material for making baskets, fish putching and waffle fencing.

SANIGAR

Swonhunger. This is a small hamlet, partly in the Manor of ham and partly in the Manor of Hinton, containing 13 dwellings in the time of Henry VIII; most buildings were on the banks of Sanigar Pill and were the homes of fishermen and some weavers who had their dwellings along the side of fresh water of the River Din.

Sanigar had 8 men fit for war in 1600:-

John Nelmes (Husbandman)
about 60 years Musketeer
Jermy Nelmes (Husbandman)
about 40 years Horseman
John Sanigar (Weaver)
about 40 years Horseman
Xpopoher Nelmes (Weaver)
age 20 years Horseman
Edward Lewis (Husbandman)
age 20 years Horseman
Maurice Denninge (Fisherman)
age 60 years Musketeer
Robert Denninge (Fisherman)
age 20 years Horseman

STONE

In Saxon times called Stance, it was noted for its small stones to repair walls and it had a tythe barn near the Chapel. Gividoe de Stone lived here as freeholder. He helped to keep the peace between Roger de Berkeley and Robert Harding and he lived at Old Court which was moated with a drawbridge. A mill was situated here called Blade Mill. A corn mill for hundreds of years it then turned into a paper mill. Here also was a remarkable inn called "Stone Inn" which was well used by travellers and kept by a landlord by the name of Thomas Gunne.

Freeholders:- Vron Wise, Thomas Bowser, John Graile, Thomas Mons, John Mallet, John Wade and John Clutterbooke.

There were 35 men at arms, among them:-

Thomas Morse (Clothier)
about 40 years Musketeer
Robert Wilson (Taylor)
about 40 years Horseman
Sam Malpass (Labourer)
about 40 years Horseman
Arthur Brewton (Weaver)
about 20 years Musketeer
Francis Parnell servant
to Thomas Morse Horseman

ULEY

Written and spelt 20 different ways:- Vley, Ewly, Euwely, Euweley, Euielye, Hewueley, Iwely, Iwuly, Iumley, Iueling, Ywely, Yweleigh, Youlay, Uly, Ule, Uleggh, Viuely, Eweley, Ulay, and Uley. The name seems to come from the French word Ewe meaning water and the saxon word Lei or Lega also meaning water. The spring rising in the village is the River Ewelme which flows through Dursley and changes its name to Cam as it reaches Cam. Smyth wrote "For sweeter springe and sweeter stream both rising and running through the whole town is rarely to be found".

Two Manors were held in this town, one called Baffet and the other called Whites - as written in the Domesday Book. The two hides of land were held by Henry II and granted to Robert Harding of Berkeley. White Court had two Parks both running with deer.

In the promontory of a steep hill at the outer edge is an ancient fort, manned throughout the ages, first by early man and from Dobunni's to the Romans. Earl Godwin camped here on his march from Beverston to Gloucester and Cromwell's soldiers made use of it in the Civil War. Here was dug up a man's tooth, some say 3" square, in any case it was very large and was kept by the Baffet family in the palour window for 40 years for all to see.

WOTTON UNDER EDGE

The first mention of Wotton was in 940AD to be found in a Charter by King Edmund of Wessex who leased land there to Edric. Written under the name Wudetum it meant a settlement in the woods. In the Domesday Book it was written as Vuture or Vilture and ruled by the Earls of Berkeley.

There is no evidence of Celtic occupation - the nearest settlements were at North Nibley, Ozleworth and Charfield. The Romans lived at the Coomb Romano-British settlement, working the land there. A much larger settlement was found at Wortley. Romano-British again, it was mostly farming people who lived there for many years because foundations of buildings have been found, built over earlier Roman buildings; with the coming of the Saxons the evidence shows the smashing up of floors, fire hearths and walls by Saxon axes and hammers as they journeyed down into the Berkeley Vale. The Saxons' first settlement was on the site where the parish church now stands. It was fortified taking in the Clould, Potter's Pond and Dyers's Brook. The first church built of timber, about the year 750AD, was on the site of the old town meeting house and came under the control of the Hinton Monks.

By the year 1,000 the Old Town was established mainly around Berkeley Close. Another church was built by the Gloucester Monks about 1,100 situated in Ludgate Hill. This church was burnt down with the rest of the Old Town by King John's soldiers in 1216 in revenge for Robert II of Berkeley's part played in The Barons Revolt in 1215 which lead to the signing of the Magna Carta. The present day church was built in the 13th Century and was called 'St. Mary the Virgin'. It was consecrated in 1282; built by the Berkeleys it was retained by them until after the reformation when it was granted by the Crown to Christ Church, Oxford.

Parcels of land were High Street, Saxland, Chiping or Market Place, Chiping Lane, Bradley Street, Hax Street, Church Lane and Sym Lane. John Duant held land and a house in Wotton. John Clerke had a Manor House in Synwell, Robert Hick held an appartment and Thomas Holams was landlord of a inn in High Street under the sign of the "Goat" which in 1611 was renamed "The White Lion" with a year's rent being six shillings and eightpence (34p).

Persons in charge to find horses for trained soldiers in time of war 1624:- Sir William Hicks, Thomas Chefter and William Baffet.

Near Potters Pond stands the oldest house in Wotton - known today as the "Old Ram Inn", it now is a guest house. It was not always an inn and only since about 1860 was it converted, before that evidence shows it was a weaver's home. The deeds of this house read thus:- "Know all men present and future that I Maurice of Bath (de Bathe) sone and heir of John of Bath and Helen my wife have given granted and this our present charter have confirmed to Peter Cook (le Couk) and Margaret his wife of Wotton under Edge ("onder Egge") their heirs and assigns, all that our tenement which is situated opposite Sinwell ("le Sonewell") near the mill of Wotton, the whole aforesaid tenement with all its appurtenance to had and held by the aforesaid Peter and Margaret his wife their heirs and assigns freely quietly well and in peace for ever, paying in respect of it twelve silver pence annually to the chief lord of that fee at four principal terms of the year in equal portions for all secular services whatsoever asked, And we truly the aforesaid Maurice and Helen my wife our heirs and assigns will warrant the whole of the aforesaid tenement with all its appurtenance to the aforesaid Peter and Margaret his wife their heirs and assigns and defent it against all mortals for ever, saving only spiritual and royal service, as much as pertains to any free tenement in the same fee. In witness of which we thus append our seals to this present charter, these being witnesses, Eli de Berley, Adam Legat, Wilfred Neal, William Heyn, Walter Glover, Adam Colewich and others. Given at Wotton on the day after St. Mary Magdalen in the twenty fourth year of the reign of Edward III after the conquest."

(23 July 1350).

THE BERKELEY VALE THROUGH THE AGES AND TIMES OF THE FITZHARDINGS.

Other towns and villages throughout Gloucestershire developed slowly over the centuries. Wherever there was a stream, brook or river there grew and flourished trade. With the help of water power, Uley, Dursley, Cam, Wotton and Stroud had corn or cloth mills and later pin mills and light industry. But the Berkeleys, behind their thick turreted walls, would have none of this development. Berkeley was lost in time, it had the use of the waters of the Little Avon, but had only two mills, one for the people of Berkeley who paid their dues to the Lord of the Manor for the use of it. The Berkeley's kept much of the vale for the pleasure of hunting, fishing, shooting and pleasures of the flesh!

Robert Harding son (Fitz) of Harding, was granted the Berkeley Henness between September 7th 1150 and October 25th 1154. When Henry II became King in 1154 "he gave unto Robert the Barony of Berkeley, which the Barony Roger de Berkeley, Baron of Dursley, held of the King in fee farme." Robert Fitz Harding established the foundations of the castle. The first building contained no more than three gates and the keep, the form is a circle of which the continuous line is broken by projections of semicircular towers. It is not known if the Castle was finished in his lifetime. Robert retired to Bristol's religious community about 1165 after founding the Abbey of St. Augustine there, becoming a regular Canon there and on his death in 1170 was buried there in a monk's habit and cowl.

MAURICE I 1170-89

Married Alice, daughter of the deposed William Berkeley and taking the title Berkeley styled himself Maurice de Berkeley. Maurice was born in Bristol and served his education under a Matthew - a school master. He founded Lorrenge

Hospital (on the A38 at Berkeley Heath) and also founded Longbridge Hospital of St. Trinity at the North end of Berkeley standing amidst the banks of fish ponds. (Mobley, on the left side of the road leaving Berkeley before the Pike House) where the ruinous walls of the Chapel were still standing in 1600AD.

Maurice made improvements to the keep and the towers. Smyth (Vol I) says - "When this Lord Maurice and shortly after somewhat enlarged his castle of Berkeley, and had for the better fortification thereof by making a ditche on the north side cut a little of the ground of the church yard belonging to the church of Berkeley (which on that part adjoineth) the Abbot and Convent soe pursued him by ecclesiastical censures, that they make himself to cast durt upon his owne face, and life a schoolboy by his deed to saye - for redemption and pardoning of my offence committed by mee upon the churchyerd of Berkeley in making the ditch about my Castle I doe give into the Church of Berkeley five shillings rent for ever issuing out of my mill under my castle, and I give also to the said Abbot and monastery - the tithes of the pawnage of Michaelwood and Appleridge and Oakeley and of Wotton Parks - in alms for ever".

Maurice made improvements to the keep and the towers by quarrying a tough redstone from an island in the River Severn off Sharpness Point - a stone that has stood the test of time, wind, rain and tide. He also quarried stone from the cliffs on the Point itself. The stone was all carried by flat bottomed barges to Berkeley by way of the Pill. Maurice built a mill under the Castle wall called Towne Mill (bottom of High Street).

Lord Maurice died on the 16th June 1189 and was buried at Brentford, Middlesex. He was most noted for his building work, and the altering of the course of the River Doverte to bring it into the pools and ponds about the Castle. Controlled by the sluices they were well stocked with fish and he also laid out walks and gardens around the Castle.

ROBERT II 1189-1220

He was called Robert Lord Berkeley - Robert de Berkeley-and was educated by the Court of Henry II. He nearly lost his Barony by joining the conspiracy against King John. Berkeley Castle was one of the places of rendezvous and part of the drafting of the Magna Carta took place on his land at Tortworth under the shade of an old chestnut tree in the churchyard (one of the oldest trees in this country and still standing to this day).

In 1211 and again in 1216 King John seized the Castle and imprisoned in its dungeons all who he had had found there. King John took his revenge by burning down the old town of Wotton. King John stayed at the Castle for four days in 1216. Robert succeeded in making his peace on stringent terms after the accession of Henry III to the throne in 1216.

THOMAS I 1220-43

Thomas was the younger brother of Robert II. He began by the deforestation and enclosing of the land in the Vale. In Michaelwood "he granted in the fee to many diver man at 3-4-6 pence per acre." He attended the Parliament of Merton in 1236 - the famous gathering at which the Bishops pointed out that children born before wedlock of their parents were recognized as legitimate. By the Canon law of the Church, under the feudal influence, the English law treated them as bastards. The Bishops called for reform but the Barons refused to change the law and this law stayed the same for 700 years until 1926. Lacking prophetic forsight Thomas could not forsee that one day one of his own descendants wished he had helped to change the law.

This Lord paid money to two other Lords who had stuck fast to King John to work a reconciliation with Henry III and so gain favour with the Court. One Reginold - a priest, killed one called Mark Agnes and was imprisoned in Berkeley Castle. Thomas was blamed for keeping the priest too long in prison and henceforth had to deliver his prisoners to the sheriff of the county.

MAURICE II 1243-81

Called Maurice de Berkeley - Lord Berkeley, son of Thomas. He married a daughter of Richard Fitz Roy, one of King John's bastards. He carried on the work of his father in improving the estate. He converted Whitecliff Wood into a park and stocked it with deer. Before the death of his father he served two years with Henry III in the wars in France (Poitus 1242), and the King gave him 20 marks to buy a horse.

In an assize for a house in Berkeley, brought by one called Russel, Lord Maurice brought in John de Ewa, his champion, to decide it by battle. But Russel, being a poor man, could not afford a champion and so lost his home. Another trial by battle was in the year 1250. William Fourd demanded of Lord Maurice half a hide (80 acres) at Est-Hay, Devon. "Issue was upon battle and the demandent's champion was overcome . Judgement for this-Lord Maurice."

In the year 1256 King Henry III was entertained at Berkeley. "William, brother of Maurice, on the Sunday before the Battle of Evesham (1265), came to Mynheld (Minehead) before Dunster with a great number of Welshmen to rob Somersetshire against whom Adam Garden Keeper of Dunster Castle came with strength and slew many of William's men." The rest fled back to their boats at Minehead. William Berkeley was held in the Tower of London and was brought to Court by Henry III. William promised to join the religion of St. John of Jerusalem and go to Jerusalem and never return to England.

By the year 1275 in the reign of Edward I:-

Wheat per Quarter was 3 shillings (30p).
Barley per Quarter was 2 shillings.
Beanes per Quarter were 2 shillings.
Oats per Quarter were 20 pence.
An Oxe cost 10 shillings, 11 shillings or 12 shillings.
Cow and calf - 9 shillings.
Bacon Hog - 5 shillings.
Fat Porker - 2 shillings.
Fat Sheep - 17 pence.
Lamb - 12 pence.
Goose - 3 pence.
Hen - 1.5 pence.
Duck - 1 penny.
Four Pigeons - 1 penny.
20 Eggs - 1 penny.
Labourer's Wages were .75 of a penny per day.

The household of Berkeley Castle consisted of 200 servants from
Knights, Esquires, Pages, Cooks to Kitchen maids. Provisions drawn from the Manor of Ham were annually sent to the Castle kitchens. 8,000 eggs, 442 pigeons, 84 pigs, 45 calves and 315 Quarters of wheat were sent. Milk, butter and cheese were delivered daily. Most of the Lord's wool was yearly put out to spinners as also was wool for clothing the poor. Most farm houses were used as inns, but no guest could be received without the permission of Lord Berkeley.

On the coming of the war, Lord Berkeley and all his power of horse and foot, it was said, must be in London within ten days of war. All fish taken on a Friday belonged to the Lord Berkeley and the rent for the land was sixpence (2.5p) per acre a year.

In the year 1279 Roger de Mortimer held a joust at Kenilworth. 100 Knights were well armed and many ladies singing joyful songs set out from London for Kenilworth. Maurice the eldest son of Maurice II of Berkeley was killed at this joust and Edward I forbade any further tournaments. Whitecliff Wood at Ham was made into a park.

THOMAS II 1281-1321

Second son of Maurice, he also improved the estate by dewooding some hundreds of acres of Michaelwood. Born at Berkeley in 1245 he was also educated there. The Lord kept a large number of Manors in his own hands. He had horses for draught and service mares for breeding and labour, oxen for draught and stall, bullocks, steers, cows and calves, sheep for butchering and wool, swine, geese, hens, chickens, ducks, mallards, peacocks, pigeons, goats and kids, bees, wheat, barley, peas, oats and rye. Each second or third year the seeds were exchanged from another Manor and the cattle were moved from one Manor to another at certain seasons.

Much of the Lord's wool was put out to spinning for the making of cloth, and for the clothing of the poor. Many people were employed in sorting, picking, beating, oiling, pulling, carding, spinning, weaving, shearing, dyeing and dressing the wool. Farmhouses were used as inns for travelling Abbots and other Lords and the Lord Berkeley granaries were their hostelries.

In the year 1290 Thomas was taken sick and was removed from the Castle to the Grange of the Abbot of St. Augustine in Canonbury Street until he recovered. Richard Wicok, servant of Thomas, took William Goyll and killed him with an arrow for setting a net to catch his hares in his master's wood. Wicok was outlawed for felony but was reinstated after two years. William Harvey an under-keeper slew a man named Clif with a forker out of his crossbow. He got off by the statute against Trespassers in Parks Act 1291 in the reign of Edward I.

At this time:-

A Sturgeon cost 26 shillings and 8 pence.
An Ox - 20 shillings.
An Ox Hide - 3 shillings.
Sheep - 17 pence each.
Lamb - 12 pence each.
Goose - 3 pence.

Wine was 3 pence a gallon and the labourer's wages were still .75 of a penny a day and a Page's wages were 1 penny a day.

MAURICE III 1321-26

Son of Thomas, born in 1281, he was married at eight years old and a father before he was fourteen. He went into the fourth battalion with the Prince of Wales when he was seventeen and newly bearing arms. He could muster a troop including one Baronet, six Knights, thirty-two Esquires, thirty Archers on horseback and two hundred on foot. It appears that each Captain had for most part his tenants with him.

Less fortunate than his father, having joined the Barons' Revolt against Edward II he was captured and died a prisoner in Wallingford Castle. Hugh Spencer held the Castle during the imprisonment of Maurice.

THOMAS III 1326-61

More successful as a rebel than his father he married a daughter of Roger Mortimor and fought in the wars between the Barons and Edward II. The Queen of Edward II, Isabella, passing by Berkeley restored the Castle to Thomas, together with the Honour of Berkeley although, just before, the King had ordered the custody of the Castle with all its men to Thomas de Bradston (Breadstone).

The Earl of Lancaster's men, travelling with Queen Isabella, took away from Slimbridge and Hurst all their hens, ducks and geese, whereby they lost all their breeding birds, and had no eggs to breed from and their horses ate all the hay and oats. The Reeves of Ham complained that they had carried away their swine and other cattle. It seems that Lancaster's men were stationed in all the villages around Berkeley. The Queen sent great quantities of wheat, oats and other provisions to fortify the Castle and estate.

The King was deposed and held in Bristol Castle, but the people of Bristol disliked the King being there and he was removed to Berkeley Castle under the cover of darkness on the night of April 5th 1327. He was made to travel in light clothes with his head uncovered and he was not allowed to rest or have food or a drink. They did everything they could to kill him without violence. They took dirty cold water from a ditch and shaved his head and beard wherewith he burst into tears. When in the dungeon, he was forced to eat rotten mutton and drink foul water. Carcasses of decomposed sheep were thrown down into the dungeon but he still did not catch any disease. When on the throne he was called a weak king but his constitution was strong for he would not die and became an embarrassment to Queen Isabella and to the Berkeleys. He moved his keepers and the family to pity but the Queen was afraid of the Church and urged his death. On the night of September 21st 1327 a Knight named Gurney joined Lord Maltravers as a gaoler and Edward was cruelly murdered. A cow horn with the point removed, thus making it into a tube (the horns of the Vale cattle, longhorns, grew straight out sideways), was inserted into the anus of the King and a red hot plumber's iron was pushed through the cow's horn and up into the body burning out his entrails. The deed was done, the iron was removed and then the cow's horn, thus leaving no visible marks on the body. As there were no post mortems in those days, the gaolers had hoped that death by natural causes would be the accepted thing. However, they forgot one thing, if they had murdered the King in the dungeon or behind some thick castle wall his screams would not have been heard throughout the town of Berkeley but he was killed in some outer building, probably a toilet overlooking the moat! The good folk of Berkeley made a complaint to the Church, the only people they could turn to, but it was ten days before John Thokey, Abbot of St. Peter's, Gloucester, arrived in Berkeley with a cart to remove the body for burial in Gloucester Cathedral.

When the crime was investigated, Thomas Berkeley produced an alibi signed by twelve Knights stating that he was ill at Bradley Court,

Wotton, five miles away at the time of murder. His statement was accepted by the jury and he was cleared of the murder.

Smyth, the local historian in the early 1660's, found household papers in the castle and on examination found that Thomas did not go to Bradley until the 28th of September, one week after the murder. Thomas Berkeley concealed Gurney with great secrecy until after the trial and then sent him to Beverston, and for the rest of his life and also that of his wife, furnished him with money and other requisites.

Thomas fought for Edward III in the battle of Halidon Hill against the Scots in 1333 and at Poitiers in 1356. In between wars he found time to build and beautify the Castle. His second wife Katherine was a very rich widow and is remembered as the founder of the still flourishing school at Wotton that bears her name.

In the year 1342 Thomas rebuilt the ruined great high tower in the north part of the keep of the castle called the Flag Tower, later to be called Thorpe's Tower after the guard captain who had his quarters in that tower. Again, stone was fetched from the island at Sharpness Point (not very far from the entrance to the Old Dock). It could only be excavated at low tide; with the amount of stone needed to rebuild the tower the island soon disappeared. The new tower was not built back to the original lofty height for lack of stone. Another stone, with not the strength of Severn stone, was also used. This stone came from Newent's quarries near Dursley but it was not used for building walls that had to resist attacks. (The Northern tower or fourth tower was at one time an ancient chapel and is now the Evidence Room. It once contained a well and has been altered by a number of Earls over the centuries. Various courses appear in the masonry work showing later alterations and a vault was found and a subterranean passage was found in 1700 - written by Rt. Hon. The Earl of Berkeley F.R.S. between the years of 1917 and 37.)

In 1348 Bubonic Plague swept across Europe and into England. Half the population of Bristol was killed in this epidemic. The country areas seemed less likely to carry this terrible disease but in the year 1351 it reached Berkeley. The Manor of Ham seems to have been worst hit and so many people died that most of the harvest of corn was lost through lack of labour. To strengthen his navy Edward III took from the River Severn all the ships of thirty tons and upwards.

Cost of living in the year 1358:-

Wheat - 5 and 4 shillings per Quarter.
Barley - 4 shillings per Quarter.
Beans - 4 shillings per Quarter.
Oats - 2 shillings and 8 pence per Quarter.
An Ox - 14 to 24 shillings per Quarter.
Sows and piglets - 5 shillings.
Boar - 4 shillings.
Calf - 2 shillings.
Stone Pig - 12 pence.
Pigeon per dozen - 3 pence.
A sack of wool - 6 shillings and 8 pence.
Onions - 8 pence a bushel.
Eggs - 20 for a penny
(which neither rose nor fell for 160 years!)
A Salmon - 10.5 pennies.

Michaelwood Chase (Forest) - subjects of the Berkeley Hundred were not allowed entrance. A herd of goats, some 400 strong, was grazed there, goat hunting being the sport of the day. Oakeley Park (Alkinton) was made into a park and Shobenasse Park (Sharpness) was a park in the reign of Edward III. The River Din was dammed to make the marshes into a series of lakes and ponds in which were carp and other fish. Wild fowl were also attracted there, with the ducks and geese ending up the victims of the arrows of Lords and Kings. New Park was enclosed by Thomas in the year 1327.

Parliament of the day passed in 1360 the Statute of Labour Act restricting the movement of labour and fixing the wages of labour. This act, together with a Poll Tax levying One shilling (5p) on every person over the age of fifteen (nearly a week's wages) brought on the Peasants Revolt under Tyler in 1381.

MAURICE IV 1361-68

He was knighted at the age of seven, married at the age of eight to Elizabeth, daughter of Hugh, Lord Spenser, who was also eight years old. At the age of fourteen Maurice was sent to Granada to prevent his cohabitation with his wife. He fought in the war (1356) at Paitiers, France, where he was wounded and taken prisoner and ransomed for the sum of £1,000 of English money. In the year 1367 he sent to Edward III six lampreys which cost him 6 marks 7 shillings and 2 pennies; the cost of carriage to London was 6 shillings and 8 pence.

Maurice had a ship which carried wool out of Berkeley to foreign parts and brought back to Berkeley wines from Portugal. However, never fully recovered from the wounds he head received fighting under his father in france, he died at the age of 37. The Bailiff of Hinton spent three quarters of beans on the fattening up of 100 geese towards his funeral feast.

THOMAS IV 1368-1417

Son of Maurice, he was contracted at an early age to marry Margaret, daughter of Warrin, Lord Lisle, while she was eleven years of age. Thomas acquired by this marriage some 24 Manors scattered over many counties, of which he leased out most instead of farming them.

The Peasant's Revolt under Wat Tyler and also the spread of Plague brought the troubles and toils of servants and hired servants to a head. The peasants asked King Richard II for four things.

1. That they should no longer be made slaves to any man, nor be compelled to give their labour without payment.

2. That the rent of the land they lived upon should be paid in money, and that they should no longer be compelled, as they often were, to do work as payment for rent. They frequently found that the work they were made to do was really worth much more than the rent which they owed.

3. That none of them should be punished for the rebellion.

4. That they should be free to buy and sell where they liked and be able to take their goods freely to market.

The King gladly promised to grant these things. (As to the promises - some were fulfilled but most of them unfortunately were broken and forgotten).

On March 1st 1404 it was agreed between the King and Thomas Berkeley, that Thomas should have with him ready for war upon the sea - 300 men at arms, 5 Baronets, 11 Knights, 285 Esquires, 600 archers, 7 ships, 7 barges and 7 Balingers double manned with marines (in the time of Henry IV). Thomas kept at Berkeley his own barge and bargehouse. He also bred fighting cocks, greyhounds and hawks for both field and river sports.

Thomas died on the 13th of July 1417 leaving his only child, a daughter - Elizabeth, who was contracted for marriage since the age of seven to Richard Earl of Warwick. By law she could not claim her father's estate, the barony descending to Thomas's nephew James.

JAMES 1417-63

Elizabeth, Countess of Warwick, refused to recognize this diversion, claiming the whole estate, and as both she and her husband were in Gloucester when Thomas died, immediately seized the Castle. Thus began a bitter struggle between James and the Warwicks which led to a hundred year quarrel between the two families.

After the seizure of the castle, James paid 1,000 marks to Duke Humphries of Gloucester as a go-between. A compromise was effected by which the Manor of Cowley, Symond Hall and Wotton were allowed to the Earl of Warwick for life. Upon Warwick's death the quarrel was renewed by his daughter, Margaret, who was married to John Talbot - Earl of Shrewsbury. When the Talbots tried to have a subpoena served on James by David Woodburne and others, Lord James not only beat the party but forced David to eat the Parchment, wax seal and all. Neither party shrank from violence and the streets of Berkeley were burnt to the ground in 1422 and again in 1455.

James kept at his Castle a great number of evilly disposed, unlawful and riotous men trained in the act of war. This riotous mob came to the Earl of Shrewsbury's Manor at Wotton breaking down the gates and doors pulled down the rafters from the roof and chopped up the doors and windows which hung from their hinges. They ripped out the lead from the roof and threw rubbish down the well. The repair bill cost Shrewsbury 4,000 marks. James settled the issue by marrying the Earl of Shrewsbury's daughter, thus securing peace in his lifetime.

WILLIAM 1463-92

William was James's eldest son. When the old Countess died, she left her property to her grandson, Thomas Viscount Lisle. Thomas Talbot was at the time living in his Manor at Wotton and between him and the Berkeleys and their servants quarrels broke out. Lisle wrote a letter to William calling for him "to come forth with all your carts of Gunnes, bowes, with oder ordinance that yee set forward to my Manor of Wotton to beate it down upon my head". It was sent on the 19th day of March 1469. Lord William returned his answer the same day; "I shall appoint a day and meete in the midway between my Manor of Wotton and my Castle at Berkeley, for to excheve the scheddinge of christen mens bludd, faile not too morrowe to be at Nyblelies green at 8 or 9 of the clocke I will not faile with Godds might and grace to mete thee at the same place."

After the exchange of letters, the two opponents met on the field of battle. The Battle of Nibley Green was about to start - March 20th 1469.

Viscount Lisle and his men of Wotton, 350 in all, 36 being on horse, camped overnight on land that is now known as Nibley House. Lord William Berkeley had 450 men, 6 being on horse which included William himself, his two brothers Maurice and Thomas, James Hiet, Richard Hilp and John Caffey of Slimbridge and nine other principal officers on foot. Camping at Michaelwood overnight, their camp fires lit the evening sky and could clearly be seen by the Lisle's guards as they patrolled the hill overlooking the Vale. In those far off days Michaelwood was very much larger, in fact it covered Upper Wick to Huntingford and out towards Nibley as far as Bushstreet Farm, but this region was not too heavily wooded. The fires Berkeley's men had lit were decoys, they had moved much closer to the foe in the still of the night and sat huddled under the bushes and trees with no fires or noise as they waited for dawn to break and the sun to rise over Nibley Knoll.

William Berkeley had in his troop some 70 of the finest archers in the country. These men were foresters, fresh out of the Forest of Dean, only ferried across the Severn the day before. The men were used to hunting deer and were deadly shots with the bow. They were promised land and money in return for their services. Just before daybreak, under the cover of darkness, William moved these archers into a forward position, hiding in trees and bushes at the bottom of the hill on the common called Nibley Green. Nibley Green, like Michaelwood, was much larger then, reaching from West of Nibley Church to Snitend Bridge, to the Isle of Rhe and on to Bassett Court.

The Berkeley Vale

Lord Lisle had the advantage of the slope of the hill. His troops were gaining momentum quickly and were urged on by Lisle shouting orders for he could see the unreadiness of Berkeley's men as they made a show of forming up slowly and crudely. Thinking the advantage was his, with his beaver still up, he was still shouting orders when he was hit on the left side of his face with an arrow fired by the hidden archers. As he fell from his horse a forester by the name of James Hiatte rushed out of his hidden position and thrust a dagger into Lisle's left side. Seeing their commander fall, the Wotton men lost all heart for battle, they turned in disarray and fled towards Wotton chased by Berkeley's men. William Berkeley lost 27 men. Lord Lisle and 52 of his men were also killed; all were buried in a common grave near the road junction at Bassset Court giving rise to the belief that the battle was fought near the Court.

So ended the last private battle fought on English soil. William traded between Berkeley and Bordeaux with the ship he called "The George of Berkeley". Returning with wine, William kept 200 tons, while the Master of The George had the remainder to sell and to pay his crew's wages. William had two children, Thomas and Catherine - both died as infants.

MAURICE V 1492-1506

Maurice V was the younger brother of William. He inherited the borough of Tetbury and his wife brought him an estate in Thornbury.

Maurice spent most of his time repairing the havoc his brother had caused. He spent years in the law courts at Westminster. The seventy year old lord with snow white hair, his papers under his arm, could be seen walking morning and night to and from the law courts with his eldest son. He was fighting not for himself but for posterity. When he died, he left more than 40 Manors to his son, Maurice.

MAURICE VI 1506-23

Born in 1467 and adapted to a military life, he was brought up under his father at Thornbury. He and his wife had no issue and with her consent he spent much time abroad and became a great soldier.

Henry VIII, in 1523, created him a Baron. In the year 1514 King Henry VIII granted to Maurice the park called "The Worrdy" or "Castle Park" and also the keeping of the red deer there. There was a sharp deterioration of winter temperatures and this was the start of many severe winters - a mini ice age.

THOMAS 1523-33

Maurice's brother and heir was knighted on the field of battle at Flodden Field in which the armies of England and Scotland met on September 9th 1513 and where no less than 6,000 Englishmen and 9,000 Scots lost their lives. In the ten years that Thomas held the castle he became the perfect Cotswold shepherd living a kind of grazier's life, moving his sheep from one district to another according to the season and selling his wool at great profit. This was the time in history when the Cotswold wool trade was beginning to develop.

THOMAS VI 1533-34

Thomas, son and heir of Thomas, died before he was 30 leaving one son, Henry, born nine weeks after his father's death. He died from eating too many cherries.

HENRY 1534-1613

The most Smyth could find to say about Henry was "he is harmless". He ruled at Berkeley for 79 years where family quarrels often broke out. During one such squabble Maurice Berkeley, Nicholas Payntz and others with their servants, raided the park of Lady Anne, mother of Henry, killing her deer and setting a hayrick on fire. They were hoping to burn down the house with Lady Anne and her young son inside. Then said Giles Payntz to Maurice "Thou shalt be heire". But by chance there was another party of hunters in the same park, stealing the Lady's deer. Hiding near a hayrick they turned and fled when Maurice and his men appeared. Thinking they were the Lady's keepers Maurice thought likewise and his party also fled.

Lady Anne fled to her old master, Henry VIII, who granted her a special commission, whereupon she was made a judge at Gloucester and sat on the bench there. She judged Maurice, Payntz and others for riots and disorders and fined them all.

Lord Henry spent much of his time in London at Tower Hill playing bowls, cards and dice games. He also hunted daily from Gray's Inn Field with a pack of hounds that he kept there. He had 150 servants there all dressed in a livery of tawny coats.

Henry VIII with Anne Boleyn visited Berkeley in the year 1535 arriving at the Castle Wharf by royal barge. Deer shooting in Whitecliff was one of the many amusements laid on to entertain the King.

William Tyndale was born about the year 1485 at Hurst Manor. (Hurst Farm, Slimbridge Lane.) He translated the Bible into the English language. William Tyndale was burnt at the stake in the Netherlands in the year 1536, for his stand against the Pope and the Roman Catholic church.

In 1559, at the coronation of Queen Elizabeth, Lord Henry dressed in the following:- one doublet of crimson satin laid with silver lace and silver buttons; his breeches of crimson velvet were lined with crimsom satin and his hat was of crimson silk and silver. The scabbards for his two rapiers and daggers were one of crimson and the other of white velvet leather and his shoes of crimson velvet.

Sent yearly from the Castle to the Queen were lamprey pies, salmon and venison. At Christmas 1560 the Lord and his guests sat down to a whole boar with all its gilt and trimmings.

Berkeley was under a perpetual haze of blue woodsmoke from the fires of the charcoal burners that surrounded the town. Charcoal was still used for the smelting of the iron ore from the Forest of Dean. In Michaelwood in 1596 a wood of fine great oaks and slender birch was guarded by a ranger and two game-keepers. Running well with deer it was a haven for poachers who used hounds to chase the deer. One day the ranger set a trap by driving the deer into a funnel of thick thorns and when the poachers arrived they were cornered. With help from the estate workers who were armed with staves, they set about the raiders, killing one man and wounding many others.

Henry outlived the heirs to the Countess of Shrewsbury's claim on the estates of Berkeley and came to terms with their nephew Robert Lord Lisle in 1609 and so ended a feud which had lasted for 192 years and cost more than four times the value of the land involved.

There were at least 19 very severe winters between 1550 and 1559. In the winter of 1564-65 the temperature dropped dramatically and large ice flows formed in the Severn causing a menace to shipping. Severe winters were 1550, 1566, 1584 with hard frosts continually for two months and in January the lakes and ponds were used by skaters, with the spectators lighting fires on the ice to keep warm. A savage winter occurred in the year 1607-8. Snow fell in the last week of November to the depth of 2ft. and stayed until the end of February and some villages were completely isolated for that period of time.

Queen Elizabeth visited Berkeley in the year 1572. Henry Berkeley was away at the time and Elizabeth demanded amusement. Head keeper Henry Ligon offered her a trip to Sharpness Park for either fishing, boating or the shooting or harking of wild fowl., Elizabeth declined the offer, she demanded a vigorous sport and wanted to impress the twenty or so young courtiers who were dancing attendance on her. From her window overlooking the little park she saw a herd of 27 stags, said to be the finest herd of deer in the country and Henry's pride and joy. She ordered Ligon to prepare the hounds and mounting a horse she told the keeper to release the deer out into the countryside. She killed many stags that day and many others in the days that followed. Soon, tired of the sport, she and her party moved on to find fresh amusements. Poor Ligon was distressed at the destruction of the herd and he sent a message for Henry to return posthaste. On Henry's return, he flew into a rage, and chased after the Queen's party and a row developed between him and the Queen. Now, no one quarrels with Royalty, and certainly not that particular Royal, for one could be soon parted with one's head! The Queen took revenge on Henry's outburst and deparked the Sharpness Park. This beautiful park of ponds and lakes was to revert back to its bogs and marshland, where wildlife could return free from the hunting of man.

At the time of the Armada, 1588, a famine raged in Gloucestershire. Men who normally produced food were set to work felling the great trees to satisfy the need for timber to build "Men of War" ships. Woolaston, on the Lydney bank of the Severn, was one of the shipbuilding yards. Berkeley Vale as well as the great oaks of the Forest of Dean suffered greatly. Drake lodged at Gatecombe to supervise the felling of the trees and the house became known as the "Sloop Inn" and is now called "Drake's House". Sir Walter Raleigh stayed at Purton Manor (West Bank) not a stone's throw from Drake's House. A Man of War ship named Woolaston after its birthplace played a prominent part in defeating the Armada.

While men were employed felling trees, the cultivation of land for food was neglected and the production of food was next to nil. Gangs of men whose families were starving raided the food ships trading up and down the Severn - grain being the most needed commodity. The ships that were captured were driven ashore and stripped not only of their cargo but of everything not too heavy to move. Fighting often broke out with their counterparts from the Forest of Dean. The Queen's men were otherwise detained on the South coast and by the time anyone in authority arrived on the scene the gang had long disappeared. Some gangs worked the shoreline waiting for a ship or barge to become fogbound, windbound or tidebound. Boats took several tides to travel a few miles and when the tide ran out they were beached near some habitation, be it a farmhouse or a river side inn. Wading ashore through the mud the crew were always made welcome. The local brew of cider was offered to the seamen and getting the crew drunk was no great task. While this was happening the gang, led by farmer or landlord, would raid the boat and carry away the cargo or what was of any value to them. The drunken crew were then drowned in the nearest pond and dumped back on board. With a hole smashed in the hull, the boat was then set adrift on the next tide to drift up the River to founder on rocks miles away from the scene of the crime - just another accident in the River Severn!

Another means the wreckers used was to change the positions of the lanterns that hung in trees to aid the navigation of the river by night so driving boats onto the rocks. One such light was situated in a massive oak tree on a hill above Sharpness. By day it was a landmark and at night the lantern was lit by the farmer on whose land the tree grew. Parkend Farm was the name of the farm (known today as Luggs Farm and the field we know today as Oakfield Way). The farmer was paid one penny per ton for every English ship passing his light and foreign ships paid double. When the wreckers were caught and they often were, they were hung from the branches of that great tree and left hanging there for weeks as a deterrent to others.

In the time of Henry Berkeley, a man who is the outstanding figure in the history of English literature - William Shakespeare visited the Vale. Although not a lot is known about his private life it is pretty certain that he knew and spent some time in Gloucestershire. There is some reason for thinking that he was once a resident of Dursley and travelled through the Vale as members of his family were still there in the early 1800's. Some passages of his writings show an intimate acquaintance with Dursley and its inhabitants; "I beseech you sir to courterance William Visor of Woncot against Clement Perks on the Hill" - Act V Scene I in the second part of Henry IV. (Woncot, Womertcot, Womet or Woodmancote was still pronounced Woncot by the people of Dursley in the early 1800's. The hill was then the name for Stinchcombe Hill and on it was then a house in which a family named Perks lived - it was burnt down in the late 1800's. "How far is it to Berkeley, and what Sir keeps good old York there with his Men of War ?" (Hotspur). "There stands the Castle by yon tuft of trees" (Berkeley Castle) - Richard III Part II.

GEORGE 1613-58

Grandson of Henry, he spent most of his time in foreign travel which was no doubt the safest employment open to him in the time of civil war. He was 13 years old when he married Elizabeth Stanhope, she being 9 years old.

The Castle and town of Berkeley were at first occupied by parliament troops but were evacuated to reinforce the garrison of Gloucester in 1642. Berkeley continued in the royal possession until its capture in 1645. Soldiers garrisoned at Berkeley played a great part in the siege of Gloucester by stopping the trade of ships to that city. As they lay tidebound in the Severn, they were boarded by royalist troops, plundered then set on fire. King Charles I stayed at the castle on August 8th 1643 on his Rally of his Troops tour.

After the raising of the siege of Gloucester, the Governor (Massey) marched with his troops and 200 musketeers to Berkeley. The musketeers kept up a fire on the Castle and kept the enemy within whilst the horse troop rode into the countryside to fetch in some principal persons but instead met with Lord Herbert's troop, with a hundred and forty horses, which was on its way to relieve the Castle. Massey slew a few as they crossed the

River Cam near Coaly (Waters End Farm). The Royalist then had no footing in the County except for Berkeley Castle and Lydney House.

On September 28th 1644 Price Rupert sent an Irish Commander from Bristol to be Governor of Berkeley Castle. The present Governor told him that he was able enough to keep it for the King's service. The Irishman returned to report to Rupert, who sent the Irishman back again to Berkeley with some horse troops to force the Governor to give up his command. The Governor told the commander that he would fire his ordnance at him if he did not withdraw. The Irish troop went into the town of Berkeley and plundered it before returning to Bristol. Massey again marched on Berkeley; he commanded a party of horse dragoons who fell upon the guard in the town. "He beat them back into the Castle slaying 10 men and taking prisoner Captain Sandy, one lieutenant, one ensigne, one sargent and seven common soldiers, likewise they brought out 40 to 50 arms and from the Castle took 50 horses and other cattle."

Towards the end of Massey's time as Governor he marched from Ross on Wye and crossed the Severn at Elmore Back then marched on towards Berkeley. The garrison of Berkeley moved forward to meet Massey and at Slimbridge Massey's men fell upon them and they retreated back towards Purton leaving behind 12 dead and 24 prisoners.

On September 11th 1645 Sir Thomas Fairfax sent a considerable force out to reduce Berkeley Castle, 1,000 men to join with Colonel Morgan and the Gloucestershire forces. On September 19th all was in readiness to storm the Castle. On September 20th - "The siege of Berkeley Castle goes well, having taken the town and church by storm and are now playing hard against the Castle wall with battering pieces from Gloucester." Sir Charles Lucas, Governor of the Castle, was called on to surrender, whose answer was that he would eat horse meat before he would yield and man's flesh when that was done. After the church was taken, the assailants applied scaling ladders to the walls of the church and stormed up onto the flat lead roof. Pulling their ordnance up they opened fire down into the Castle. When the wall of the Castle was breached the Castle surrendered (September 26th 1645).

Governor Lucas moved out with his arms and 50 marks in money. Under the article of surrender every field officer with 2 horses, foot officers 1 sword and 7 marks, common soldiers 5 shillings each, 11 pieces of Ordnance and 6 months provisions fell into the hands of the captors. Afterwards, the Castle was given back to George Berkeley and, to render it thenceforth incapable of defence, a large gap or breech was made, which still can be seen to this day.

"On one occasion the forces of Thomas Fairfax, on a march from Bristol to Gloucester, camping overnight on the old Roman camp at Tortworth, the soldiers raided the local villages for loot and women, forcing the women and girls at sword point back to Tortworth camp. On returning from working in the fields at dusk the menfolk were told by the old people and children what had happened. Gathering together what arms they could find, be it pitchforks, knives, scythes or axes, they advanced on the camp where they found the soldiers lying about the camp in a drunken stupor. Setting about the soldiers, who were in no fit state to offer any resistance, they cut their throats and hacked off their heads and soon the blood bath was over and known for ever after as the "Bloody Acres".

We are indebted to Smyth for the names of the men at arms. He emphasised the number of men available in the Berkeley's armed forces but he also gave us their villages and their occupations. For example Alkington had the largest work force, most taking their living from the water power provided by the Little Avon and the brooks that ran swiftly down through the parish; many men were weavers, fullers, clothmakers and papermen.

Hinton must have held vineyards, for living there were a number of barrel makers (coopers). Halmore had a miller (John Haller) who probably owned a mill there. Wanswell seems to have had mostly farmers. Stone had its share of weavers and clothiers. Berkeley had its tannery and there were tanners, shoemakers, cobblers, millers, weavers and tailors.

GEORGE II 1658-98

Son of George, he helped to promote the restoration of King Charles II and the disposition of James. At the of 40 he published a religious text. In 1679 he was created Viscount Dursley and Earl of Berkeley.

The plague had already caused much death in the Vale for many years but now it was reaching epidemic level. Again, Ham was to suffer. It is best told of how it would spread by the following story:-

John Nelmes, his wife Mary and two sons John and Samuell moved from Breadstone to Ham, John Nelmes taking a new position as overseer for the Berkeley estate. In the year 1662 Mary was heavy with child and knowing no one at Ham had asked her sister in-law Elizabeth, wife of James Nelmes of Pitbrook, to be the midwife and to help with two boys. John Nelmes was busy loading a barge with beans at the castle wharf. Mary gave birth to a son on June 2nd and named him Thomas. On June 5th both boys, Sam and John, died. The Black Death had arrived. John's wife Mary died on the 10th of June and baby Thomas on 15th of June. The barge from Bristol had brought the disease to Berkeley. Meanwhile, Elizabeth had hurried back to Pitbrook, Wanswell. On the 12th of June her son John was suddenly taken ill, broke out in large blisters and died. Elizabeth also died two days later and one week later James was dead; the only survivor was 10 year old Richard.

Another brother of John and James, Thomas of Sanigar, took young Richard into their home - a beautiful and merciful but foolish action, for they were inviting trouble. Thankfully neither

Richard, Thomas nor his wife caught the plague but their next door neighbours Maurice and Margaret Denninge were both found dead in bed three days after the arrival of Richard. John Nelmes the original carrier of the disease married again and was Mayor of Berkeley twice. He died in bed of old age on his 80th birthday. (All the families were kinfolk of the author).

Tobacco was grown locally at Berkeley in 1652. It seems that the farmers neglected the growing of food for this new profitable crop and so this caused a famine. Parliament prohibited the growing of this crop but it was still grown on the Berkeley estate for many years after.

CHARLES 1698-1710

Charles was the second Earl and went to Ireland as the Lord Justice. In the next year 1703 on November 26th in a great high wind, the Severn beat down the sea walls and the sea flowed into the parish for about one mile and did great damage to the land and the buildings. It carried away one house that was by the sea wall and carried a stable with a horse in it to the next field. 26 sheets of lead weighing 40 tons were ripped from the middle aisle of the Church and were taken up in the air in one piece and then scattered over a wide area of Berkeley.

In the Severn estuary 7 ships were wrecked and 70 seamen lost their lives. In the lower reaches of the Severn many men and cattle were lost. 15,000 sheep were also lost.

Again we are indebted to Smyth of Nibley for the Proverbs and Sayings of the Vale folk in the middle ages; The letter f is frequently used for 'V'- as fewed for viewed, fenifon for venison, farnifh for varnish. Also note that the letter f was also used for the letter 'S'. 'V' is frequently used for f as in varthing for farthing, vire for fire, vat for fat and vafting is fasting. G is often used for 'C' as in guckowe for cuckoo and grabs for crabs.

Some Sayings may be a bit crude but that was country folk of the Seventeen Century:-

Thicke and thucke - this and that.
Putton Vp - put it up (here V is used for U).
Cutton of - cut it off.
Fetton Vp - fet it up -set it up.
Wenchen - girls.
Hur goes too blive for mee - she goes to fast for me.
Hur ligs well y bed y this morne. - her lay well in bed this morning (she likes her bed).
Fhee fleepes a napp of nyne hours - she sleeps for nine hours.
Wil'by piff a bed - will you piss your bed.
lick many - like many.
To tett - to chase; Hee tet my fheepe.
To Loxe - to steal.
A Penston - coin.
Thick cole will y not y tind - this coal will not burn.
Fader and Moder - Father and Mother.
A Gofchicken - a goflin - young goose.
A piffe glaffe - a urinal.
Hee is an hoflis man - he is an angry man.
The cow's white - butter and cheese.
Wone, Iwa, Three, Voure, Vire - 1, 2, 3, 4, 5.
Hee wants boots a beame - he wants money to spend.
Thuck vire don't y bran - (an easy one to work with.)
Ga'as zo'm of thuck bread - give me some of that bread.
Moder, Gyn will not y wafhen the difher - Mother, John will not wash the dishes.
Hee's like an Aprill Fhoure thats wets the ftone 9 times in a houre - applying to an unconstant man.
Hee feekes for flubble in a fallowe field - He seeks for a needle in a haystack.
Hee that fears every graffe muft never piffe in a meadow - a faint heart never won a fair lady.
"He thats cooled with an apple, and heated with an egge, Over mee fshall never fpread his legg!" - A widow's Proverb.
Hee is very good at white pott - white pot was a custard or pudding baked in a bag - a good eater.
A great houfkeeper is fure of nothing for his chear, save a great turd at his gate.
My catt is a good moufhunt - an unusual fpeach when husband comend the dilligence of his wike (the husband maintaining the orthodox position) hence the saying - That hee thatfometimes flattereth not his wife canot alwaies pleafe her.
Money is noe foole if a wife have it in keepinge - that a foole and his money are foone parted.
When wheat lies longe in bed, it nifith with a heavy head.
Hee mends like fowne ale, informer.
Hee growes from nought to worfe.
As head thats grey ferve not for mayden's play or An head thats white to mayds bringe noe delight.
When the daies bgin to lengthen, the cold begins to ftrengthen.
A man may love his houfe well though hee ride not upon the ridge, or love well his cowe though hee kiffe her not.

The Berkeley Vale

As nible as a blinde catt in a barne.
Two hungry meals makes the third a glutton.

If thou louft mee at the hart
thou'lt not loofe me for a fart
When thou drinke beware the toft
For there in lyes the dange moft
Hee that will thrive rife at five
But hee that hath thriven my lye till feaven
The backe of an herring
The poll of an tench
The fide of a falmon
the belly of a wench.

A sowe doth fooner than a cowe bringe an ox to the plowe
- meaning more profit doth arise to the husbandman by a
  sow than a cow.
Hee that fmell the firft favour is the faults firft fathers -
meaning that hee firft fmell the fart that lett it.
Neerefit to the church, furtheft from God.
Hee never hath a bad than hath a good night.
The cup and cover will hold together.
Birds of a feather will flocke together.
A woman, fpaniell and walnut tree,
the more they are beaten the better they be,
Thing ne'ere goe ill,
When Jacke and Jill.
Piffe in one quill.
Much fmoke little fire - much ado about nothing.
When Wotton hill doth weare a cap,
Let Horton towne beware of that.
 (Meaning that rain is likely).

JAMES 1710-36

James entered the navy and became Vice-Admiral of the "Blue Fleet" and in the war against Spain in 1718 he commanded the Channel Fleet.

AUGUSTINE 1736-55

Augustine is memorable solely for his elopement with the scandalous Lady Vare. He died at the age of 39 killed by quack medicine which he took for gout.

FREDERICK AUGUSTUS 1755-1810

He was ten years old when his father died. Shooting a highwayman and the encouragement of Edward Jenner were about the only good deeds that can be credited to him. A sportsman, gambler and rake he said he would never marry but in his 41st year he seduced an attractive 17 year old girl named Mary Cole. When she became pregnant he took her to live with him in the Castle. She completely dominated him, so much as to not only rule the household, but to manage the estate as well, in fact far better than the earl did before her. Finally in 1796 and 8 children later he married her. The eldest of the children born out of wedlock was William Fitz Harding. Now ten years old the earl could have made him his heir but the title would inevitably pass to the fifth male child born in wedlock - Thomas Moreton. Thomas never claimed the Earldom out of respect for his parents. (If Thomas I in the year 1236 had helped to change the law, William would have had no problems).

T'was Berkeley fair and natures smiles,
Spread joy around for many a mile,
The rosy milkmaid quits her pail,
The thresher now puts by his flail,
His fleecy charge and hazel crook
By the ride shepperd are forsook,
The woodmen too, the day to keep,
Leaves echo undisturbed in sleep
Labour in O'er - his rugger chain
Lies resting on the grassy plain.

The sun drove off the Twilight gray
And promised all a cloudless day,
His yellow beams dance o'er the dews
and changed to gems their pearly hues.
The song birds met on every spray,
and sang as if they knew the day,
The blackbird piped his mellow note,
The Goldfinch strained his downy throat,
To joint the music of the plain
The lark pour'd down no common strain,
The little wren too left her nest
And, striving sung her very best,
The Robin wislsey kept a way
His song too plaintive for the day.

These verses were written by a young man of Berkeley in the last quarter of the eighteenth century. Born on the 17th of May 1749, the son of a local Vicar, Edward Jenner became the town of Berkeley's famous son.

The Berkeley Vale

Jenner's father was Vicar of Berkeley from 1729 until his death in 1754. His mother, Sarah, was daughter of the Rev. Head, vicar of Berkeley from 1691 to 1728; she died in the same year as her husband.

Living in the depths of the countryside, surrounded by nature and men of the country, Edward Jenner loved his native Berkeley in particular, and Gloucestershire in general. As a boy he could recognize the cry of every bird and the name of every plant that grew along the banks of the Castle brooks and streams watching the dragonfly hover from lily to lily and the trout jumping for the evening fly and to see the kingfisher busy among the reeds and rushes. To him observation came naturally and before long he was turning his knowledge to good account.

Beauty of nature was his delight, disease and sickness were alien to him but he was determined to fight against diseases and studied under Doctor Daniel Ludlow, a surgeon of Sodbury. It was during this time that he noticed a local belief - that if once a man had had the disease known as Cow Pox he did not suffer the effects of the more deadly disease Small Pox. Cow Pox was usually caught from sores on a cows udders when milking. Knowing that these old country sayings had a ring of truth to them, he was determined to prove his theory. He made ceaseless enquiries among his medical colleagues. Most doctors seemed to think that his notion was just "Old Wives Tales". Still Jenner was not satisfied. He had gone to London to study under the physician John Hunter but still kept on with his research and investigation. He returned to Berkeley in 1773 and by 1780 he had discovered that there were really two different forms of Cow Pox but only one acted as a defence against Small Pox.

At that period of time, Small Pox was at a low ebb in the Vale and it was some considerable time before he could put his theory to the test. After twenty years of research he seemed to prove his point. On May 14th 1796 he inoculated an eight year old boy, James Phipps, with the Cow Pox visicles from the hand of a cow maid named Sarah Nelmes of Newport (she was an ancestor of the author). Sarah was described as a Berkeley milk maid but in fact she was of an old highly respected local family and certainly no peasant. Her father was a prosperous farmer and she assisted with the husbandry of the family acres. She was also a distant relation of Doctor Jenner.

Some of Jenner's medical colleagues awaited the result with excitement while others condemned him for the risk he was taking. As he predicted James Phipps escaped the Small Pox disease. Even after receiving a dose of Small Pox virus, James lived to a ripe old age.

Sir Walter Farquhar said to Jenner that if he chose to preserve it a secret he might make £100,000 by it but Jenner was determined to give it to the world and he was as good as his word.

In 1798 Jenner published his "Inquiry into the cause and effect of Varicolae Vaccine". No sooner had he published the results than every kind of Doctor - genuine or quack - took up the practice. The Fairgrounds throughout the country were infested with quacks offering 'genuine vaccines' in the name of Jenner and people were infested with innumeberable diseases.

Jenner's fame spread throughout the world, even Napoleon became an enthusiastic patron. Jenner wrote to him asking for the release of some English prisoners of war, to which Napoleon replied "We can refuse nothing to that name". Parliament finally voted him a grant of £20,000 in 1808. His wife Katherine died in 1815, a year after Jenner left London to return to his beloved Berkeley. He devoted his time in retirement to his boyhood pursuits of natural history and geology. In 1823 he also presented a paper to the Royal Society on the migration of birds.

Many is the time the good folk of Berkeley looked skywards to see strange flying objects over the town, for Jenner built the first balloon to fly over Gloucestershire. Not only did Frederick

The Berkeley Vale

Lord Berkeley encourage Jenner with his practice of medicine and ornithology but he also helped him launch his balloons from the keep tower.

On January 24th 1823 Jenner was found unconscious on the floor of his library. His right side was completely paralysed. The next day this goodly man of nature, poet, doctor and benefactor of the poor was dead. He was buried near the altar in Berkeley Church.

WILLIAM FITZ HARDING BERKELEY 1810-57

He succeeded to the estate but when he claimed the Earldom, the House of Lords rejected his claim. He was known as Colonel Berkeley and grew up to be one of the most repulsive cads and ruffians of the peerage. By political service to the Liberal party he obtained a Peerage in 1831 with the title of Baron Segrave. Ten years later he was made an Earl. These peerages died with him.

In 1816 the harvest was poor and to supplement the larder both farmer and peasant took to poaching the deer, pheasants and fish of the Manor. One such venture turned into a tragedy when a party of young men, mostly sons of the farmers, planned a raid on Calgrove, near Hill. With blackened faces and deceptive dark and camouflaged clothes, many carrying guns, they were met with a wood full of gamekeepers instead of a wood full of pheasants. They called on the poachers not to use guns and the fight that followed was with sticks and fists until one the poacher's guns accidentally fired. The men from Hill, thinking that Berkeley's men had hidden guns, opened fire killing a game keeper. The frightened men then fled back to Hill. Colonel Berkeley himself led a large force to Hill to apprehend the men. Allen, the ringleader, was confronted on the door step by Colonel Berkeley who hit Allen about the head with a cudgel. Hitting him and his servant to the ground Berkeley then apprehended eleven of the poachers. Allen and John Penny were hanged - the last public hanging in Berkeley. The others were transported to the convict camps of Australia. Colonel Berkeley was brought before the House of Lords and was censured for his actions and was told in future to uphold the law of the land.

In the summer of 1987 I was handed a small leather book with brass hinges and a brass clasp. The writing was in beautiful copperplate and was written by George Smith, the custodian of Berkeley Castle in the time of Colonel Berkeley (the book was found in a dustbin in Berkeley!). It was the diary of Smith from August 1821 to the 31st December 1823 - a treasure of information giving accounts of wages, jobs, occupations, and above all it gives us an insight into the character of William Fitz Harding - Colonel Berkeley (see Appendix A).

I took extracts from a number of different items, from names of workmen, their trades or professions, where they lived, their wages, their place of work and dates of interest. For example we know from the diary that the canal was full of water on December 16th 1823 and that Colonel Berkeley did not reside at Berkeley but at Cheltenham.

Colonel Berkeley, as he was called, seemed to have spent most of his time in the fashionable town of Cheltenham and the running of the Castle and the Castle estate was left to George Smith. Smith twice a year went to Cheltenham to settle Colonel Berkeley's massive bills - money taken from a well managed estate - £100 in 6 months for chocolates for the ladies of Cheltenham, the same amount one of his game keepers would earn in two years. It appears he only came to down to Berkeley for the foxhunting and pheasant seasons or to find pleasure in evicting a tenant who was unable to pay his rent on time, for he was always at the farm or cottage with George Smith and his minder William Long to either evict or to seize cattle and stock. He was in the habit of borrowing 20, 30 or 50 pounds from the accounts of George Smith but never seemed to pay any back - Smith must of have quite a problem balancing the books!

According to the diary the Berkeley Pill was being widened and the banks shorn up with stakes at that time. Also, the Castle had its own ships in the Pill - there is no doubt because entries in the accounts regularly show wages paid to John Dowell and his crew - so why would William Berkeley, in the year 1821, have the express desire to build a boat house at Sharpness Point which had a rugged coast line jutting with rocks and a swift current instead of using the slow leisurely Berkeley Pill? One reason springs to mind - the building of the canal from Gloucester to Sharpness; the Berkeleys were against the building of the canal from the very onset but an act of Parliament gave the canal company the rights and the land was bought from the Berkeleys. A boat house built near the entrance from the Severn to the canal would be a hazard to shipping or was he establishing his right of way and ownership of the foreshore?

On January 2nd 1823 a dispute arose between the canal company and Colonel Berkeley. It was reported by Farmer Jones of Purton that company men were excavating on his land. Smith and Long arrived in the afternoon at Purton and saw the men digging on estate land. They were ordered to quit and Smith went on to confront the canal contractors. After arguments and threats Mackinzie withdrew his men and Smith rode on to Dursley to consult with Bloxsome and Player, the estate solicitors. With the advice given, Smith despatched Will Neale, a messenger, to Cheltenham with a letter for Colonel Berkeley. On Neale's return Smith again visited Purton where the company men were back on Jones's land digging holes. Smith and Long arrived back at Purton in the afternoon with a gang of estate workers who pulled down the hut that was being erected there. By 7th January the situation had worsened. Again Smith left Berkeley with a force of men; this time a much larger force set out and stopping on the way they were fortified with beer. It was either a very large gang of men or they were very heavy drinkers for it cost George Smith 8 shillings for beer at either the Salmon Inn at

Wanswell or the Wayfarers Arms at Halmore, or at both, for at less than half a penny a pint a considerable amount of beer must have been consumed.

On arriving at Purton, the Berkeley men quickly set about demolishing the huts built along the Severn shore. Whether there was a skirmish or not Smith never mentioned. I would hardly think a gang of Irish labourers would stand idle and let their homes be pulled down around them. All the huts were knocked down except one and under no amount of threats from Smith with their fear of dismissal from the Colonel's service would they go anywhere near that hut, which was an isolation hospital hut for smallpox and other contagious diseases and held many infected victims.

By the end of the year 1823 another incident happened concerning the canal. The canal was full of water by December 16th when Smith visited Mr Fletcher, the Canal company's engineer, to check the flooding of the Newgrounds from a breach in the canal. Fletcher admitted to injury and the company paid compensation. Mackinzie and the crew denied any fault of workmanship and set their own enquiry. Their findings showed that explosive substances had been used.

Farmer Cowley admitted that he had caused the damage, trying to cut a sheep wash into the canal bank. It seems that Cowley took the blame but afterwards Colonel Berkeley never again came into conflict with Cowley. Farmer Cowley paid his rent on every quarter day, and the very next day Smith would arrive at Cowley's farm with an amount of money corresponding to the rent that Cowley had paid. He said that it was for work done on the estate such as repairs to the sea wall, fencing, hedging or ditching.

Fox hunting and pheasant shooting took much of man's time both in terms of work and pleasure. Hay, oats, barley and other fodders were traded, for example - "July 8th 1823 Paid Turner for oats and oat meal - £136.2.0. and November 6th 1822

Paid Tho'd Manning for horseshoe nails - £61.18." Berkeley employed 29 game keepers and earthstoppers.

Thodore and William Gough had many entries in Smith's diary for 'foxes taken'. At between £1.11.0. and £2.10.0. for a fox they made a good living when the game keeper's wages were about £1 a week. These foxes were released in covert or woods where foxes were depleted. Fed by gamekeepers until they were old enough to fend for themselves they ensured the population of foxes in the Vale for the next season. Villagers were not slow to cash in on this sport of the rich; pulling the heads off a few old hens and ruffling up the feathers, they presented these at George Smith's office, complaining that master fox had killed them. They were given 5 shillings for a hen, 8 shillings for a goose and they still had the dead poultry for a roast or stew!

An interesting entry dated August 5th 1821 stated "Two men came to me about Job Davies stealing a horse". Some five years before Colonel Berkeley had personally hanged two men at Berkeley for poaching at Catgrove Hill. For that act he was reprehended by the House of Lords and now a case of horse stealing arose which could be a hanging offence. The case was taken out of Berkeley's hands and the Constable of Berkeley was ordered to take Job Davies. On October 6th Tho'd. Nelmes took Job Davies; Nelmes, a game keeper, received 10 shillings from the estate accounts. It seems that Colonel Berkeley's game keepers acted as a private police force. January 3rd saw Smith and the Constable at Alveston to prosecute Davies who was committed to prison on January 11th. Job Davies pleaded not guilty to the charge saying that the horse had wandered into his field and that he was "set up". That is the last we hear of Davies; he was sent in chains to a convict station in Australia. On the 8th of February his home, stock and effects were sold in a sale under the direction of George Smith who went to inspect the sale.

Mayors of Berkeley from the mid 1600's to the time of Colonel Berkeley are listed below. Some of the names are familiar to us and have descendants living in the Vale today.

James Roberts - 1664
John Edwards - 1648
Josias Edmonds - 1650
Clemwell Woodward - 1651
Thomas Pearce - 1653
Richard Trotman - 1656
Richard Pallmer - 1661
John Nelmes - 1671
John Somers - 1683
George Lewis - 1696
Daniell Clarke - 1709
Thomas Denninge - 1711
Thomas Varham - 1714
William Hooper - 1722
Nickolas Hicks - 1756
John King - 1770
William Neale - 1781
John Bick - 1793
John Phillips - 1809
John Spiers - 1829
Stephen Alpass - 1849
Col. F W Berkeley - 1857

MAURICE VII 1857-67

William's next brother, unlike William, was well liked and a respectable naval officer. In the year 1861 Maurice was created Baron Fitz Harding of Bristol, a title he transmitted to his son.

FRANCIS 1867-96

At this period the family estate consisted of the Mayfair property, 20,273 acres in all, 18,264 acres of which lay in Gloucestershire with an estimated gross rent of £33,718. At this time the history of the vale changed dramatically. The Gloucester - Sharpness canal was in full use, a new dock was built to take the over spill of traffic in the Severn, the railway had cut the Vale into two halves and a bridge was built across the Severn which linked the Vale with the Forest of Dean.

Randal Mowlray Thomas Berkeley, 1896, the great grandson of the fifth Earl's young brother, established his right to the Earldom of Berkeley, despite the opposition of Francis Lord Fitzharding, whose last attempt to prove that Frederick Augustus had indeed married Mary Cole in 1785, failed. Francis Fitzharding was succeeded by his brother Charles.

CHARLES 1896-1916

Charles was the last male descendant of Frederick and Mary; he too left no children and at his death the Fitzharding Barony became extinct.

RANDAL EARL OF BERKELEY 1916-1942

Randal was the heir of the legitimate line who now returned to his ancestral home. He was renowned both as a golfer (he had a golf course laid out in Little Park) and an expert on the measurement of Osmotic pressure. He also wrote intensely on the alterations of the Castle carried out by his fore-fathers. He sold the Mayfair property to modernize and repair the Castle. He left no children and the Earldom died with him.

ROBERT GEORGE WILLMOT BERKELEY 1942-68

He was a junior descendant of James (1417-63) and the Roman Catholic branch of the family.

JOHN BERKELEY 1968

Taken from Berkeley Parish and Church Records - Berkeley Church Bell Ringers on April 4th 1763 were:

Henry Knox, Thomas Hicks, John King, Richard Croone, James Phillips, Nickolas Corkonk, William Wade, Thomas Wiltshire, Robert Pierce, John Jones, James Watts and Nickolas Hicks.

Thomas Pearce, watchmaker and Mayor of Berkeley five times, was interned in Berkeley Churchyard in the year 1665. A watch-maker known throughout the world. The late President F D Roosevelt possessed a clock of wooden construction made by him. Pearce's epitaph on his tombstone reads:

Here lyeth Thomas Pearce whom no men taught,
Yet he in Iron, Brasse and Silver wrought
He Hacks clocks and watches (with art) made
And mended too when others works did fade
Of Berkeley five times Mayor this artist was
and yet this mayor this artist was but grasse
When his own watch was downe on the last day
He that made watches had not made a key.
To wind it up, but useless it must lie
Until he rise again, no more to die.

At the east side of Berkeley Churchyard lies the tomb of Dicky Pearce who was the Earl of Suffolk's fool. He was lent to James Berkeley to entertain at one of the many parties held in the great hall at Berkeley Castle. A drunken orgy developed and got out of hand and while Dicky rolled up like a ball and rolled around on the floor one of the drunken guests aimed a kick at him. Soon others joined in and Dicky was used as a human football. After the laughter had died down Dicky was found to be dead. He had been kicked to death by a party of drunken louts. He was buried at Berkeley on June 18th 1728 aged 63. His epitaph reads:

Here lies the Earl of Suffolks Fool
Men called him Dicky Pearce;
His folly served to make Folks laugh
When wit and mirth were scarce.
Poor Dick, alas! is dead and gone
What signifies to cry?
Dickeys enough are still behind
to laugh at bye and bye.

In the year 1765 a new clock was fitted to the church tower. £5.5 shillings was paid to Robert Clarke for putting up the clock; the money was paid by William Bennett the Church warden. On April 23rd 1777 Berkeley Church was robbed of the commission plate valued at £60. It was stolen by Hugh Price, a chimney sweep, and a boy named William Smith and was taken by William Jayner.

Rev. John Fisher wrote in 1856:

"That at the junction of the four cross roads in Berkeley stood a market cross, and in High Street there was a high cross - opposite the west window of the church (built in the middle of the road where the main Castle entrance meets High Street). It was a shrine for all travellers passing through Berkeley."

"In the market place near the market cross was a well, used by man and animal alike. It was later to be covered over and an iron pump fitted. Beneath the pump was a stone cattle trough and it was overshadowed by a massive elm tree that grew by the High Street turning."

The new market house was built in 1824 consisting of a number of archways over which was built the Town Hall. In the archways straw was laid down for the laying out of cheeses on market day. This practice ceased in 1850 owing to the use of the building by beggars and tramps. Bedding down in the straw was bad enough but they also used it as a toilet. The stench was so bad that local people complained to the Parish Council and for a number of years after it was fenced off and used only by storage carts. Later the archways were fitted with windows and doors and became the Town Hall the upstairs rooms were daily in use by the British School for Young Men's Society as a school for the boys of the town. On October 5th 1696 by the Last Will and Testament of Samuel Thurner of Thornbury he gave certain lands for the education of poor boys and girls of the town of Berkeley at the Free School.

In 1825 Mr Alfred Pearce, a wine and spirit merchant of Berkeley, introduced an annual fair to be held on the second Monday in December. A monthly market was established on February 2nd 1859 for the sale of cattle, cheese and fowl at the Berkeley Arms hotel, on which day 90 gentlemen and farmers sat down to dinner. (In the 1800's farmers could not be counted as gentlemen). The first fair in Berkeley was held on Holy Rod Day - May 3rd and was held until the year 1856. The same year saw the last interment in the churchyard of Margaret Browning, widow of Berkeley. Aged 71 she was buried on December 31st 1856.

Despite modern medicine and the general knowledge that people live longer today, the folk in the 1800's lived to a great age could it have been the lack of stress and strain of modern life, clean air, clear water and good wholesome plain food?

The following people all died over the age of 80 in the Parish of Berkeley (some may be your great grand-parents!):

Mary Millard	Woodford	August 25th	1813	age 82
Mary Wilts	Bevington	February 16th	1814	age 84
Jane Denly	Alkington	November 24th	1814	age 93
Mary Ford	Ham	February 28th	1816	age 90
Josiah Fryer	Purton	March 13th	1817	age 84
Hannah Ponting	Berkeley	June 9th	1818	age 82
Catherine Wood	Sugar Loaf	January 23rd	1819	age 92
Edward Curtis	Sanigar	January 26th	1820	age 98
Jane Nelmes	Berkeley Heath	March 3rd	1822	age 82
Sarah Curtis	Sanigar	January 4th	1823	age 90
Mary Woodbourne	Sanigar	September 18th	1824	age 97
Sarah Cole	Ham	May 15th	1825	age 80
Anne King	Ham	December 22nd	1826	age 98

John Trotman	Breadstone	July 11th	1827	age 92
Mary Pead	Ham	April 20th	1828	age 91
Thomas Reynolds	Berkeley	April 16th	1829	age 86
Deborah Haviland	Sharpness Point	July 25th	1830	age 82
John Denning	Newport	December 25th	1831	age 88
Anthony Kingcott	Halmore	December 30th	1832	age 86
Mary Andrew	Browns Mill	January 31st	1833	age 87
Sarah Creese	Purton	March 15th	1834	age 90
Elizabeth Gaston	Sanigar	February 10th	1835	age 81
Edward Cook	Wanswell	January 10th	1837	age 80
James Hinder	Halmore	April 1st	1838	age 84
Mary Gainer	Swanley	September 7th	1839	age 88
Ann Alpass	Wanswell	September 2nd	1840	age 88
Elizabeth Purnell	Berkeley	January 27th	1841	age 86
Hestor Heaven	Newport	May 1st	1842	age 88
Susanna Fryer	Hinton	December 13th	1843	age 82
Ann Fryer	Brookend	February 2nd	1844	age 84
Joshua Ball	Hinton	September 9th	1845	age 85
Jane Mallet	Berkeley	September 2nd	1846	age 96
Ashfield Shipway	Heathfields	March 21st	1847	age 99
James Phillip	Wanswell	March 9th	1848	age 83
Ann Hinder	Berkeley Heath	May 11th	1849	age 94
Sarah Mallet	Berkeley	January 16th	1851	age 96
John Pick Vinefarm,	Wanswell	June 7th	1852	age 100
Thomas Gale	Wanswell	April 3rd	1853	age 92
Thomas Alpass	Wanswell	December 25th	1853	age 97
Hannah Croke	Breadstone	September 27th	1854	age 84
Henry Matthews	Wanswell	January 13th	1856	age 81
Thomas Griffith	Berkeley	March 24th	1856	age 85
Ann Trotman	Berkeley	October 18th	1857	age 85
John Taylor	Wanswell	January 13th	1858	age 81
Hester Ruthur	Wanswell	March 10th	1858	age 92
Frances Matthew	Wanswell	September 12th	1858	age 82
Hester Webb	Purton	November 30th	1859	age 99
John Powell	Halmore	April 9th	1860	age 89
Sarah Powell	Halmore	February 13th	1861	age 81
Hester Kemmett	Halmore	January 27th	1861	age 87
Sarah Woodward	Halmore	July 19th	1861	age 95
Sarah Eddle	Wanswell	June 11th	1861	age 82
Mary Taylor	Wanswell	February 14th	1862	age 80
Samual Grafton	Halmore	October 9th	1862	age 87
Hannah Smith	Wanswell	November 29th	1863	age 85
William Cooper	Berkeley	June 20th	1863	age 85

Note the number of inhabitants of Wanswell who lived to a great age; 13 people in all between 1837 and 1863, a span of 26 years with a total age of 1,214 years and with not many more than a dozen houses in the village at that time. History seemed to repeat itself for one hundred years later or so, we had Mrs Tanner of 100 and Mrs Everett, Mrs Tanner' childhood and life time friend and neighbour, who died aged 98. (Mrs Everett told me that they had a bet on who would live the longest - I don't know how the winner would collect the bet!) Others in the village who had reached over 80 years were Mr Bird, Mrs Lord, Mrs Greatrix, Mrs Gaston, Mrs Johnson, Mrs A Denning, and Mrs Workman to name a few (and some are still going strong!)

A week in the life of 'Honest Tom':

"Season 1885.

Important to breeders of Heavy Carthorses.

That young grey cart stallion - "Honest Tom" will serve mares this season at 25 shillings each and 2 shillings and sixpence the groom. The groom's fee to be paid the first time of serving, and the other on or before the 1st day of August when an abatement of 4 shillings will be allowed but at no later period."

"Honest Tom is a rising 6 year old who stands 17 hands high. On remarkably short fat legs with immense bone and substance, sound and of good constitution he is the property of and bred by Mr J Weeks of Grange Farm, Kingswood near Wotton-Under-Edge. He was awarded the 2nd prize of £10 at Gloucestershire show held at Cheltenham. He is a sure foal getter and his colts are very promising. Honest Tom was by "Hartbury" the property of the late Mr William Allen of Hartbury near Gloucester. His dam is a very wide boney and old fashioned carthorse. Further pedigree on application. (No mares taken by colt).

Honest Tom will attend the following places (fairs and sickness excepted):-

Monday
Leaves home through Charfield to "The Crown Inn" Wickwar to feed. Thence through gate to the "Porter Stores" Chipping Sodbury for the night.

Tuesday
Through Horton and Hawkesbury to the "Cullis Inn" Hillsley to feed. Thence through Kingswood and home for the night.

Wednesday
Leave home through North Nibley to the "Bell and Castle Hotel" Dursley to feed. Thence through Cam and Coaley to the "Lion" at Cambridge for the night.

Thursday
Through Slimbridge to the "Bell" at Berkeley Heath to feed. Thence through the village to Woodford and home for the night.

Friday
Leave home through Cromhall to the "Crown Inn" at Iron Acton to feed. Thence through Latterbridge and Earthcott to the Old Beauford stables at Thornbury for the night.

Saturday
Through village to Falfield to feed. Thence Through Tortworth and home till Monday morning."

INTO THE NINETEENTH CENTURY AND THE INDUSTRIAL REVOLUTION

Trade in the Vale of Berkeley was mainly agricultural. Ninety per cent of the population lived off the land, whose cultivation rarely gave them much rest. They relied on primitive methods to keep themselves and the rest of society from food shortage or even starvation. Berkeley town was the centre of the Vale and the character of its shops showed the nature its people relied on for their existence. Scythes, reap hooks, sheep shears, bill hooks, spades, mattocks and hoes were sold at the ironmongers; bee hives, butter-ferkins, churns, milking stools and pails, field flagons and seedlips at the coopers; cart rope and plough harnesses at the saddlers; horse embrocation at the chemists; hedgers glovers, thatchers kneecaps, ploughmens leggings, villagers pattens and boots from the leather cutters.

Most people had to be content with the position on the social scale into which they were born; "The rich man in his Castle, the poor man at his gate". At the top were the ruling nobility for whose comfort society existed. Their country houses with the surrounding gardens and parks were oases of opulence in what was for the majority a desert of poverty. The Berkeley's ran their estates largely in their own interest. They controlled the church and acted as general benefactors when it suited them. The mass of labourers toiled to earn rather less than they needed to support themselves and their families.

In 1764 Watt completed the first steam engine. In 1825 the Stockton and Darlington Railway was built.
In 1819 the first steam boat would cross the Atlantic. This was the start of the Industrial Revolution. The first steam ships were paddled by wheels resembling those of a water mill. Made

of iron some 20ft in diameter, each of them was composed of two circles 3ft apart between which were fixed planks of wood 2ft wide. Driven by steam from one steam engine fixed amidship, the speed of these steam boats was 6mph. These were the first power driven boats on the River Severn. The first screw steamer was built nearly 300 yards in length and capable of speeds up to 25 knots.

Great as was the change brought about by the steam boats even greater was the invention of the locomotive engine, and by 1830 the Liverpool and Manchester Railway was opened. But all this meant nothing to Berkeley. Time stood still for centuries with the Lord in his Castle, slumbering behind the thick walls; he would not tolerate such intrusions. Even with the coming of the railway to the Vale, the station for Berkeley had to be three quarters of a mile away on the fringe of the Parish and that was the way it stayed until the building of Berkeley Power Station in 1950-60. Looking back, perhaps the old Earls were right in preserving the beauty of the Vale - but then again beauty does not feed empty bellies!

But progress had to come eventually if not to Berkeley then to Sharpness three miles to the north on the banks of the Severn, in the form of a canal. Canals were a quicker means of transport and definitely a smoother journey than by road. The Romans had built a network of fine roads during their occupation of the British Isles. They were good engineers and they build well but without maintenance or periodic reconstruction even their roads could not hope to survive. Road travel in the 18th century was slow, dirty and dangerous. A coach could overturn in a rut, be bogged down in mud or be robbed by highwaymen.

The Berkeley Vale

Defoe wrote in 1726 of highways "Not passable but just in the middle of summer, after the coal carriages had beaten the way, for the ground is a stiff clay so after rain the water stands as in a dish and the horses sink in up to their bellies." A system of private enterprise called Turnpike Trust was set up whereby a board of trustees was granted the right to construct and maintain a particular stretch of road.

The old Berkeley Toll gates in the Vale were used for this purpose but like most toll keepers throughout the country some cheated by pocketing the toll money and so very little was done to repair the roads. Not until the early 1800's did the roads improve, thanks to men like John Metcalf (1717-1810), John Mcadam (1756-1836) and Thomas Telford (1757-1834).

The Gloucester - Berkeley canal (as it was then called - to suit the vanity of the Lord Berkeley or should I say Colonel Berkeley) was not built to subsidise the roads but to help ships navigate to Gloucester and beyond safely but not swiftly. 16 miles in length and without a lock throughout the whole distance, it is spanned by 15 swing bridges. With an average breadth of 90ft on the surface, vessels with a carrying capacity of 1,000 tons can navigate to Gloucester Docks. With three basins, two at Gloucester and one at Sharpness and with its two sets of locks until the opening of the Manchester Ship Canal, the Gloucester - Berkeley Canal was the largest in the country. It served Gloucester and the network of canals through the Midlands. The Canal had been no less than 34 years in the making but from the end of the eighteenth century until 1817 it was abandoned with only five miles of the canal dug at Gloucester and two basins made at Gloucester and one at Sharpness. Eventually the operation was started again with Government backing. But when it was completed the canal had cost over £450,000 to build. The Sharpness basin was in operation up until 1820. It was a tidal basin used for the purpose of imports of paraffin, benzine and other oils. Dyes for the dyeing of the Cotswold cloth were transported by road to Dursley and Stroud and other Cotswold towns and mills.

Opening day of the canal was April 26th 1827. Hundreds of people gathered at Sharpness Point to cheer the vessel 'Ann of Bristol' as she entered the basin. It was not without some anxious moments for the sailing vessel Ann was arriving late and, with a lack of wind to help and the tide beginning to turn before she could reach the Point, she had to be assisted by numerous crafts; and when the ropes were thrown ashore the enthusiastic crowds helped to haul her through the entrance to much cheering and firing of guns.

Waiting were the dignitaries of Gloucester who had arrived earlier on 'Meredith of Gloucester'. With Meredith leading the way both vessels were drawn by horses with ribbons flowing from the shining horse brasses as they trudged the 16 miles to Gloucester. From 9.30am until 3.30pm the journey lasted - with crowds lining the bridges and tow path all the way.

Trade flourished not only to Gloucester and beyond but to the villages along the banks of the Canal. Purton developed into a thriving community. It was the first port of call - a place to restock on provisions, a place to quench one's thirst, to unload cargo or to load at one of the three wharf's there. A church - The Church of St John - was built to satisfy the needs of a rising population, as were shops and farmhouses cashing in on local seamen trade by opening one or two rooms as bars to serve beer and the local brew - cider. Purton had its own custom house in the village. The first school, until George Muller of Bristol built his school there, was up some stone steps to a room over outbuildings at the Berkeley Arms Inn on the Severn Wharf. Coal was bought across the Severn from the mines of the Forest of Dean by barges to unload the wharf under the shadow of a walnut tree. Goods were taken by carts to load on barges for Gloucester or on to the Stroudwater Canal which at Stroud joined the Thames and Severn Canal and so up into the Cotswolds.

As the trade grew so did the size of the ships and it was found necessary to enlarge the dock at Sharpness. With new and more powerful tugs the large windjammers could be towed up the Severn on high tides. A new dock was needed to take in the larger ships that could reach the far flung outposts of the empire, so money was found to purchase land to build a new and larger dock.

SHARPNESS DOCK

At first it was intended to extend the canal down river to Northwick Oaze but the cost was prohibitive; then the planners had a site in mind for a new dock at the mouth of Berkeley Pill but this too was found to be too expensive. By an Act to 200ft at the northern end and at a depth of 24ft 3ins on the inner sill of the lock. The Tidal Basin and entrance lock was 900ft long and the lock's width of 57ft was to accommodate vessels carrying up to 9,000 tons of cargo. The excavations were carried out by gangs of navvies operating steam shovels and labourers filling endless lines of small-gauge railway trucks pulled out of the cutting by steam driven winches and dispersed over a wide area of low lying marshland. The rock and stone was blasted out with gun powder. Bricklayers and stone masons moved in to build the walls around the dock, lock and tidal basin. Stone from quarries in the Forest of Dean was shipped into the old dock and transported on

Excavating Sharpness New Dock 1873

of Parliament in 1870 a new dock was authorised in meadow land and marshland known as Holly Hazel (the old Shobenaffe Park) in all taking in 60 acres. The dock was 2,000ft in length, 350ft wide small-gauge rails drawn by horses to the dockside. Engineers and fitters then fitted the lock gates and other machinery to complete the operation. In the deep peat bed, in many places 12 to 14ft thick, that was once forest, were found trees and stumps covered by sand and gravel deposited by the Severn when it periodically burst through to flood the lowlands. In the peat were many bones of deer, ox, horse and of man; most were found in the excavations near the low bridge.

Where did all this work force live? The contracting engineers and other dignitaries found billets in Berkeley at the Berkeley Arms and White Hart Hotel and other hostelries, while the workmen had to rough it. They had no option, there was no village, no houses that could take in lodgers. With only a dozen small dwellings in Sanigar and four houses at Oldminster the labourers had to build their own accommodation with whatever was at hand, earth, sod and turf. Huts sprang up all around the site roofed with sheets of corrugated iron held down with chunks of rock. Food was cooked on open fires purchased from the number of tin sheds set up by merchants quick to cash in on a shortage of food and other commodities. The only inn near to the dock working was 'The Oldminster Arms', a low stone building with a stone roof with long stone seats around the outside walls where thirsty labourers could sit and relax during the hot summer evenings under the shade of two plane trees that grew on each side of the inn (there is only one there now on the opposite side of the road near the 'Pier View Hotel'). With the coming of winter and the dark evenings the men would huddle around the large log fires sipping hot cider while the mud and rain-soaked clothes dried on them. Numerous small rooms each with a fireplace were available; according to the late Mr Joebert Miles of the garage Newtown when the need arose the rooms were extended by just building on another room. The landlord was a Mr Asbee and his daughter married a Mr Kidd who came to Sharpness to manage the Railway Halt at Oldminster.

At about this time another inn came into being - "The Shant" later known as the "Old Shant". It was situated on the cliffs overlooking the old dock. It catered for the needs of seamen, bargemen and dock workers at the old dock. The landlord was Mr George Turl. The new dock had a few set-backs when the walls collapsed and the water leaked from the dock and there was trouble in operating the lockgate, but finally the dock was opened.

On Wednesday November 25th 1874 the first ship docked. She was a sailing barque with the name "Director" - from St. John, New Brunswick, Canada and was loaded with 19,629 pieces of deal, batten ends and scantling for Nick and Co. She was assisted by the tug "Milo". The Captain of the Director was Mr Shamper. An hour later the "Protector" docked - a full-rigged Norwegian vessel assisted by two tugs "Cambri" and "Vanguard" and was ably piloted by Mr Tom Williams and Albert Everett. The ship's master was named Mr Falch. The Protector was loaded with 317 pieces of oak, 750 pieces 5ft of pipe staves, 1,200 pieces of puncheon staves and 14,747 pieces of pine deal ends all for Price Walker Ltd.

It is interesting to note that at the same time as the Protector was docking the "Fratelli" from New York loaded with 4180 qrs of grain passed by on her way to Gloucester. She was quickly followed by the "Vase" also from New York with 3,590 quarters of wheat for Gloucester. Many ships followed the Director in the following weeks.

The opening of the new dock did not mean the closing of the old dock (that did not close until 1927). Both were kept working at full capacity.

All these ships had to be discharged and loaded by the manhandling of the cargoes, there were no cranes or other mechanical power. Lifting the cargo, be it bags of grain, peas, or lengths of timber, was done by stages or platforms, each gang of dockers lifting up a stage until the deck was reached; then the cargo was humped on the backs of dockers to the shore or over the side of the barque into a barge.

Sharpness Old Dock 1895

But where did this manpower come from? There was the small hamlet of Sanigar, the nearest village was Wanswell and there the population would be perhaps a dozen able bodied men. There were no Newtown, Brookend or houses at Sharpness. Most of the workforce were the men who built the dock. Some brought their families to live in the turf huts and others walked great distances (from Frampton, Uley even Nymphsfield and beyond) arriving at Sharpness at 6am on a Monday morning to be picked out for work. They lived rough all week and returned home on a Saturday. Men left the land to work in this new environment where the wages were double those on the land, but they had to forfeit their tied cottages and this led to a housing problem. Houses had to be built and quickly, not only for the ex-farm workers but also to re-house the people living in the turf huts. The dock company built houses on the dock to

accommodate their own workforce - the company servants, but made no provision for the casual labourforce.

Here was the biggest movement of population in the Berkeley Vale since the Saxons moved into the villages; a complete new community formed - the villages of Newtown and Brookend mushroomed; in a few years other villages were enlarged to take the influx. On the dock, Severn Road, Great Western Road, Dock Road, Dinmore Road and Bridge Road came into being and of course this new population had to be fed and clothed. Shopkeepers and many trades and professions moved in to satisfy that need.

The life of the dock worker was a hard one. They had to work in all winds and weathers and if there was no work there was no money, no dole, no handouts. The workers living locally were lucky, but some had great distances to travel. They would arrive at the low bridge by 6 o'clock in the morning and if there was no work that day they either had to walk back home again or hang around for days until ships were due. Some lived rough, sleeping in the sheds and warehouses or on the barges taking their meals from numerous tea rooms or coffee houses that had sprung up around the dock.

William Birch had a refreshment room at the back of what is now known as Severn Ports. Matthew Gardiner had the bridge coffee house and refreshment room near the low bridge. There was also a café near the lockgates.

Many of the local footpaths can be attributed to these early dock workers. Many led to Sharpness from many miles away. Some led to inns where the landlords rose early to serve a 2d rum or a mug of hot cider on a cold winter's morning or on a summer's day a cold pint of beer to those walking from home at 3 or 4 o'clock in the morning.

Sturdy and tough they were; they had to be to meet the conditions. They started work at 6 am until 6 pm, carrying timber on their shoulders or across their stomachs, sacks of grain over 2 cwts in weight humped across the shoulders and back. Loose grain and coal had to be shovelled. The dockers food for the day would be wrapped in red neckerchief and was mostly bread and cheese and a raw onion or a piece of cold rabbit and a lump of bread pudding, washed down with either a bottle of farmhouse cider or a bottle of cold tea. After the day's work was finished the day was not over because the garden or allotment needed to be cultivated to help supplement the food supply in the lean winter months when the Canadian and Baltic ports were icebound. If these hardy men worked hard they certainly played hard; football teams for both rugby and soccer were formed in most villages - Brookend, Halmore, Berkeley, Sharpness, Slimbridge and farther afield Dursley, Cam, Nibley and Wotton. With road improvements and transport available, even if it was only horse and carriage or bicycles, the dock

workers finished work at 12 noon on a Saturday, had a quick wash and a bite to eat and were away to the match. They played ninety minutes football, washed the mud off after the match in the local duck pond, sometimes a tin bath was provided in an outbuilding of the local pub but after the first one or two had washed the duck pond water was cleaner than the bath water! They would have a few pints of beer or cider and then go "out on the town". Some spent the evening drinking or visiting all the inns in turn while others went to the local Saturday night "hop" to find the local girls. Many a girl found her way back to Sharpness or Berkeley as a bride after the end of the football season!

And what of these women? Like the menfolk they too were strong and tough, the rigours of the environment called for nothing else. Many came from the quiet but hard life in the Cotswold villages and some had never been farther than the next village, before marrying and moving down near the Severn in a new environment of dock life with its noise and bustle of trade and commerce. They cooked on gas stoves, having gas lighting in the home and on the street. Shops and stores nearby bewildered many a young housewife. If she was bewildered by the modern standards of the day she was overawed by her first encounter with foreign seamen, with their dress; many a housewife locked the door and hid under the stairs at the sight of a black man standing on her doorstep. These seamen subsidised their pittance of a wage by going from door to door selling the wares of their country - peacock feathers, beads or wooden carvings from Africa, ornaments, fans and silks from the Orient.

SHARPNESS AND NEWTOWN

The first family to move into Great Western Road, Sharpness was the family of Mr Sam Grove into Number 8. Sam and his wife Elizabeth moved from Gloucester to become manager of the new brick warehouses known as "Severn Ports". One of his jobs was to supervise the discharging of the grain cargoes. Mrs Grove (Bessie) was the daughter of one John Payne owner of many longboats down the canal to the docks. (An account was given by Bessie to her grand-daughter Mrs D Greatrix of Wanswell - a grand old lady with a wonderful memory).

Bessie Grove, unlike most of her neighbours, was a much travelled lady. Born on a longboat she spent her childhood on the canals of England, going to school whenever they stayed a while in one place. Her education did not seem to suffer. Her father, John, worked the canals all over the Midlands up from Gloucester to Birmingham, Bradford and Leeds. Bessie helped to work the longboat through the tunnels by lying on her back with her feet on the tunnel roof and pushing the boat through. When in winter time the canals froze over Bessie would run over the ice to tie up the longboat. Longboats would trade in coal from Walsall District Colliery down to Sharpness. Also salt was brought down from the Midlands for export from Sharpness and the boats returned back up country with grain, cotton seed, lotus beans, timber and cocoa beans. Early steamers were bunkered with coal from these longboats. With the prairies of Canada and the USA producing vast quantities of wheat, the trade in grain flourished at Sharpness.

New red brick warehouses changed the skyline and a new feature arrived - a ship called the "Leitrim" a grain sucker to quicken the discharge of the ships.

Sam Grove took over the duty of discharging officer. While the dockers were away at lunchtime quenching a thirst brought on by the dust from the grain (an insuperable thirst handed down from generation to generation of dockers!) Sam climbed aboard a ship to check how much grain had been discharged but alas Sam must have looked into a hold once too often for he slipped on the loose grain on the deck and fell head first into the cargo of Indian corn. When the dockers returned to work at 2 pm and the "Leitrim" started to discharge the cargo Sam boots came into view. The dockers rushed to uncover him but they were too late - Sam had suffocated in the grain.

Timber ships carried large lengths of timber in specially built compartments, the timber lying on wooden rollers in ducts built throughout the lengths of the ship (not unlike torpedo tubes in a submarine). The entrances to these ducts were in the bow, the height of a man and about 8ft in width. Loaded with oregon pine logs, a tug would drag them out through the bow then, floating in the dock, they were chained together and towed to Gloucester by tug. One such ship was a three mast barque called the "Sally" which docked in 1895.

The following extracts are from a former lockgate man's diary;

January 27th 1880 SS "Anglo" ashore at Sharpness.
February 9th 1880 Hodder, Winfield, Cook and Smith shops destroyed by fire
1881 A Greek steamer aground on Bull Rock
April 9th 1881 New Coal Tip opened. Barque "Idea" load with coal.
April 26th 1881 "Cassandra" capsized.
November 13th 1881 "Silkworth" aground on Chapel Rock.
December 8th 1881 Barque "Hercules" docked stern first.
1887 Barque "Victor" capsized. Tug "Prince Victoria" lost in sand at Chapel Rock - never found.
May 16th 1888 Two fishermen drowned in the Severn.
1889 Henry Denning a boy of 10 years drowned in the new dock
(unfortunately the first of many child mortalities).
May 23rd William Everett dock the ship "Warrior" drawing 23ft.
1891 Tug "Resolution" blew up on September 13th killing one man.

The Berkeley Vale

(This tug was tied up in the old dock when the boiler blew up. The blast blowing a crew member over the western pier on the sand. The late Bill Smith (Longboat) told me he was a small boy at the time and was carried on his father's shoulders down from Purton to see the mast and funnel sticking out of the water (R T Denning)

1893 SS "Ragna" lay aground in the dock entrance.

SS "Northern" ashore.

1894 Hydraulic working.

1895 Dock wall completed.

October 12th 1895 "Aloedene" discharged with federation logs.

1896 SS "Topane" aground at Ackthorn.

October 8th High water - 34ft 6ins - south-west wind.

November 6th SS "Tafa" on Chapel Rock, pilot W Everett.

Barge "Thames" aground at Sanigar Pill.

November 19th SS "Tafa" docked. Capt. Field - new entrance master.

December 17th Earthquake.

1897 "St Gathand" ashore at Ackthorn. Harold Dowdeswell drowned.

August 11th W Gray killed.

September "Atbone" aground on Ackthorn. Barque "Madras"
laden with pine logs ashore just above the north pier.

1897 "Northgate" ashore at the new entrance. J Blinkworth was the pilot.

1898 Thomas Williams died (Harbour Master).

February 12th 1899 Tide 35ft.

February 19th Smith Shop, Post Office and Chemist Shop all destroyed by fire.

April 9th W Palmer drowned.

June 6th W Sumsion and Charles Browning drowned.

August 19th The "Great Western" docked after sailing from Gloucester USA to Gloucester England.

1900 "Leitrim" arrived (a grain sucking ship) - ex Irish ferryboat.

1901 Sam Groves killed.

1903 Deals carriers strike.

1904 George Williams Dock Master.

1908 New Coal Tip opened.

1909 William Willis drowned.

15 incidents in the Severn in 17 years 1880 - 1897.

8 drown in river and dock.
1 incident in the old dock.
3 men killed.
2 fires to the same owners in 19 years.

WHY?
Did man have the ability to adapt to this new environment or were the steamers too big for the pilots to handle? Were the tugs under powered? Were the pilots more used to the slow leisurely sailing ships? And what of the dockers - were they too slow and untrained? were they more used to the slow life of walking behind a plough than working a steam winch?

RIVER AND CANAL PILOTS 1865 - 67
Joseph Ashford, Purton: William Bruton, Wanswell; Frederick Dowdeswell, Canal Pilot, Purton: Albert and John Everett, Wanswell: Edward Gaston, Canal Pilot, Purton: William Matthew, Wanswell: Thomas Hadell, Purton;

George Morgan, Purton: Thomas Price, Wanswell; William Price, Wanswell: William Price (Jnr), Wanswell: Henry Smith, Wanswell: Henry Smith, Canal Pilot, Wanswell: William Smith, Wanswell: Edward Williams, Purton: George Williams, Purton: Thomas Woodward, Canal Pilot, Pilot Inn, Purton.

River Severn Pilots in 1885.

Albert Everett, Wanswell: Samuel Everett, Wanswell: James Biddle, Wanswell: Enoch Brinkworth, Wanswell: John Brinkworth, Wanswell: Thomas Hill, Wanswell: William Smith, Wanswell: Harry Pick, Wanswell: Henry Price, Wanswell: Henry Smart*, Wanswell: Charles Smith, Purton: Daniel Smith, Wanswell: George Smith, Wanswell: William Smith, Canal Pilot, Halmore: Thomas Woodward, Canal Pilot, Purton:

1906.

John William Dowdeswell, Pilot, Purton: Richard Morgan, Brookend: Thomas Morgan, Wanswell: Thomas Organ, Purton: Albert Price, Brookend: and Frank Price, Brookend.

*Henry Smart was killed while walking over the railway track at 9 pm on his way to Severn Ports to board a ship leaving the Port. He was not found until daybreak the next day. His legs were severed from his body by a passing train. The time of the accident was known because his pocket watch stopped on impact with the engine.

These river pilots each had his own cutter and crew. They were stationed in the tidal basin and would race each other down river to the ships riding at anchor off Portishead; the first to arrive had the picking - probably the largest and so the most profitable. The wreck of the last survivor of the old pilot cutters lay until recently like some prehistoric monster, with its iron ribs sticking out

Tall Ships

Dockers 1930
Jack Long, Frank Lewis, Sid Eaves, Alec Denning, Stuart Hick, Alf Short, Ken Turl,
Val Portlock, Reg Parsons, Tiny Morgan.

of the sand and mud near the old dock entrance (according to the late Mr Albert Lane, the last survivor of the old pilot days). This once proud and graceful ship, some fifty feet in length with mast stepped well back from the stern was built to ride the open sea or to skim through the shallow inland water channels, so easy to handle that one man could sail it single handed. These vessels were still on active service until 1914 war.

The Severn Trows and Schooners of past years have long disappeared from the waterways of the Severn. With the coming of iron and steel ships powered by steam engines they lost their place to progress and now lie rotting in a graveyard at Purton. Their holds once full of valuable cargoes of coal, grain and timber now hold black slimy Severn mud or are so submerged that only the bows protrude through the grass.

These vessels had wonderful names like Ada, Shamrock, Britannia, Nomarch Higre, Orby, Severn Bridge, Severn Collier, Emma-Louise, King (a barque) Haman, Selina-Jane, Flower of the Severn, Exilorsor, Peterross
(a wrecking barge) and Harriett of Bristol. Beautiful names for some beautiful ships - even now playing a part in the fight against the mighty Severn if only to stop the erosion of the Severn banks.

The following are some of the Pilot Cutters and their Pilots in 1890:-

"Bee" - William Matthews: "Elizabeth" - Thom Addle: "Eliza" - George Morgan: "Hope" - William Smith: "Star - Henry Smith: "Industrious" - William Bruton: "Little Bet" - George Williams: "Wave" - Thomas Price: "Glance" - John Everett: "Sunbeam" - Charles Smith: "Lily" - Thomas Hill: "I'll Try" - Henry Pick: "Wreath" - Henry Smart: "Lizzy" - Stephen Dowdeswell: "Florence" - John King: "Agnes Annie" - George Smith: and "Reynard" - William Everett:

The Trow "Lavender" captained by Mr Meadows and Mr "Baller" Fryer as mate, traded up the Berkeley Pill in the 1920's. Coal barges discharged Forest of Dean coal at the wharf behind the "Brewers Arms" (bottom of Park View estate). The "Finaty" and the "Mary" also traded up the Pill both now lying beneath the Severn mud. The Trow "Industry" as well as the "Lavender" carried stone, quarried at Chepstow to the Newgrounds, Slimbridge to reinforce the Severn bank, each carrying forty to fifty tons of stone and each manned by a crew of three.

One of the last three mast schooners to work the Severn was the "Haldon" in 1944. The last man to take a Trow up the Severn to Gloucester was the late Mr Sam Aldridge of Saul. He took three day-time tides to reach Gloucester from the Bristol channel.

BERKELEY AND ITS PEOPLE 1850 - 1993

The coming of the canal, railways and road improvements due to the Industrial Revolution took large trunks of land from Berkeley Estates.

Dursley turned into an industrial town with at first pin making and clothmaking and then heavy industry (Listers) and broke away from the agricultural yoke and became independent. Cam also, with the use of the new steam engine, relied less on water power for its cloth industry. Wotton too moved into the new industrial age and again steam power came to the rescue; wool mills, silk mills and elastic mills sprang out of the old grist mills. But for Berkeley there was no such prospect. The Berkeley's had to suffer a canal and

a dock on their doorstep but they would not allow the shadow of a factory chimney to fall across the keep of their Castle. So Berkeley remained much as it had always been, the centre of the Vale life with small cottage industries, shops and ale houses, with one exception - brick and tile making. The clay from Oakhunger, first used by the Romans, was used mostly for roof tiles. The brick industry in 1850 was at its peak.

Charles Smith 1865 of Lynch Lane, Charles Ayliffe 1879 of Salter Street, Miss Sarah Smith 1875 of Oakhunger, Thomas Clark 1885 of Oakhunger and William Smith 1889 of Marybrook were all brick makers. Farmer Clark owned some of these pits but after the pits were

Market Place Berkeley 1903

closed (I think they were worked out) they were used for dumping the town rubbish and are now all filled in.

Another trade that flourished was tanning, with its connections with the Berkeley Hunt, for saddles, harnesses and riding boots. Oak bark was brought via the Pill in barques from Purton and elsewhere to John Croome's Tannery in Marybrook Street to tan the leather.

A list of some of these tradesmen is at Appendix B.

NEWTOWN

Newtown, a village of no beauty, was built hastily in the late 1800's to accommodate the influx of the labour force required to operate the dock. It is served by a road that ran from Berkeley which we now call "Old Lane" (the monks road to Berkeley). It was called Oldminster before the name Newtown was adopted. Oldminster could boast of an inn and four cottages in a small cobble stone square. Four or more houses, or rather cottages would be a better word, were in a field now called Baylands and there was a cottage where Miles garage now stands and down the lane a little way was Sanigar with 12 dwellings.

The Baylane road from Wanswell was not in existence then. The lane finished at Bucketts Hill Farm; from there to Newtown there was only a muddy cart track which finished at a gate where the garage is now situated.

This trackway and its hill was called Begger's Hill which was shown on an old map. (I think the correct name was Bugger's Hill but for obvious reasons the name was changed!).

Later when the dock trade developed, this trackway was made into a lane which was dense

Oldminster Road Newtown

The Berkeley Vale

with elm trees and the branches hung so low that high sided carts found it impossible to pass under. There was no road linking Newtown to Sharpness, only a footpath across a level crossing. Later (about 1902) a footbridge was built over the busy railway track.

The small inn at Oldminster was inadequate for the needs of a developing village and port trade, so the old inn was sold and a railway siding called Oldminster Halt was built in its grounds. Mr L.O. Kidd became Station Master in 1879.

"Pierview Hotel", Newtown.

The Pier View Hotel was built opposite to the site of the Oldminster inn. It was a new modern hotel in every way.

Landlords:

1875 Alfred Neale.
1885 Mrs Sophia Fear.
1902 Thomas Dimery.
1914 Alfred Hoare.
1923 Arthur Johnson.
1927 Major Budd.
1931 Mr Ward.
1935 Snowdon Hickman.
1939 Charles Edwards.
1950 Harry Whittem.
1960 Doug Kempster.
1980 Vernon Spencer.
1987 Mike Breen.

Co-op Shop Newtown Sharpness.

By the year 1885 commerce was well established and was amiably served by the landlady Mrs Fear (Widow) and her staff. Lunches, evening meals and full board were offered.

As houses grew into streets and streets grew into villages the need for shops arose. The first Co-op was built out of sheets of corrugated iron and stood where Thomas's Butchers now is. The building later became a union chapel and later still union offices and a bandroom. The Co-op moved to new premises, now the Newtown Post Office, and the need arose for a much larger building so the present building was built. It had its own bakery, grocery stores, boot and shoe department and drapery store while the rooms upstairs were used as meeting rooms and a concert hall. The Police Station, with its one cell, was built on the local children's playground, where local children played on swings and see-saws.

Local farmers were not slow to cash in on this new influx of people. Hardings at Sanigar Farm turned their stables into a slaughter house, killing their own cattle, sheep and pigs, providing not only the inhabitants but also the shipping community with fresh meat. Other farms sold milk, butter and eggs while others grew vegetables; and the breeding of horses both for transport and pleasure was undertaken.

The Severn Bridge brought a considerable amount of traffic and trade to the Port. It shortened the distance to South Wales to 30 miles and the Forest of Dean coal could now be exported from Sharpness, as well as bunkering the steam ships.

The railway bridge, opened by the Earl of Ducie on October 17th 1879, took four years to build and cost £200,000. It was 4162ft in length, the viaduct of masonry on the north side of the River being

Building Severn Railway Bridge 1877

70ft high. The swing bridge spanning the canal was 200ft in length, the bridge proper consisting of 21 openings, constructed from bows and girders carried on piers formed of cast iron cylinders sunk deep into the rocky bed of the Severn; later these were filled with concrete as the amount of traffic caused more wear and tear. 14 of the spans were 134ft in width and 5 had a width of 171ft and the two spans over the navigable channel were 327ft each, with a headway of 70ft above high water on ordinary tide.

Station Masters:

1875 Thomas Bedington - Berkeley Road.
Henry Hunt - Goods Manager, Sharpness.
Joseph Sturge - Berkeley.
1879 William Chorley - Berkeley Road.
William Mabbett - Berkeley.
L.O. Kidd - Sharpness.
1885 Henry James Mabbet - Berkeley Road.
John Mabbet - Berkeley.
Leonard Kidd - Sharpness.

Severn Bridge on completion

The first train over the bridge was drawn by an engine named "Maid Marian" from Lydney to Sharpness and the first passenger service followed a year later on August 1st 1880, joining Lydney to Berkeley stations with a loop line.

By the year 1885 a new hotel opposite the Sharpness Railway Station was opened - named "The Severn Bridge and Railway Hotel".

Its first landlord was Pearce Thomas Taylor who held the Berkeley Arms Hotel in 1879.

Landlords:

1889 Mrs Jane Taylor.
1902 Mr Tom Taylor (Farmer - Luggs Farm).
1931 Mrs Emma Varman.
Pre War George Varman and Post War Bill Petheram, Pope, Wally Goulding, Tich Butler and Basil Curtis, Pete Hogan.

The Hotel took its trade mostly from rail travellers. Sea Captains' wives would stay there while waiting for their husbands' ships to arrive. Shipping agents and ship owners settled business deals over a drink in the Tap Room while down in the Station yard cattle were auctioned in their pens after arriving. by cattle boat from Ireland.

A staff of 20 people helped to attend to the needs of the public. The only road to the dock passed by the front door of this Hotel from Brookend. It was a narrow road that took its name from the horses and coaches that travelled to Sharpness Point in olden days (Coach Road). It passed Luggs Farm down Turf Hill onto the new viaduct bridge and on to the dock. Later a path made of black cinders from the gas works joined Newtown to the top of the dock.

SHARPNESS

On the dockside business was brisk. Albert Curtis opened a chemist shop next to Lancelot Marling. An "iron" church was built next to the chemist shop and Post Office (1877). By the year 1885 Sharpness had its own Dock Chaplain - Rev. Herbert Ault who was followed in 1889 by Rev. Arthur Browne. Rev.William Thomas Campion became Vicar in 1902.

Down at the dock entrance Mr Leopold Coppola, Ships' Chandler, had a shop and so did Johns and Sons Ships' Chandlers. Thomas Gasser was a Provisions dealer and grocer and Mary Evans's newsagents completed the row of shops.

Other businesses:-Francis Barnard-Lloyds - Agent; Godsill Brown and Sons - Sack Contractors; William Galway - Poultry and Game food; M.S. Carr - Agent; John Chadborn - Steveador, Charles Cox - Customs; Jesse Gardener - Timber Merchant and Saw Mill; Lane and Williamson - Ships Engineers (and Ship Owner); Hodder - Butchers; William Smallwood - Shoe Maker; Hartly Hodder - Ship Owner, Ship Broker and Farmer; Hudson and Co. - Sack Contractors; Smith Brothers - Outfitters; Richard Smith - Outfitters; Captain James Calway - Harbour Master; Alexander Jones - Ships Smiths: W. C. Lucey and Co - Corn Merchant; Severn Ports Warehousing - Alfred Woodward was Managing Director: Gas Works - Henry Wakeman was Manager; R.G. Round and Thomas Sturge - Corn Merchants; Elizabeth Withers - Shopkeeper and F.F. Fox and Co. - Petroleum Merchants.

The Elementary Education Act of 1891 made free the education for all children, thus superceding the Education Act of 1870 which stated that all children must either be properly educated at home or be sent to school. The cheapness of paper and printing had led to the publication of thousands of cheap books. Books were now within the reach of everyone. The chance to learn and the opportunities gaining for knowledge gave the common man much which was denied his forefathers. In the Market House in Berkeley the rooms above were in daily use by the British School and Young Men's Society in 1850. The Master's name was William Dunstall.

In 1866 The Free School at Berkeley had three teachers - George Shepard, Robert King and Fanny Slatldie. Miss Louise Copeland had a boarding and day school in High Street. John B. Evans had a boarding and day school at Woodford, while Mrs Hannan Hill held classes at Halmore. 1875 saw Miss Limbrick's Ladies' Day School at Stone and Mrs Mills' Day school at Bevington. Amos Moss was Master of the Fitzharding School in Canonbury Street.

The Berkeley Vale

Miss Fanny Reynold was Mistress of the Fitzharding Infant School which held 184 boys, 126 girls and 56 infants.

In 1879 Purton Public Elementary had an average attendance of 85 boys and girls and 55 infants. John Paige was Master and Miss Mary Bennett was the infants' Mistress. It was built and supported by George Muller of the Orphanage at Ashley Down in Bristol. Children walked from Sharpness, Newtown, Wanswell, Brookend and Halmore in all winds and weather, many using the footpaths their fathers had made.

Sharpness Dock Company provided a temporary wooden building at the back of the dock offices for a school for employees' children only. Purton School was rebuilt in 1898 and also acted as a Sunday School which closed in 1930. Sharpness mixed school was built in 1885 at the end of Great Western Road and was enlarged in 1897 to take the large influx of children. The average attendance was 150 and Miss Elizabeth Stockham was Mistress. Later a new school was built in Newtown; Sharpness School became St. Andrew's Church.

October 30th 1888 saw the opening of the New Rooms at Newtown. Coffee was served at 8pm and present were large numbers of men and boys. On February 1st 1889 a Magic Lantern show was held at the Dock School and the following night at Halmore Institute.

The building in New Street was erected in 1883 as a chapel for Roman Catholic sailors but as it was never consecrated it was admirably suited for the purpose of a Parish Room, the want of which had long been felt. But if at any time the services should ever enlarge it could be used as church.

Sharpness Iron Church

In April 1889 there were six lending libraries in the Parishes of Berkeley, Chanty, Wanswell, Newport, Sharpness and Halmore and there was the Berkeley Institute. The need for knowledge, the search for the truth and the willingness to learn were now within the grasp of all men - for example in Religion.

For two thousand years man had been told what to do, he had no rights, he could not read and he could only believe what was preached to him - from the time of the Druids and the monks of Oldminster to the times when the early Lord Berkeley installed a monk in their church and later still a Vicar.

Man was compelled to attend the church, he had no way or means to doubt the words of the religious teachers. The fear of God or Gods was instilled in him, the fear of hell fire, the Devil and the wrath of God if he did not obey his masters.

The people were not told of the Love of God. Even the sick and dying were brought to church and propped up against the wall at the back of the church - hence the saying "backs to the wall" or "the last stand" (there were no seats in a church in olden days!). Many died from the affects of standing in a cold and draughty church; the soul was saved but the body lost. Man began to build his own churches; independent Churches and Chapels sprang up even in the most remote villages such as Bevington, Pitbrook, Wanswell and Berkeley Heath. There were Wesleyan Chapels at Halmore Newport and Canonbury Street. Wick Chapel was built in 1875 and Breadstone's "Iron Church" in 1878. In 1877 Sharpness "Iron Church" was opened and the Congregational Church at Berkeley was built in 1875.

Places of worship grew as did the inns and public houses. On the dock at Sharpness a new hotel was built in 1885. "The Sharpness Hotel" (The "New Shant") replaced the "Old Shant" of Mr George Turl whose small wooden and brick inn nestled under the cliffs of the Old Dock a hundred yards away. (The Turl family lived there until it was demolished in the late 1950's). The first landlord of the Sharpness Hotel was Henry Hall 1881 then Mr Albert (Blommer) Reece 1903 and in 1914 Charles John Hall (Rugby International); Pre and Post War landlord Ted Webb and Post War was John Innes. It then became a night club called "The Papillon" and is now the Dock Workers Club.

For a further list of landlords see Appendix D.

TRAVEL IN THE VALE

Travel in the 1800's was by horse back, horse and cart or carriage or by walking. Long journeys by stage coach were dangerous; the roads if one could call them roads, were of rough stone deep in mud in the winter and dry and dusty in the height of summer. Travel was not cheap either for one could not move freely about the country without paying tolls at the turnpikes.

People living at Sharpness and near the canal were fortunate for they had a bus service to Gloucester - a water bus. The first two vessels to operate were horse drawn and although slow they gave the passengers a smooth passage and a safe journey.

The "Wave" and the "Lapwing" both traded on the canal for many years and only stopped with

Trows on the Canal at Purton

With the coming of the railway, parliament stopped the tolls on the roads and passed an Act whereby the railway companies could not charge more than one penny per mile for third class travel.

the arrival of a road bus service. In 1925 Captain Curtis had a crew of four on the Wave. She could carry 240 passengers and has been known to carry over 300 on a bank holiday with the Captain giving orders for the passengers to stay seated and not rush to one side of the ship for fear the ship would capsize. Fares were two shillings and six pence - First Class, from Sharpness high bridge with fare reduction at each bridge stop. Reaching Gloucester in two and half hours, allowing for bridge stops, these ships must have made very fast speeds, with the bow waves pushing water over the banks into the fields beyond.

There seemed to be no speed restrictions in those days. Goods were also carried; salmon caught at Purton and wrapped in reeds from the canal banks were loaded on board destined for the fish market at Gloucester. Calves were also carried, they were tied in sacks which were tied to the handrail with only their heads sticking out of the top of the sack. Using 10 tons of coal a fortnight, the first class seating was astern and second class passengers sat forward paying one shilling and ninepence from Sharpness.

In fine weather the ladies sitting on the top deck under an awning would drink tea or lemonade and eat fresh baked hot scones provided by the Captain's wife, while the men folk stayed below playing cards - it was a leisurely way to travel, no haste, no traffic and no fumes to inhale.

When the shopping in Gloucester was completed, the goods were parcelled, with a label giving the owner's name and the name of the ship and were delivered by errand boy to the ship.

This left the shopper free to move around unhindered by parcels to dine in one of the many good class hotels. For one shilling (5p) one could buy a three course lunch of soup, lamb and two veg. and a sweet.

The late Mr "Crump" Collet of Purton as a boy was a member of the crew, cycling to Gloucester by way of the canal tow path early in the mornings to light the fires for the boilers in readiness for the Wave's first trip down to Sharpness laden with holiday trippers for the Plantation Pleasure Grounds at Sharpness Point. Picking up passengers for Gloucester, returning in the afternoons and taking the day trippers back at night.

After cleaning up the ship he would cycle back down the 15 miles of tow path to Purton.
(The "Lapwing" helped in the evacuation of Dunkirk in June 1940).

The women in the outlying villages were less fortunate than the women living at Sharpness and Newtown; for them there were no modern gas stoves or gas lights, many lived down muddy lanes or even in a cottage in the middle of a field.

They had to carry water by pail from the village pump, well or even a stream, trudging down the lanes to Newtown or Berkeley for their weekly shopping. The said lanes would be covered in mud in the winter and dust in the summer. Cooking was on an open fire or a black-leaded grate with the blackened sooty kettle singing on one hob while on the other hob stood the "Skackle Pot" simmering with its rabbit stew or scragend of mutton. Whatever was in the pot was most welcome to the homeward bound traveller on a cold winter's evening. Paraffin lamps or candles were the only form of lighting, the womenfolk having to carry cans of paraffin from either Newtown or Berkeley.

The women of the Vale were good housekeepers, they had to be, their very existence and that of their family depended on it. When they became pregnant, which was very regularly, there was no pre-natal clinics to attend and the old wives tales frightened many a young housewife. The midwife was anyone with the experience of having had children herself and there was no anaesthetic, just the strong arms of the midwife. Families of ten or twelve children were commonplace and in small country cottages with only two small bedrooms sleeping accommodation was a great problem.

The Berkeley Vale

There would be as many as eight children to a double bed - four at the top and four at the bottom, and when the boys grew older they had to sleep in outbuildings or sheds. The girls were "farmed out" at the age of thirteen or fourteen, going into "service" as it was called (and perhaps other names unmentionable here!)

Farming out the daughters of the poorer households was the accepted thing; it was a way of life and it saved another mouth to feed and it saved on room space. Work at the "big house" was hard and strenuous. Wages were 13 shillings a month (65p) and they had to provide their own clothes and uniform.

They had to work from 6am with the lighting of the kitchen fires, scrubbing the flagstone floors, preparing food for the day and waiting at table. They had only two Sunday afternoons off a month and then had to be back in their attic bedrooms by 9pm. Many a servant would retaliate on a vicious mistress by spitting in the soup (or worse!) before serving and then standing back and watching the lady of the house enjoy her meal.

Not all big houses were indifferent to their servants. Some households were a pleasure to work for and kept the same servants for many years; even when they were old and retired they were still visited and wanted for nothing.

Breadstone House in the days of Mr Crew Jackman, a Berkeley Magistrate, was one such household. Work was hard and long according to the late Mrs Emma Ackinson of Newtown, but the conditions were good with 15lbs of beef on the table - it was carved by the master and the servants' meat was also cut off the same joint and they all shared the same food, but the gardener, groom and indoor staff all ate in the kitchen.

Cider was made on the premises. Mr Jackman had his own barrel and other barrels were shared among the staff.

STEAM WINCHES

Sailing ships by far outnumbered steam ships in those early years of Sharpness New Dock.

A sailing vessel had no power in port other than manpower, so a barge fitted with a steam engine operating a winch fitted on the deck went alongside the windjammer, a head of steam was made and the winch pulled out the cargo from the hold using the sailing ship's block and tackle.

A similar thing occurred in later years with steam ships; if the engines or boilers needed repair or cleaning, a supply of steam was piped aboard and connected to the ship's steam pipes, so taking over the running of the ship. Here is a copy of the letter John Chadborn sent to ship owners:-

Sharpness Dock 1879

John Chadborn - Steam Winch. Information to Ship owners likely to be of service in the event of their vessels visiting the port.

"I John Chadborn have discharged here with the aid of my winch over 600 steamers and sailing vessels. I introduced these winches here in 1879 when exorbitant rates were paid under the process of hand labour. I only ask for a continuance of this support and I can guarantee you the same efficiency and that the work will be under my personal supervision.
JOHN CHADBORN
Gloucester. "

PRICING OF CARGOES ETC.

"Export - at two shillings per ton freight from Cardiff or Newport. Owners can stipulate to load at Sharpness when chartering for Welsh coal. Salt in bags to Sydney, Adelaide and Melbourne in bulk to Calcutta, USA and Newfoundland, dock dues inward one shilling and sixpence (7p) per ton. Ballast one shilling and sixpence per reg.: ton. Steamers four pence per reg: ton. Outward sailing ships seven pence per ton to Penarth Roads, eight pence to Cardiff and Newport. Pilotage from Kingsroad to Sharpness 800-1,000 tons registered £6-5 shillings and £1 for every 200 tons over up to 1,800 ton less one fifth if towed or propelled wholly by steam power."

"Dry Dock Dimension - 350ft + 50ft and 15ft on to the sill: Entrance Fee 500 tons registered £5-5 Shillings advancing 12 shillings and sixpence per each 100 tons or part of 100 tons.
Sharpness Dock Master - Captain Colway. Manager for coal tips (Bunkering) Mr Thomas, Severn and Wye railway office, Sharpness. Canal towage - Sharpness to Gloucester and back first 150 tons, eight pence per ton, over that 5 pence a ton. Steamers above 200 tons pay half the towage rates but must take a tug."

Local tradesmen of Sharpness were more interested in the rich pickings of the shipping trade than serving the community.

These tradesmen had their own cutters and crews (similar to River Pilots). They would race down to Kingsroad (Portishead) to secure the trade of the five-mast windjammers and schooners.

The first one there would board the biggest ship lying at anchor and take orders for supplies and measurement for suits and coats, boots and shoes from the Captain and crew. Then they would race back to Sharpness on the next tide, work day and night to make suits and boots etc., and all would be finished before the ship departed from Sharpness. On the day of sailing, the Captain bought clothes etc. from the tradesmen and would keep them in a slop chest. After being at sea for a considerable time he would open the chest and resell them to the crew, making a handsome profit.

Many a young local lad had his first taste of sea after joining a ship at Sharpness. Some signed on for the one trip while others served the full five years before the mast. Some stayed on the sea all their working life and even ended up being Captain of their own ship. Old seafaring men have told that on Joining a ship at Sharpness they would have to buy from the local trader at the trader's extortionately high prices, his own mattress, pillow and blankets, his sea boots, oilskins and other sea clothes, even having to buy his own cooking and eating utensils.

Two well known characters who could always bring a crowd to the pier head were Mrs Thomas and Mrs Willis, both washerwomen, who raced to the pier on the sighting of a ship in the River. First aboard had the contract for the ship's washing.
They always fought tooth and nail much to the enjoyment of the crowd of dockers. These wonderful ladies, hard working and honest, would carry large baskets of washing home which they would wash, dry and iron and have back on board within three days, weather permitting.

Sailing ships arriving empty or with part cargo, carried earth as ballast, and before loading would discharge the earth.

This was spread around the dock area either to fill in a dip or level off a piece of land - which accounts for the many strange and beautiful plants and flowers to be seen growing on the dock side in spring and summer. Seeds were carried in the soil from all parts of the world, not to be seen anywhere else in the Vale. The same would apply in reverse, ships leaving Sharpness empty would ballast up with the soil from a field near the dock entrance - known locally as the ballast hole.
Later when ballast was no longer used, the hole was filled with water and used as a swimming pool in the summer and a skating rink in winter.

A railway bank of hundreds of tons of soil from the front of Sunnybrook Railway Cottage completely disappeared into the holds of the windjammers and there are to this day English wild primroses, violets, dog roses and other plants growing on Australian or South African docksides.

The Berkeley Vale

Trade at Sharpness was given a boost with the arrival of Messrs. Cashmere Ship Breakers, in 1910; they gave employment to many local families. The first vessel of any importance to be broken up was "HMS Tribune", a cruiser. She was broken up behind the North Pier. The masts of this ship were salvaged and put to good use as markers of the channels and rocks in the shipping lanes between Aust and Sharpness and were lit at night with oil lamps.

After the Great War some of the old four funnel destroyers were also scrapped behind the Pier, before Cashmore's moved to the River Usk at Newport.

SECRETS OF THE SEVERN

As told by Mr. W. H. Savage,
Master of the steam tug - "Resolute".
(1927)

"Of my 53 years sea going I have served 52 on Severn Seas. I served my apprenticeship in the Lydney Pilot Cutters and for the past 42 years have held a Lydney Pilot Licence. I am the last of the old Lydney School. During the last 31 years I have commanded deep water tugs of the Sharpness and Gloucester dock authorities and prior to that I served in tugs of private ownership. But in this company's service alone I have made more than 20,000 passages between Sharpness docks and Avonmouth and Portishead or rather 10,000 round voyages - the service being tidal twice daily each way. The purpose of the service is to assist and tow barges and sailing craft, providing an unfailing service between Sharpness and Lydney to Portishead and Avonmouth and vice-versa.

"I am beginning to get familiar with the River, but I have not yet dared to reach the stage of familiarity that breeds contempt. The Severn commands a big respect from her familiars and I do my best to show her such respect and in so far as I understand her wishes she is responsive in her aid.

"The vessel "Resolute" and I are old friends, for I took her over in 1903 and she is as good today as she was then and a credit to her builders - Stotherts of Bristol. Here comes her engine man, he also must be very fond of her, he took over from the builders in 1897 and has been true to her ever since, apart from his inordinate appetite for lampreys and lamperns.

"Before we get underway I am going to talk about old times, or rather before my time, about the River above the Severn Rail Bridge so that you can appreciate what vital and welcome improvement the Gloucester Ship Canal and the Sharpness Docks have effected on the Severn both for large and small craft.

"Above Sharpness the going must have always been bad at best. You young people these days take much for granted but I want you to realise the problems that faced our forefathers in these reaches between Sharpness and Gloucester, now circuited by the canal which opened in part to Hardwicke in 1827 (the canal was opened full length on April 26th 1827 [R.T.D.]). Before this date there was an extensive trade done in the upper reaches, and the navigation of any vessel drawing over 6ft called heavily on the resourcefulness of the shipmasters of those times and the small craft even of less draught had infinite trouble in encountering these difficult intricate, ever shifting channels; they had to be mastered with the sole aid of heavily manned rowing boats, keeping the vessel's head to the tide. In those reaches the period of high water is very limited, and in the highest reaches we can almost call it a matter of minutes.

"From Sharpness to Gloucester must have often taken a week or a fortnight or even more, under exceptionally favourable conditions with a following wind. I do not believe this section could have been accomplished in less than six tides. Daylight or bright moonlight were essential every tide giving at most 1 hours working on each tide. To illustrate my argument, they would be lucky to pass the Nooze at Frampton on the first tide. It might take all the next tide to get to Framilode; on the next tide, (it would have to be a big one) they would clear Bollo Pill and then they could breathe a bit. I think there is one more stopping place before they would see Gloucester. After losing the Spring tides, adverse or light breezes would cause incalculable delays on this section.

The Berkeley Vale

Gatcombe, above the bridge, had a small regular trade in my day, owner Prout's vessel of 50 tons burthen. Bollo Pill was dockised in the early days of industrial era. It was fed in pre-railway days by tramlines. I remember it shipping coal to Bridgwater and Bristol. The Dean Forest coal and iron masters, the Crawshoys, used to ship coal there and pig iron for transhipment at Worcester and Stourport for the Black country. The family used to lay up there their two cutter-rigged yachts, the "Arrow" and "Forest Queen".

"In bygone days Newnham and its limb Broadoak were important ports at a very early date in the Irish trade, and handled oak timber for Britain's wooden walls and a big coast-wise trade in Oak bark for the tanning industry. These three way ports could have been made on one tide from Sharpness given a spring tide with strong south-western. A sailing boat ferry, with an ancient franchise was operated from Purton until the opening of the Severn Bridge. It carried passengers, sheep, pigs and calves but cattle and horses were forded at low water. The construction of the Severn Bridge so increased the already onerous difficulties of going up-river, that only a few die-hards have since its construction braved the older way.

"I was once asked to take the tug "Speedwell" up to Broadoak to tow a lighter to Gloucester or bring her back to Sharpness at my discretion, but I declined. The tug that went in my stead took three working tides to get her to Gloucester. This should explain the difficulties our ancestors must have experienced with larger craft which knew not steam power.

"In my time, winch or salt barges of 90 tons burthen, but only five feet draught, would bring salt from Droitwich to Bristol and load back with deals and generals. Under most favourable conditions they would navigate the old River to Worcester in three days. You asked me just now if I remembered any craft in my early days that might be the successors of development of the

wood bussors or bushes of the Stuart period. I wonder if the Withy barges of my youth were their lineal descendants? They were miserable cranky craft at best, as nearly as I can recollect 70 feet long 12 to 14 feet beam, and between three and four feet draught. They used to cruise down from Ironbridge with pottery, and from Brockweir and Bigsweir out of the Wye with withys for Bristol and wait sometimes weeks for favourable weather to get in and out of Bristol. No gear in them, four of a crew of five would pull a towing ahead. If a wood buss was like a Withy barge I can quite understand her foundering with all hands at the benches as Daniel Defoe describes it.

"One thirty pm. It is now time for us to get underway, so come along up on deck. We draw blank tonight here. We will see what Lydney has got for us, and blank at Lydney, eh? That buoy on the starboard hand marks Bull Rock, but we treated him to dynamite some years ago and reduced his measurements.

"On the left bank there Hogthorne. The sea was badly broached there 53 years ago. Two hundred and fifty large elms were cut down for piling, so that the massive stone wall could be erected. There lies Berkeley Pill, sadly neglected these days as a navigable waterway. Schooners of 120 tons burthen used it in the olden days and formerly small barges went up to the bridge at Berkeley and brick trows used to load out of there for Cardiff. Times have changed, and I shall point you out several other creeks en route from which such trade has likewise departed or shrunk, to wit, Oldbury, Littleton, Aust and Chessle Pills.

"There lies Shepperdine. This was a roadstead much used in the days of sail, generally by outward bound vessels. The prevailing wind of the River would be adverse to them. They would lie on that mud bank, hence the name of the inn "The Windbound". This site was considered for the dock-scheme which materialised however in the 1874 Sharpness extension. From here ran a very ancient ferry, though not recorded in English history as a franchise ferry. This ferry provides an ideal passage to Wollaston on the flood . The Narewood Rocks provide shelter from seaward. According to records, the country hereabouts in olden days was not a nice place to live in. The people of the right bank had peculiar ideas about the property and lives of the people on the left bank, and they certainly harassed the shipping industry. Apart from seizing vessels at anchor, casting crews adrift, spiriting cargo inland and breaking up their vessels they had another trick of blackmail, of coming out armed and insisting on transfer of cargo at rather heavy rates, to their own smaller vessels for the up river ports. Legislation had to be invoked to deal with them. But I feel after what I have said about the upper River, that you may agree with me they were only being cruel to be kind in avoiding the bigger vessels the heavy risk of the upper reaches.

"There is Littleton Pill. A large whale once entered the Pill and stranded, but I don't think the Littleton people were ever optimistic of the business being regular enough to justify founding a whaling industry there. We are now in Slime Road, a good road too. In the days of sail it was much used for resource by the windburned mariners to the "Three Salmons" in Beachley hamlet. Ahead is Beachley, an ancient place of passage, described in old-time books as "the only commodious passage over Severn". The customs used to board all vessels for up River here and search them in Slime Road. On our port hand is the World's End Sand. On Good Friday 1887 the barque Prince Victor, with barrel oil, touched and capsized. Her crew were saved but the Captain's wife and child were drowned. She capsized her attendant tug The Victoria. Beachley taught Bristol the export slave-traffic. At any rate, the business was transferred there at an early date. At a much later date Bristol captured from Aust the Irish cattle trade. This traffic was carried on at Aust under conditions at which the R.S.P.C.A. would shriek today. Just imagine the suffering of cattle carried under sail on a protracted voyage.

"If on arrival off Aust, the tide did not serve to put in to the North Pier, of which you can see a few remaining piles, the cattle on fasting stomachs were swum ashore led by boats with ropes around their horns and heads. Some of the Irish cattle-pens are still at Old Passage. Portishead secured this traffic from Aust, but Bristol then awoke to the possibilities and built the lairs at Cumberland Basin. Now Fishguard has outstripped Bristol.

"Between Beachley and Old Passage lie the Benches - a submerged reef which has the effect of an overall causing, particularly on the ebb, about a dozen very nasty short seas. Of the Benches there is a legend that nine jolly fiddlers were returning from a party, and on encountering these troubled seas the boat foundered and drowned them all. Today rough seas on the Benches are described as 'The Fiddlers turning up'.

"I am told that in Aust there is a strongly held tradition that the ancient landing place was one and a quarter miles upstream at the Folly. Such a landing place would avoid the Benches in crossing and provide a more sheltered course, but offhand I do care to express any further opinion without viewing the suggested landing place in regard to its low water possibilities. Over there in deep water you see the Northwich Ooze buoy. My company lightens big vessels there on neaps, if grain laden with their powerful self-propelled elevator with carrying capacity 1,000 tons, SS "Leitrim" with a tug (sometime yours truly) and lighters in attendance.

"There is the ancient Port Skewett, a place with several pasts, not dead but dormant, and bound from its situation to rise again. Its more recent activities were the New Passage Steam Ferry, the Severn Tunnel construction and Walkers Sudbrook Shipyard-a venture by the Tunnel contractors to utilise the housing of the tunnel workers. Several of Bristol's steam barges were built there. The lighthouse abeam is Charston

The Berkeley Vale

Rock or New Passage Light. Forty five years ago above this point the river was unlighted. We are now in the Shoots, and are just going over the Tunnel. There is Sudbrook Camp Shown on the map as a Roman Camp, but some say a British Camp. One of those pills round the point they say the Romans made navigable right up to Caerwent, and I can believe it of them.

"This race of tide we are now passing through is caused by the wreck of the SS R M "Hunton" about 41 years ago. She was lying in Kingroad with cotton seed with hatches open for ventilation. A southerly wind swung her off and she touched by the stern on the Cockburn Rock. The flood tide coming up under her caused her to heal over and list so heavily that she sank.

"We are going to lie off Portishead Pier by the pilot-cutters but I shall first head for Avon River to see what I have waiting for me tomorrow morning. There is my lot in the Drain four including the old "Twea Gesusters", a Dutch built craft. You will see how beautifully she nurses the waters on our way up tomorrow.

"Now when we have anchored, some supper, a yarn, turn in and turn out again at 4.30am to get under weigh and pick up out tow for the home port."

(British Waterways, Gloucester Docks, 1980)

Captain "Bill" Savage, born in 1863, was one of the best known pilots on the Severn waters. Captain "Bill" retired in 1934 at the age of 71. He was guest of honour at a supper at the Pier View Hotel, Sharpness. He spent 60 years afloat on the Severn; first serving on Hodder's paddle tug-boats at the age of 11, he joined the dock company in 1897. Captain Savage was presented with a "Berkeley Chair" on behalf of his many friends at Sharpness. Supper was served under the direction of Mr S C Hickman and during the evening excellent musical entertainment was provided by Mr Harry Phillips, Mr J Portlock, Captain Brinkworth, Mr Bill Nash; Mrs Francis was the pianist. The presentation was made by Mr A J Cullis (General Manager) and in support was Mr E Perry (Engineer), Captain Owen (Dock Master), Captain Brinkworth (Deputy Dock Master), Mr J R Evans (Severn Ports) and Mr Wollard (Dock Engineer and Chief Officer of Sharpness Fire Brigade).

Captain W H Savage died on 16th of February 1937 at the age of 74 years.

An isolation hospital was built for the cases of small pox that broke out among the labourers, while the new dock was being built. It was situated on the fore shore south of the Severn road house. It was later a dwelling house and was demolished in the 1950's. When the dock was in full operation a new hospital was built to accommodate any sick seamen suffering from contagious diseases. According to Bessie Groves, who worked there, the long black wooden building only ever held one patient - a seaman suffering with the symptoms of VD. Bessie said that they refused to treat him and sent to Berkeley for Doctor Awdry. When he arrived in his pony and trap the seaman had dressed and walked out of the hospital, disappeared and was never seen again either in the locality or back onboard ship. Future patients were either taken to Berkeley or Gloucester Hospital. If the hospital was idle, the mortuary, a corrugated iron shed in the hospital grounds, certainly was not. The death rate was fairly high, mostly from drowning's.

The seamen after a night ashore in the local public houses, probably drinking their first drink after many months at sea, in the darkness of the dockside slipped and failed to climb the rope ladder to get back on board ship. The Master of the ship would deliberately not report a missing seaman - it saved paperwork and extra time in port for an inquest and funeral. Weeks after the ship had sailed a body would float to the surface sometimes with no identification to prove who it was, or from what ship he came. The dock police had the job of laying out the bodies. Berkeley cemetery holds many of these unknown graves.

The Dock Hospital was later used as a Seamen's Mission and was called "Salty Sam's" after the old seaman who ran the mission. It was used mostly by out of work dockers.

MARSHFIELD 1900

Known locally as "Timber Pond" it was dug out of marshy pools some over nine feet deep (the left over of the River Din). Irish labourers working in bare legs and feet dug out the mud. Some carried it in buckets on shoulder yokes while others pushed pram-like burrows loaded with mud. Some labourers would disappear in the deep mud holes and had to be hauled to safety by other work mates. All this was witnessed by a small boy who lived nearby. He spent the summer sitting on the canal bank watching the men at work. That small boy was Mr Albert Lane (the old River Pilot). The pond was used to soak Oregon pine logs to stop them from splitting. A tough wood having the highest resin contents of all wood, it was used in stead of steel girders in the building trade. There was a large import of this timber during the 1914-18 war when steel was in short supply.

Sharpness had it's own lighthouse out on the point (again, according to Albert Lane). It was a stone - built tower some 18ft in height adjacent to the lighthouse keepers stone cottage. It had a steel ladder on the outside of the tower which gave the keeper access to the lamp for cleaning , trimming the wick and refilling with paraffin. If he had another occupation it is not known. One name is known from records in 1885, that of Thomas Sturge - Sharpness Point Keeper (whether this means keeper of the light or game keeper is not known). Situated on the red sandstone cliffs above the rocks of Sharpness Point the light gave warning to olden day mariners of the dangerous rock below (it was pulled down well before the First World War).

Evidence of a beautiful garden can be seen in the Spring and Summer. Snowdrops, Daffodils, Iris, Lilacs both blue and white and passion flowers can be seen. The Rose bushes have reverted back to dog Roses. Ostricha fern and Tongue fern still flourish in the undergrowth but each year chunks of this garden are eroded away as the cliff crumbles and falls into the Severn.

Another interesting item was a ferry across the canal at the canal junction with the dock. Again we are indebted to Mr Lane. This ferry served to take out the journey down to the Old Dock via the towpath, across the lockgates and back up the cutting to the high bridge. A cable across the canal could be raised or lowered according to the needs of shipping. A punt would ferry people across with the operator pulling the punt hand over hand across the canal. This was about the year 1908.

THE PLEASURE GROUNDS, SHARPNESS POINT

Known as the Plantation it was about eight acres of woodland and was the last remains of the old Sharpness Park. It was set in the headland jutting out into the Severn and was thick with Chestnut, Beech, massive Oaks, Plane, Cedar and Pine trees. One could lean on the railings and look down the cliff face and watch the incoming tide pound against the rocks below, or just sit on a bench seat and admire the magnificent view up or down the River, or take in the panoramic view of the Forest of Dean and its surrounding countryside.

Opened in 1888 there is a lovely account of that event :-

"The day was fine, though somewhat cold and after a short service in the church the children preceded by Berkeley Drum and Fife Band marched to the Pleasure Grounds.

"They seemed to enjoy thoroughly the various amusements provided for them, especially the races, jumping etc., instituted by several Captains of Ships who provided themselves with large stores of silver and copper for the youngsters benefit. Tea was served for the children at four o'clock and for their elders at five.

The Berkeley Vale

The Berkeley Brass Band had by this time arrived and their performance throughout the evening gave the greatest of pleasure to several hundred people. Dancing was kept up with considerable vigour until nine o'clock when a number of rockets and blue lights were sent up by Mr Thomas, and the company gradually dispersed."

Prices at that time;
To hire of the Pleasure Grounds £1.10 shillings
To hire Berkeley Brass Band £1.15 shillings
To hire Berkeley Drum and Fife Band
5 shillings
Hire of crockery 5 shillings
Grocery and cakes etc £2.10 shillings
Printing shillings and six pence

The Pleasure Grounds , Sharpness Point

For many years the "bun fights" as they became known were the highlight for the children both from School and Church. The procession of decorated farm wagons and carts led by Sharpness Silver Band would leave Newton and proceed up the Station Road, over the dock bridges to the Point, where in the Pleasure Ground the children competed in track and field sports etc., just the same as their parents did in that year 1888.

Tea, cakes, buns and home-made ice cream were provided by the Sturge family, and gallons of lemonade were consumed by the thirst competitors, while their elders sat and relaxed in the cosy tea rooms.

These tearooms were ex-French ambulance carriages from the Western front, brought to Sharpness by ship after the Great War. According to the late Mr Adolf Sturge, they were unloaded on to railway lines and pulled by horses to the Plantation.

As the carriages Passed over the track, the lines were pulled up and laid down again in front of the carriages - a long laborious task.

Dotted among the trees were life boats of the old schooners and windjammers (long ago lost to the breakers yards). Cut in half these life boats were up-ended and looking like soldier's entry boxes, they were fitted with seats and tables, and were used for families to hold picnics. Children's swings hung from the low lying branches of the Oaks and see-saws made from a plank balanced on a fallen log provided endless entertainment, while their parents sat around the band stand listening to one of many local bands.

The Pleasure Grounds not only gave pleasure to local people, but to people as far away as Birmingham. A cheap day return ticket on the train brought crowds to Sharpness. They took a drink at the Railway Hotel, before walking over the bridge to call at the Sharpness Hotel on route to the Plantation where they held their festivities. The highlight was a firework display at dusk and the release of small hot air balloons.

Even before the railways ran their excursions the "Wave" and the "Lapwing" ran trips down the canal from Gloucester. This was the nearest many people were able to get to the sea.
In the summer of 1902 Sharpness welcomed home from the Boer War her only returning soldier. Crowds gathered at Sharpness Station and flags and bunting flew from the platform as the train pulled into the station. As Mr Weaver descended from the carriage Sharpness Band struck up the tune "See the conquering hero comes" and the children, dressed in their Sunday best, cheered and waved their Union Jacks.

Mrs D Greatrix, a small girl then, dressed in her white pinafore was one of the many children who gazed in awe at that soldier dressed in his best dress uniform with a row of medals gleaming in the sun. The band marched in front of the procession down the black ash path to Newton,

with the crowd dancing and singing in the rear. The flags were again in evidence as Mr Weaver marched through the village and people waved from their doorsteps.

Later, tragedy overtook Mr Weaver. After surviving the battlefields of Paavdeberg and Elandslaagte, and the welcome home celebrations, he started back in his old job on the dock and whilst working he stepped between two railway trucks while they were being shunted and was crushed between the buffers. Mr John Evans and Mr Alf Groves rendered first aid but decided he was beyond their help. The only means of transporting an injured person was a two-wheeled stretcher, two large pram-like wheels in the centre of the stretcher with handles at both ends. The dockers took charge of the stretcher, carrying it over the railway track to Newton and running with it all the way to Berkeley Hospital. Dozens of dockers took their turn at the stretcher. The condition of the rough road added no comfort to Mr Weaver, for just as they pulled up at the Hospital door he expired.

SHARPNESS BAND

Founded in the year 1898 it was known as "The Union Church Temperance Band" and its founder members included many dockers and port workers, but after two years the name was changed. The word "Temperance" was deleted from the big drum. To Bob Portlock, George Francis and George Millard blowing a cornet, trombone or euphonium was thirsty work and no amount of lemonade could quench a thirst that had built up during work - busheling barley at Severn Ports. If the name "Temperance" had not been erased there would not have been enough members left to form a band.

Members of that original band are as follows;

Alf Groves, Frank Wilkin, Matt Francis, John Heaven, Bob Portlock, A. Phelps, Bill Portlock, Dan Thomas, George Millard, Sam Groves,

The Berkeley Vale

Arthur Wilkins, Alf Bick, Bill Wimbow, Fred Merret, George Francis, Harry Phelps, Neil Haliwell and Tom Drinkwater. The band was disbanded during the First World War.

After the War the band was reformed under the Bandmaster Fred Smith and the band room was the corrugated tin shed which was once the old chapel. Members of that 1921 Band were:- R.Fryer, A.Williams, F.Merret, G.Barnfield, G.Earl, M.Palmer, T.Fryer, C.Priday, J.Portlock, G.Haward, T.Phillip, W.Cole, F.Smith, G.Portlock, A.Denning and S.Price.

The band played for many charities with the members giving much of their time and energy. Berkeley Hospital benefited greatly from their efforts. They gave pleasure to many people when life was at a low ebb.

WORLD WAR ONE - August 14th 1914

The Vale of Berkeley in the County of Gloucestershire was far removed from the horrors of war. The battlefields were on some foreign soil and aircraft were not yet powerful enough to penetrate into the depths of the country. The Zeppelins raided the East coast, as did the hit and run surface raiders. The West country was ensured of its safety. The coming harvest in the Vale seemed far more important. The weather giving far more concern than Belgians, French and Germans lying in crowded ditches. Farmers hid their best horses, carts and hunters from the army, hidden in out of the way sheds and barns through-out the Vale. A farmer, coal merchant or timber haulier had little or no compensation for a horse killed on war service.

Here at home posters were everywhere - 'Your King and Country needs you". Reservists joined their units and the Territorials marched to the local railway station from village and hamlet. They said their good-byes to wife, mother or girlfriend and embarked for the training camps. All too soon they were across the channel. Kitchener's boys were going to war, joining the Belgian and the French in the trenches, their blood mingling with that of their allies.

War with its horrors had come to the British at Mons, retreating in defeat, struggling across France were whole units - units of men, brothers, friends and work mates many from the same village, cut to pieces and dying to a man. Soon the local press had Roll of Honour columns running into many pages - a list of the dead and wounded.

July 1st 1916 saw the start of the greatest battle man had yet known, a carnage that was to wipe out a million men - men in their prime both British, French and German.

Five hundred thousand men of the British Army fell in that agony we called "The Battle of the Somme". The finest in physique and intelligence and courage, a whole generation of men both German and British was left on the barbed wire or in shell holes. Battalions, brigades and divisions, wave after wave of troops, were just thrown into battle to gain a few yards of mud. Sixty thousand were lost on that first day of July. Thousands were lost in the first few minutes and it took seven days for the last of the wounded to stagger back into the trenches. The skeletons of the dead lay in rows or huddled in hollows and heaped against the barbed wire not until the following spring when the Germans retreated were they recovered.

After the Battle of the Somme conscription was the order and conscripts went forward to battle like driven sheep and never again was man heard to sing as he marched to the front. (There never was an enquiry into the massacre at the Somme).

Schoolboys left school at the age of 12 to replace the labour force called up for war. Women for the first time were taking their place in industry, driving buses, trams, trains and working in factories and on the land. Sharpness docks had its most industrious time since the dock opened, with a quick turn round of shipping. Grain from Canada and U.S.A. was a priority. Also the repair of ships damaged by enemy action and the conversion of sail to steam required an import of skilled labour from other shipyards - from South Wales to the Northern shipyards, men were drafted to Sharpness to work at the Dry Dock.

Ships were being hit frequently by German surface raiders in the Western Approaches. One such ship was the "Carman" a sailing vessel with a wooden wheelhouse. The masts and wheel-house were shot away and she was put in the "Gully" for the debris to be removed and so clear the hatches for unloading. A dock crew was detailed for the job and soon the waiting railway trucks were loaded with broken spars, ropes, pulleys, masts, hatches and of course the smashed up wheelhouse. The railway engine shunted the trucks down a siding to a place behind the North pier where the debris could be sorted out - the salvageable from the rubbish. The rubbish was tipped alongside the railway track. The engine fireman, cleaning out his firebox, threw the hot ashes out onto the track, where a fire started. There was an almighty explosion bringing people rushing from their houses in Dock Road, Severn Road and Great Western Road to see a man staggering about clutching his throat. By the time the first aid men Mr Alf Groves and Mr John Evans reached him Mr Wilkins was dead. His jugular vein had been cut through by a piece of flying metal thrown up by the explosion. Apparently an explosive charge from an unexploded enemy shell had been among the debris and the hot ashes had ignited the charge.

Saturday the 10th of September 1914 saw the largest ship to dock at Sharpness. Lockgate men under the skilled leadership of Captain Brinkworth edged the great ship inch by inch through the entrance gate. It was the SS "Assyria" - a steam ship of 6,370 gross tonnage and 4,105 tons net, with a length of 450 feet 6 inches, 55 feet 2 inches in beam and a depth of hold at 30 feet 1 inch - her dead weight carrying capacity being 12,000 tons. She carried part cargo and having discharged 5000 tons of cotton seed at London she discharged 1,998 tons at Sharpness and then proceeded to Glasgow to discharge the rest of her cargo - 1,200 tons of general cargo. The record was previously held by the SS "Pindari" of the same owners - T and J Brockebank Ltd-which docked in 1905. Built in 1891 she was 5,713 Gross, 3,696 net, length 446 feet, 49 feet 2 inches in beam with a draft of 20 feet.

On the evening tide of that same day, September 10th 1914, the Docking Master and his crew again had their skills tested, for another large ship was docked - the SS "Clan Macpherson".

Not so large a ship as the Assyria but she carried a heavier cargo - 6,419 tons of which 3,219 tons

were cotton seed and the rest 3,200 tons in Manganese ore, her dead weight carrying capacity was 9,000 tons, length 400 feet, 51 feet in beam, draft 23 feet 6 inches and Net Register 3,041 tons.

The people living in the Vale were luckier in most respects than others living in towns and cities - a garden or an allotment supplemented the food larder (it always did even in peacetime). From the unloading of the very first grain ship in Sharpness Dock householders kept chickens. A hen coop on the backyard with 3 or 4 hens provided a widow with her needs (someone would bring her a bag of wheat or barley).

For the docker with a chicken run on his allotment, his pen of fattening cockerels for the table were all fed on waste wheat, barley or maize - spillage from ships' holds. The dockside residents had only to let their hens run loose to roam freely and help themselves to what took their fancy.

One such place was Birch's Coffee House, situated behind the Severn Ports grain warehouses. Dockers out of work and broke would corner one of those fat hens, hold it by its neck and dunk it several times in the dock. Then holding it tenderly he would present the hen to Mrs Birch at her kitchen door, saying that he had saved it from drowning in the dock! For his reward Mrs Birch would give him sixpence (always a sixpence). Turning away with a big grin and clutching the sixpence he would set his sights on "The Shant" and with a determined step make his way up to the pub with a vision of three pints of cider lining up on the bar! One often wondered why Mrs Birch never rumbled that trick; perhaps she did and it was her way of showing kindness.

Rabbits were kept for the table and most households with plenty of ground or allotments kept a pig to fatten for pork and bacon. Wild rabbit, pigeon, rooks and even blackbirds often made a delicious pie. Fish was plentiful from both dock and river. Fat freshwater bream, some bigger than a dinner plate, were caught near the

Port warehouses and eel baskets were set out amongst the rocks in the River. A jack fish (a young pike) from the ice-covered timber pond in January stuffed with sage and onions, baked in the oven, helped to supplement the wartime rations and of course elvers were caught by the bucket load in the Spring. They were cooked, put into stone jars and boiling lard was poured on to the elvers thus sealing the jars air-tight. With lids screwed firmly on, this source of food put in the cool cellar would keep for months.

The humble potato was the main diet in peace time and was even more so in time of war. Every village and hamlet had its allotments, sometimes more than one, owned or leased by the parish. They were cultivated to the last square foot and up to a ton of potatoes could be harvested, enough to last an average family until the new season's potatoes came in the following June.

Potatoes went into the making of bread and beer. Inns and public houses that enjoyed unrestricted hours of business were now enforced by law to limit hours of opening (A law that is still in operation to this day).

Butter was rationed to 2 oz's a week, as were lard and cheese.

The people of Berkeley would go to the dairy (at Berkeley Station) where they could buy a quart of skimmed milk for a penny; cracked eggs were sold at 3 pence a dozen.

A soup kitchen was opened at the Castle, where every Friday afternoon jugs and basins that were left by the school children in the morning were filled ready for the children to collect after school.

THE STORY OF A GREAT WAR SOLDIER

The day after the Aberfan disaster (October 21st 1966) when a mountain of mud engulfed a school, trapping the children inside, I was sitting with Albert Sumsion in his kitchen drinking tea when on the TV screen came the scenes of children being dragged from their classrooms.

Memories came flooding back to Albert - memories of the mud at the Somme. It is very rarely one can get old soldiers to relate their experiences; their minds to the horrors of war. The sight of those children covered in mud upset him immensely.

Albert would not have thanked me for calling him a hero, but one he certainly was, they all were, those soldiers who went "Over the Top" to certain death or to suffer horrifying wounds of body and mind. Albert Sumsion was born on August 14th 1891, the son of one of the pioneers of Sharpness - his father was one of the first to settle in Newtown; by the very virtue of his birth Albert was destined for the killing fields of Flanders. Albert, like his father and brothers, worked on the dock carrying deals and sacks of grain. When war came, with thousands of other young men he joined the army. 1915 saw Albert in the Gloucestershire Regiment; his brother Arthur, a regular soldier in the "Glosters", was already in France.

On November 16th 1916 Albert Sumsion marched six long miles to the front at the Somme, along a muddy track once called a road. Having many times to step off the road to allow ambulances both motor and horse- drawn to pass, passing columns of wounded soldiers stumbling back was demoralising enough, but the thing that stuck in Albert's mind was when they passed rows of neatly packed wooden boxes stacked along the roadside and realised that they were empty coffins. It was late afternoon when they reached the rear trenches and were welcomed with a mug of hot tea but no food was on offer. The officers went to a briefing and they knew that they would soon be winding their way up the communication trenches to the second line trench, where they would wait while the officers and NCO's held another briefing. The time was midnight; Albert and two other soldiers were to form up with the detachment to reconnoitre and cut the enemy barbed wire and leave white markers for the following troops to pass through. Again they moved forward to take up positions overlooking "No Mans Land". The smell in that trench was appalling, related Albert; the smell of urine was everywhere and soon they were adding to it as bladders weakened with nervous tension as they waited to go over the top. The worst part was the waiting. A rum ration was issued to help steady nerves but it did little to melt that block of ice in the pit of the stomach. Time was getting short; a Captain moved forward to look through a slit in a plate of thick steel that protruded above the trench, a look at his watch, a wave of his arm they were on their way into the unknown.

The British shelling had stopped, all was quiet in their section. Albert's platoon covered the first 100 yards without incident. A splutter of machine gun fire away to the left died out. The stillness of the night made every little sound seem like a clap of thunder. Still they crept on, even their breath seeming to roar from their lungs. 60lbs of equipment made every movement laborious; again there was a splutter of gun fire - jerry was getting a bit nervous. Suddenly the night sky lit up in a brilliant white light and all hell was let loose. Shells came screaming in. Albert remembered lying to the right of his two comrades when a shell exploded to the left with a blinding flash throwing Albert into the air. There was a great rush of air and noise like an express train roaring through a station and that was all he could remember. When Albert came to, all was quiet and of his two mates there was no sign. Gone too was his pack, webbing, greatcoat, rifle, steel helmet, all blown away. His tunic hanging in tatters, Albert tried to stagger to his feet; his intention was to make a dash back to his own lines but when he tried to stand up he fell over as if drunk. He was in no pain, he felt his head, no blood - his arms and hands were OK and he felt on down his body. His right leg was fine he could move it, but when he felt for his left leg his hand felt a mass of pulp, a sticky warm mess of flesh, bone and blood. His leg was gone - blown away, yet he felt no pain.

German shelling had again erupted, aimed at the British lines. There was no retreat and to find cover was his main concern. Albert dragged himself forward and eventually fell into a muddy shell hole and lost consciousness.

The warmth of the pale November sun brought Albert Sumsion to his senses. At first he thought it was all a bad dream until he took stock of the situation. A sharp frost at night had helped the mud and blood to congeal around the stump of his leg and had stopped him from bleeding to death. He dared not move, for fear of breaking that cake of blood and mud, his back resting against the cold muddy side of that crater, up to his loins in mud. There was no activity, no shelling that morning and the only sound to reach Albert was the cry of a wounded comrade somewhere near by and that ceased at about midday. Gunfire by the late afternoon stopped any attempt at rescue and as night drew on he was resigned to spending another night in that shell hole. His leg was now aching, a dull throbbing ache that would allow no sleep and although he was very thirsty he felt no pangs of hunger.

Next day, his second in No Man's Land, brought rain. Thankfully not a downpour that would flood his crater but just enough trickled down the side for Albert to cup his hands and take a drink of muddy water. By the afternoon he wondered why it was so quiet with no shelling, no whiz-bangs or machine gun fire. Soon he was to know why for over the rim of that shell hole came a trickling of yellow vapour - Mustard Gas, the dread of all soldiers. The trickle turned into a flow as it rolled down the side of the crater. That flow petered out only minutes later to flow even faster and soon ever increasing puffs came rolling in and began to fill the crater. All of Albert's equipment lay scattered over a wide area of No Man's Land, no respirator, no first aid kit not even a piece of rag he could soak in the mud and hold to his face. He knew the deadly gas burnt out a man's lungs and innards and left large burning blisters on the flesh. Gradually the hole began to fill with gas. Albert made one last desperate attempt to save his life. He covered himself in mud. Twice the Somme mud was to save him; he smeared it over his face, head, arms and body; his leg and stump were already submerged in the mud. He put his left arm across his face so as to breath through the material of his tunic sleeve. The mud and sleeve acted as a filter but the mustard gas eventually penetrated and he coughed and spluttered. Gasping for air he took the gas down into his stomach. The coughing and convulsions brought intense pain to his stump but that cake of mud held firm and there was no bleeding. A fresh wind blew into his face and told him that the gas had dispersed. Another day drew to a close, by far his worst one. His stump ached, his good leg was numbed with the cold mud and his mouth, throat and stomach were burning and blistered.

There was no sleep that night or the next day and still no rescue teams came. Although the November sun did give some warmth his mouth and throat were dry. He tried to suck some mud to give relief but only made the burning pain worse. It was now his fourth night in the shell hole. He would welcome a German bullet or at least a prisoner of war camp for anything was better than this lingering death.

Luckily for Albert he could not sleep for in the early hours of the morning he heard voices. Whether they were British or German he was beyond caring. He tried to shout but no sound came from his burnt throat. He started to clap his hands this being the only sound he could make. This brought a face to the rim of the crater, then another, and another. Albert never knew who his rescuers were, they were British and that's all that mattered. They half carried, half dragged him back to the trenches and safety and still that cake of mud held firm. Even at the clearing station after they washed him all over and wrapped him in dry blankets that lump of mud was left on his stump and not until the operation was it removed.

Shipped back to England, Albert's war was over. He spent 18 months in Northampton Hospital for operations on his stump. Not until 1923 after many operations on his stomach, was Albert able to eat solid food. Albert's brother Arthur was killed on the same section in September just a few weeks before Albert arrived there. Albert Sumsion returned to the dock to work, but no more was he able to carry timber or grain. He had a tea and coffee stall by the low bridge and served the needs of the dock workers.

With only 3 inches of stump left, a heavy thick leather harness had to be fitted around his waist to hold on a stiff artificial leg. To walk, Albert had to swing his left hip around and that would throw his leg out in a circle. For all his disability he was one of the most cheerful pleasant and kind men one could ever wish to meet. Albert Sumsion died in October 1981 two months after his 90th birthday.

There is not enough space in this book to list all the valiant deeds of those young men from the Vale, of whom all too many never came back. Here to honour all those brave men are the names of the men from my parish of Hinton- just a small country parish, yet 31 men lost their lives:

W. Arnold, W. Allen, C. Bennett, A.Boxwell, R. Boys, J. Bennett, M. Cornock, H. Bick, S. Fields, F. Gasser, E. Gasser, P. Gasser, F. Gardiner, A. Gardiner, T. Gaston, E. Paul, A. Hore, W. Henrickson, W. Kilminster, G. Lambert, S. Morgan, D. Miles, R. Philips, E. Pople, A. Sumsion, J.W. Thomas, H. Smith, F. Smart and A. Rudge.

The first Serviceman to be killed was Private Samuel Morgan of Sanigar. He was killed in action at Cheuonnes, France on the 3rd of September 1914.

The Great War is now in the archives of history and other wars have been fought since, but that war fought in France was the bloodiest and most horrifying of all wars. In the five parishes of Berkeley 120 men and 1 woman lost their lives in the four years of war.

From the first onset the goal the Germans sought was Paris and the channel ports. To prevent this many thousands of lives were sacrificed.

The heroic defence of Verdun by the French at the price of unparalleled suffering and loss; the terrible battles around Ypres, Lens, Loos, Somme and Aisne these and many other equally memorable actions formed part of the stubborn defence which at last at great cost brought victory to the Allies.

The end of the war came in November 1918. The great attack of the Germans failed and the Allies seized the opportunity to counter attack which led to final victory. The news of an armistice was rumoured for several days but no one was sure of the actual time. People in the Sharpness district were told to listen for the blowing of the dock's steam whistle, in Berkeley the ringing of the Church bells.

At 11am on the 11th day of the 11th month the people of Sharpness, Newtown, Wanswell, Brookend, Purton and Halmore heard the welcome sound of the dock hooter - a sound that for years they had prayed for. People rushed into the streets, roads and lanes shouting, laughing, crying and dancing. The School Teacher Miss Tockam let the children out of Sharpness School to rush home and join in the street parties. Inns and Public Houses flung open their doors and people drank and made merry well into the early hours of the next day. The dead lay in neat rows in war cemeteries, while stones marked their graves, some known, many unknown. Kings and Generals pinned medals on soldiers, sailors and airmen while others less fortunate spent months or years, some all their remaining years, in hospitals, and for what? Albert Sumsion summed it all up in four simple words:-

"ALL THAT FOR NOTHING!"

THE AFTERMATH OF WAR

Soon the truth dawned on the people. The stories that the returning troops told and the wounded and maimed were evidence. The lists of the war dead were shown engraved on stone in churchyards or on village memorials. The one-legged man was learning to walk again, the one-armed man was trying to roll a cigarette or dig his garden, the blind man was feeling his way along streets he once ran and played in as a child, the man with his lungs burnt up with gas was trying to live a normal life but was unable to run, play football or cricket.

The Serviceman on his discharge returned to his place of employment. The Vale was mostly agriculture, factories at Dursley and Wotton were turned over to peace time production. The docks at Sharpness were still in full use and new faces appeared to replace lost work mates. But there were men with no jobs or homes to return to who drifted from town to town, village to village looking for hand-outs. These were joined by others as Britain slipped into a recession. "A land fit for heroes to live in" was a myth - a chestful of glimmering medals produced, no glistening coins in the pocket. They became the forgotten heroes singing or playing musical instruments on street corners until they were moved on to the next town by the police.

All too soon the man with work lost his job. Sharpness docks were empty of ships, the factories cut back on production and even the farms lacked money to produce the quality or quantity of food that was required to feed the people; food was rationed by price. The out of work dock workers took over unkept pieces of land and allotments to cultivate for food and to help relieve the boredom of idleness.

Farmers needed labour but could not afford the wages. A barter system grew out of the depression whereby a docker or out of work factory hand would lend a hand on the farm, helping with the planting, haymaking and harvesting, which in those days required a great many men and horses to operate; in exchange for his labour he was given a furrow in the ploughed field in which he could grow his potatoes, also he was given milk for his children, a tot of cider - the cellar door was forever open- a load of manure for his garden, the use of a pony and trap if the family had to travel any distance, apples at Christmas, the run of the land to pick mushrooms and blackberries, the setting of rabbit wires, and if a tree fell in a gale near his home it was his to saw up and cart home in the farm cart. Looking back it was a fair system when no-one had much money.

Some new houses were built for rent after the war but they lacked many domestic facilities - no running water, gas, electricity or drainage; lighting was by paraffin lamp, cooking was on a coal fire, there were no sinks and the waste water was thrown into the nearest ditch and there was certainly no bath. But the worst health hazard and the cause of many diseases such as diphtheria, scarlet fever and poliomyelitis was the toilet bucket which was emptied into a hole in the garden late at night (that's if one had a garden!). For those people living in Berkeley it was most humiliating, for a slurry cart came once a week and the bucket was carried out into the street and emptied into a horse drawn cart. If the house had no side entrance or passageway the bucket was brought out through the kitchen and living room. In summertime the smell was terrible as the flies buzzed round the open-topped slurry cart. People would turn about and walk the other way as the cart came down the road. This means of collecting sanitary waste lasted for many years throughout the Vale and not until sewers were laid through the villages and towns did this practice stop (about 1950).

In the Vale, between the two wars, there were very limited dust cart collections; in some villages there were none at all. People had little to throw away, the coal cinders were riddled and reused, the dust thrown on the garden and the problem of empty tin cans never arose as people could not afford to buy the few available products from the markets.

When anything was to be discarded, broken beyond repair or worn out, it was thrown into the nearest roadside pond or pool. People of those days were not pollution conscious and very often ditches and streams were littered with junk such as old prams, cycle wheels, jars and bottles.

One tends to forget the bad things and only remember the good and pleasant ones, and in the country the good things far out weigh the bad. The song of a thrush or blackbird on an early morning in Spring, or the nightingale in full voice at dusk, the waving grass in the gentle Summer breeze, grasses with heavy heads of seeds we no longer see in the meadows today, the smell of new mown hay, a blue carpet of bluebells under the great oaks of Tintock and Bushy Groves or a sunny bank of pale gentle primroses
(a sight all too rare these days!).

And in the Winter an elm tree glistening in the sun with a hoar-frost draping its branches, even the virgin white crisp snow that crunches under foot as one steps out to view the changing landscape after a night of snow.

Ten seconds, ten seconds the time it takes to read this sentence, and disaster would have been averted. In that ten seconds a goods train of 51 trucks would have been shunted safely into a siding at Charfield Station on the night of October 13th 1928 and the night mail train from Leeds to Bristol roaring down the track at 60 mph from Berkeley Road Station would have passed safely on its way, but fate had to play its little game. The express engine hit the tender of the goods engine as it was leaving the main line and ploughed off the track into the path of a goods train passing on the up line. The mail train landed on its side among the smashed empty wagons of the goods train and three carriages immediately behind the engine telescoped and struck the brickwork of the bridge. The hot coals from the engine were thrown along the track setting the carriages alight.

As the carriages in those days were lit by gas the gas cylinders beneath the carriages exploded adding fuel to the fire. Soon the scene was horrendous as carriage after carriage burst into flames. The passengers trapped by the legs and arms had no chance of escape despite the rescue attempts of the injured passengers, railwaymen and Charfield villagers. Screaming passengers pleaded for assistance but people had to stand by helpless, the heat being too intense for anyone to approach.

The Railway Tavern near the Station was used as a First Aid Post treating 30 injured passengers while 11 very gravely injured were rushed to the BRI Hospital. The outbuilding of the Tavern was turned into a mortuary. 16 people were killed that night and it took days before the 8 bodies already found could be identified. So charred were the remains that some could only be identified by bits of clothing a ring or some other personal item. Two children were never identified they were buried at Charfield and it will always remain a mystery why they were never claimed. It is said that as late as 1950 a woman dressed in black visited the graves once a year and laid flowers there. One man, a student, was known to be a passenger on the train but his body was never recovered. The engine driver and his fireman escaped injury mostly due to the coal from the tender falling on them and this stopped them from being thrown out onto the track.

An inquest held on October 31st cleared the signalman at the Charfield signal box of any fault and that confirmed that all his apparatus was in good order and that his signal was set at Red.

The engine driver of the express was committed for manslaughter despite his plea that the track was covered in patchy fog and he thought the lights were on green. For some unknown reason when the case appeared at Gloucester Assizes the case was dropped and he was discharged.

During the depression years of the early thirties a life line was thrown to the unemployed men of the Berkeley Vale which brought them out of the dole queue for a few pence above the rate of unemployment benefit. They had no option but to take the work; they were given a pick axe or a spade and were set the task of digging hundreds of holes across the face of the Vale - for electricity was arriving at last to towns and villages. Ugly constructions of steel frames appeared dotted across hill and dale and to the people they became known as electric pylons.

There was no objection to this from the population for they needed the power that the pylons would bring, power for home and power for factories, nor was there any objection from the conservationists of wild life and countryside, but nature herself objected.

The winters were the wettest for a number of years and floods occurred throughout Gloucestershire. Men worked up to their waists in mud and water, the holes for the footings of the pylons some to the depth of 12 to 15 feet were shorn up with timber shuttering which at times collapsed under the weight of mud, trapping men in the holes and workmates had to dig frantically to save them. Most nights the men returned home covered from head to foot in either red clay from the lowlands or yellow clay from the hills. Mud would be caked on their hair, face and body so that they were hardly recognisable. Life and limb were lost by labourers, steel erectors and cablemen.

In the Summer the weather was so hot and dry that the ground baked hard and man made little impression with the pick and spade. But West Midlands Power Company did arrive at last, though the electricity did not bring much needed industry.

Houses and shops were lit by electricity but the streets of Berkeley still had the lamplighter going around town on his bike putting on the gas lamps at dusk. There were no road or street lights from Berrycroft to Newtown except for just one lamp - a paraffin oil lamp at the road entrance to Berkeley Station. Newtown had gas lights, two on the footbridge were always alight right up until the bridge was demolished in the 1970's. The Station was lit by gas until it closed in 1967.

In the mid-thirties the timber trade at Sharpness began to improve. Throughout the long summer days one could hear the continuing sound of the dropping of timber planks (deals) sometimes on into the evening as dockers carrying timber on their shoulders ran along planks of wood supported on trestles to drop their load on a stack of timber sometimes as high as 25 feet and two hundred yards from the ship. Even with the protection of a leather pad on the shoulder the shoulder became chafed and scratched. A man was not classed as a deal carrier until he could proudly show a shoulder scarred and lumped with a large callous. Running up and down in rhythm with the movement of the planks these extremely fit men would carry in the course of a day about 5 tons of timber each.

Not many lived to a great age, they suffered from heart complaints in later life and many had hip displacements due to the hip joint wearing away from carrying such heavy loads.

One could always tell a deal carrier by his walk - his gait showing the drop of one shoulder and sometimes a limp.

Timber would also travel by rail, stacked into railway trucks and shunted into a siding. When the dockers' days work was finished the railway men took over the sheeting over of the timber with tarpaulins. The dock never fell silent until late at night. The trucks were labelled with their destination and shunted into different sidings; there was banging and clattering as buffer hit buffer, with the huffing and puffing of the small steam engines as they pushed and pulled their charges here and there as busy as a collie dog sorting out the sheep. Finally when their work was done the big railway company engines would roar in with a good head of steam and would hook up to the wagons and with the blowing of whistles and the waving of the guard's green lamp and the hissing of escaping steam, the wheels would slip as they tried to grip on the track as the heavy load was pulled up the incline towards Berkeley Road Station. The noise could be heard throughout the district except by the dockers who were asleep - the sleep of the exhausted.

THE MILK RACE

If the docker's life was a hard one, no less so was that of the farmer and farm labourer. He was up before the crack of dawn to trudge across the misty heavy early morning dew in summer or in the long winter months through thick mud or snow to bring in a herd of 30 cows to milk by hand in the draughty cowshed or even out in the open fields. The full milk churns were loaded onto milk floats pulled by the farm's fastest horse in the shafts. The farm worker would race down lane and road to be on the platform at Berkeley Road Station before 7am. 40 to 50 different types of carts would merge at the Station from as far as Dursley, Cam, Nibley, Alkington, Stone, Falfield, Slimbridge, Gossington, Halmore and Purton, all rushing at full speed down to Berkeley Road. Even in the dark winter mornings there were no lights on any of the floats.

Dead on time the Royal Mail train would pull into the Station and reverse into the loop line platform where the milk from Lydney, The Forest of Dean, Sharpness and Berkeley was already waiting (God only knew what time the Forest farmers milked to be able to have fresh milk at Berkeley Road at that time of the morning!). Empty churns were thrown out onto the platform and a mad scramble began as farm cart after cart rushed to unload their churns into the milk wagons in the few minutes allocated by the train's guard. With the blowing of the whistle the driver would release his steam lever and the engine would burst into life and in a few seconds only the red tail light would be seen as the train roared away to Gloucester and beyond leaving any late corners with their milk still on the platform or even still on the cart to be driven back to the farm and the enraged farmer.

These trains also carried livestock, cows, horses, sheep and pigs in open trucks destined for the markets of the Midlands and London.

To the farm worker the day was still young; in summer it was work until dusk when the last load of hay was brought to the rick or the last sheaf of wheat to the threshing machine.

The gentle giants, as the shire horses were affectionately called, their muscles on shoulders, legs and flank glistening with sweat, the harness stained white with body salt, heads bowed low, both horse and man near to exhaustion, the shires were led into their stables to be rubbed down with a sack or straw. They were fed on oats and hay and, when cooled down, watered, and then the harness was to be cleaned for the next days work.

In Winter the ditches had to be dug out by spade and shovel and hedges had to be trimmed and laid and manure spread over the field by dung cart with the farm worker spreading the heaps of manure by means of a dung fork.

The wages were very low, a good farm hand might get £1.5 shillings a week, a rent-free cottage and a pint of milk a day.

One of the most beautiful sights of power and beauty combined and yet frightening to see was a team of shire's sometimes as many as six horses in tandem, straining on the harness as they pulled the giant timber wagons laden with massive oak or elm trunks to the saw mills. A mare most probably led the team and with a foal dancing and running loose at her side she pranced along the country roads.

The early morning sunshine glistened on the brass of the harness and the cracking of the whips was soon drowned out by the noise of wood chopping and sawing as the woodcutters with their double handled cross-cut saws sang as they ripped through the oaks and elms.

The horses pulling the large tree trunks onto the wagons were again harnessed to pull the loaded wagons out of the fields onto the roads. The whips cracked as the horses strained at the large wooden wheels which bit into the soil and mud. The wheels were six feet high with thick wide steel rims sometimes up to the axles in mud. Teams from other wagons would hitch up to help pull the wagons clear. On the hard surface of the road the mare, led by the driver and four brake men - one for each wheel - set out on the return journey.

When the wagons approached an incline the horses were halted and chocks - large wooden wedges strengthened with iron bands - were put in front of the back wheels. If the hill was very steep chains fastened to the wagon were locked around the rim of the wheels to stop any movement of the wheel.

The front wheels had enough chain to allow freedom of movement for steering and the wagon slid down the hill with wheels locked and sparks flying from the steel rims.

A local character to be seen on the highways and byways of Gloucestershire in the twenties and thirties was "Bill" Browning of Berkeley.

Bill, now in his nineties, worked with horses nearly all his working life and he was stud groom for the Berkeley Heavy Horse Society. In 1921 Bill Browning walked his first stallion down the lanes of the Vale - a shire by the name of "Sudley King". Other shires followed over the years, shires with names Bill well remembers; "Theodore Bamrose", "Theodore Forster" and "Theodore Electric".

But Bill always had a soft spot for that first stallion he handled.

Bill Browning and his Gentle Giant

The start of the season was the 13th of April. With halter polished, the brass shining, and red and blue ribbons (prizes won in the show ring) flowing from the horse's mane, the midday feed of hay tied to the horse's back together with Bill's personal kit and bed roll, leaving Berkeley at 9am on a Monday this team of man and beast would walk 15 to 20 miles a day calling on farms wherever a mare was to be covered. They visited farms as far away as Newent, Gloucester, Stroud, King Stanley, Cam, Dursley, Yate, Chipping Sodbury and Thornbury, returning to Berkeley on Wednesday night and away again on Thursday to Saturday night staying at different farms overnight.

With the horse in the stable Bill slept in the loft; sometimes Bill had the luxury of a bed in the grooms' quarters, but not very often.

One hundred mares would be covered in a season. Mares would often kick out while the stallion was being handled. Bill had many near misses but could boast that he never had a hair kicked off his stallions and that was some achievement when one thinks of the size of those animals - 17 to 18 hands high and weighing 19 cwt.

Bill Browning's wages were good for that day and age, £2.10 shillings a week (£2.50) and 2 shillings and sixpence groom's money for every mare covered (to be paid to Bill on the day of service).

Bill could tell numerous tales of his adventures; some could not be repeated here, and others would take too much space but there is one lovely little story about Bill and his stallion.

Bill was travelling back to Berkeley after a tiring day, having wined and dined rather well (he assured me he only had two pints of cider!) and was making good time back when he spotted a gateway in Taits Hill. It was well carpeted with clover and thinking his horse could do justice to it he let the reins go and sat down with his back against the gate post. Soon Bill was nodding off to sleep and woke with the setting of the sun; his first concern was the safety of his stallion. He need not have worried for that big giant of a horse was lying by his side fast asleep.

With the coming of the Second World War, for Bill the walking of the stallions was finished. For eighteen years he had walked the lanes of Gloucestershire and now he was directed into war work at Draycott Mill, Cam. But the love of horses was too great for Bill to be without his four legged friends for long. After the war he joined the staff at Berkeley Hunt Kennels and on his retirement at the age of 65 he again took up stallion walking but by this time the age of the gentle giants had ebbed away. The stallions were now thoroughbred hunting horses belonging to Stockwood Stud Farm, Worcester.

He then walked the stallions through Worcestershire and Oxfordshire.

ELVERING

The elver season started in November after the boiling of the Christmas puddings. For during those long Winter months plans were laid for the next season's elver net. The kitchen table was hastily cleared of the remains of the evening meal, the wick of the paraffin lamp was turned up, pen, paper, pencil and ruler came into play as new ideas for a new super net took shape- light in weight, easy to manoeuvre and able to catch more elvers with less effort. New sheets of perforated zinc were purchased, a strong frame built and the net took shape with new ropes and guys rigged, and a new bucket was bought and strong bags or pillow cases were made ready. All that was needed was an early Spring, reasonable weather, a slow tide and a glut of elvers.

In those far off days elvering was a way of life, handed down from father to son. The secrets were closely guarded - What time to fish? What place to go at different times? Old Dock, Entrance to dock, lock or basin, daytime or night-time? Night elvering was an experience never to be forgotten.

A walk down to the dock at dusk, stopping in Bayhill to listen to the nightingale, owls fluttering low from the overhanging branches of the large elms, the bats flying through the rows of the highly stacked sweet-smelling pine timbers.

As one approached the dockside the smell of seaweed and the sound of the incoming tide as it lapped against the stout timbers of the piers could be heard, the winking lights of the few navigation lights broke the dark void that was the Severn Estuary

Then the lapping of the tide was broken by a low purr that grew louder by the minute, and as one peered out into the darkness first one green light appeared then another and another until the River seemed full of green lights reflecting eerily on the water. Suddenly one by one green turned to red as the navigation lights on the small river craft swung from starboard to port as they turned to enter between the piers; they were the barges and small petrol tankers of Shell Mex, B.P., Cleveland, John Harker and Severn Carrying Company.

They all came under the soft glow of the pier lights, changing the ghostly silhouettes into reality. The gleaming paintwork and polished brass and the clean and tidy appearance showed the pride that those Severn faring men had in their boats.

Of course elvering at the entrance came to a stop while docking was in progress. It was a time to stop for a thermos of tea, the elvers' bucket if full was to be emptied into a sack and left in the grass to drain out the water and running repairs were done to the net.

Elvers were cleaned and sold at sixpence a pound (2p) and were in great demand at the beginning of the season, but as the season wore on the demand grew less and elvers were taken farther afield.

The Public Houses in the Cotswolds did a roaring trade on a Saturday night as the elver "Kings" carrying their buckets of elvers on their bicycles called at "The Black Horse", North Nibley, "The Swan" at Wotton, "The Plough" at Charfield, "The Yew Tree" at Stinchcombe, Berkeley Arms" at Cam and "The Star" in Dursley.

THE COSTA SEVERN

If one took a stroll along the Severn shoreline today one would perhaps see a man exercising his dog or someone collecting driftwood. The desolate foreshore at Sharpness is littered with jetsam of this modern age - plastic bottles, old plastic buckets, sheets of white polythene brought in by the tide and deposited on the tide water mark to be blown by the western winds into fields and hedges.

break, have died of Dutch Elm Disease and have never been replaced. Now void of trees and bushes the banks stand bare and naked. The only birds to be seen are squawking gulls as they fight over the effluent deposited in the sewer beds, and the wild sea birds feeding at the end of the outflow pipe.

Sharpness Docks 1920

Old car tyres, plywood boxes, milk crates, a dump of junk is washed ashore by wind and tide. Broken glass bottles, a menace to man and beast, have smashed against the stones of the breakwater and concrete banks. With the banks strengthened and widened the old elms (planted by the Lord Berkeleys years ago) to stop subsidence of the sea wall and also to act as a wind

On the skyline stand two nuclear power stations that blot the landscape; no-one decades ago even their wildest imagination or dreams would have thought this possible.

For those people of yesteryear the Severn shore was their playground, their seaside, where they held picnics during the hot summer evenings and lit fires with driftwood in a ring of stones. With the kettle boiling on the stones, tea, sandwiches and cakes were consumed by hungry children. The frying pan sizzled with Alpass's prime (my own) sausages and potatoes baked in the embers of the dying fire (people call it a barbeque today). Cricket and rounders were played by one and all and children's swings hung from the huge boughs of the elms. Dancing took place, or if one was less energetic one just sat on the grass and listened to the new modern portable gramophone playing the latest records. The small children played in the muddy pools left by the last tide while older children explored the rocks, stones and seaweed beds for small crustaceans. With the river in flood everyone would retreat to the safety of the shore, for they all had respect for the mighty Severn and only when high water was reached and the water lost its pace did the brave venture in for a swim and the children were allowed to paddle at the waters edge.

The dark smudge on the horizon of the estuary became a column of smoke; this gave way to a moving blur. Slowly this vision took on the shape of a ship, the white upper structure showing against the backcloth of trees; then the small tugs came into focus for this would be one of the large steamers with its escort of three or four tugs on route for Sharpness, bringing trade to the port. The resulting work guarantee docker at least three weeks work if it was a timber ship but far less if it carried grain.

Crowds would gather along the shore or near the piers to watch the seagoing tugs manoeuvre the large steamer around for the bow to enter between the two piers. The rear tugs would release the tow ropes and with a blast on the whistle would steam at full speed back down the river followed by the bow tugs as they raced to catch the leading tug. With the turning of the tide, the wind freshening and the night growing chilly people extinguished the fires, packed the kettle and picnic basket into prams, collected up their rubbish in bags and leaving the place neat and tidy would trudge home contented with a pleasant day. Only the courting couples were left, lying hidden in the tall grass, oblivious to all!

THE BIG SHIPS

In 1928 the SS "Wimborne", a ship carrying 8,714 tons of grain, had the biggest cargo to discharge at Sharpness.

Her draft after lightening was over 22 feet and the tidal basin had to be flooded to give sufficient volume of water to raise the ship over the sill. This was achieved by sand-bagging the top of the outer gates to stop the overspill of water. Water pumped into the canal at Gloucester brought the water level up enough and she entered the dock. The Wimborne was 3,689 net registered tons, her length was 415 feet, beam 55 feet 5 inches and her draft was 24 feet 10 inches.

SS "Wiire" carried 2,100 standards of timber to Sharpness in July 1934 (a standard is 165 cubic feet). She carried the highest deck of cargo of timber to be discharged in the port.

The height of the timber stacked on the deck was 22 feet.

A Finlander, she returned on July 11th 1937 with 6,500 tons of wheat. Her former names were - "Charterholme", "Northway", "Tempestuous" and "Hornfels". Her length was 400 feet, beam 50 feet, draft 28 feet 5 inches and 3,525 gross tons. The SS "Essex Noble" discharged 2,202 standards of timber and the "Kastelholm" discharged 2,388 standards of timber.

Big Ships:-

	Tons	Length in feet	Beam in feet	Draft in feet
Assyria	4,104	450.6	55.2	19.6
Barenfels	3,419	416.3	53.9	24.4
Carlow Castle	3,708	400.0	53.0	19.7
Cainhill	3,296	400.6	52.0	24.0
Clan Macgillivray	3,107	430.6	53.6	18.0
Clan Macpherson	3,041	400.0	51.0	23.6
Clara Camus	4,461	435.0	54.0	17.4
Dalhanna	3,512	408.0	55.0	14.0
Essex Noble	3,893	370.0	51.7	22.8
Gleneden	3,018	350.0	51.1	23.9
Hathkola	4,318	285.0	51.2	21.0
Jeff Davies	3,797	395.6	55.0	23.6
King Robert	3,615	400.0	53.0	16.0
Kurdiston	3,863	380.1	53.5	22.6
Lavington Court	4,080	420.0	54.0	19.10
Mottisfont	4,228	400.5	52.0	22.6
Paris City	3,959	412.0	55.0	18.6
Polenzo	3,997	412.0	55.6	15.3
Seang Bee	3,784	445.5	49.1	25.0

Taibun Maru	4,099	415.0	55.5	16.5
Wentworth	3,210	401.0	52.0	18.6
Wimborne	3,689	415.0	55.5	24.10

The ship that became a part of the landscape of Sharpness was the SS "Dundrennan". She arrived on December 16th 1929 from Argentina with a load of grain. After discharging, owing to the depression she was laid up at the green bank near the low bridge. There she stayed for five years with two local men taking turns as watchmen until she was bought by the Greeks and renamed the "Argentina".

The SS Argentina arrived back at Sharpness on December 27th 1936 with 7,500 tons of grain but not without incident, for a tow rope parted from a tug and she turned and ran aground on the rocks off Sharpness Point. All efforts by the towing tugs to drag her clear failed. In the next few days several unsuccessful attempts to free her were made. Seven-sea-going tugs had lines aboard - they were "Islegarth", "Plumgarth", "Reagarth", "Corgarth", "West Winch", "Bristolian" and "Merrimac" and the Sharpness tug "Resolute" stood by in case of emergency.

The only way to save the ship and the cargo was to lighten her of some of her cargo and hope she would float clear but first her sprung rivet holes were plugged with wooden plugs - this was to stop the sea water from damaging the grain. Next, barges had to be brought alongside and the grain grabbed out and into the barges but a snag arose because the barges could not lie in tight to the ship

SS Argentina and Tugs

(the jutting rocks around the hull prevented this); men were brought over from the Forest of Dean quarries - men who were explosive experts - to blow away the rocks, then with the rocks level the barges could move into position. In the meanwhile large holes were dug in the mud on the foreshore and bulks of timber 12 feet in length and 14 inches square were lowered lengthways into the trenches with ropes attached; they ran out to the ship to secure her in case she broke free of the rocks on a high tide.

On the 10th of February 1937 at about 6am all was ready. The tugs Bristolian, Corgarth, Merrimac and the salvage tug Ranger had tow lines aboard the Greek ship. Again the tug Resolute hovered in attendance. With the tugs at full steam the Greek ship was pulled clear of the rocks, the remainder of her cargo was discharged once she was safe in the dock. An inspection was made of the damage, her bottom was found to be badly damaged, with twisted frames and buckled plates so she was towed to Newport to the breakers yard and broken up.

After the salvage operation the large bulks of timber were dug out of the mud and sold to make deck planks for the barque "King". Later she finished her life in the graveyard at Purton.

The "Stig", a three mast schooner, lost part of her deck cargo whilst docking (1931). The Captain blamed the docking crew for the accident and getting no satisfaction at Sharpness he decided to go to the head office at Gloucester. He could not get a taxi to take him there so he borrowed Mr Jack Evans' bicycle and rode there to make a protest to the dock authority.

He paid Jack two shillings and sixpence for the hire of the bicycle.

On June 10th 1937 a large crowd stood on the foreshore to watch the last of the windjammers

Viking in Dry Dock

arrive at Sharpness; even without her sails billowing in the wind the "Viking", assisted by tugs, was a graceful sight as she swung round off the piers.

Loaded with 4,000 tons of wheat from Australia, when she was on her berth at Severn Ports her masts stood higher than the new silo.

The Viking entered the dry-dock for a bottom scrape on July 3rd and on the 6th while in the tidal basin prior to sailing on the 7th she was opened to the public and when she sailed she carried seven paying passengers. The Viking is now a training ship for sea cadets in Gothenburg Harbour, Sweden.

The following are some interesting extracts from Mr Woolard's works diary - Mr Woolard was foreman engineer far the Dock Company:-

July 18th 1932
> Monday. Passenger steamer to Ilfracombe with 500 passengers, mostly from the Midlands.

August 3rd 1932
> Passenger steamer "Brittania" fog bound at Sharpness.

August 25th 1932
> Greek ship "Sty branios" lost anchor in the dock entrance.

August 28th 1932
> SS "Kia" entered basin after running aground outside the South pier.
> Struck pier, damage to repair £20.
> SS "Nicke" bunkered 260 tons of coal.
> Fitted Tanker "Paso of Ling" with flood lights so she could navigate the canal at night.
> "Paso Metford" damaged her floodlights, cost to repair £40.
> Steamer "Loke" bunkered with 400 tons of coal.

December 15th 1932
> Thursday. Steamer "Heathfield" struck South pier.

December 20th 1932
> SS "Dundrennan" bunkered.

January 3rd 1933   Severe: Gales.

May 1933
> Rise in wages, wages for sawer - one shilling and five pence per hour.
> Wages for timberman- two pounds for 48 hour week.

May 26th 1933 Friday.
> SS Dundrennan on fire. Brigade called out at 3.55.
> Fire float alongside playing on fire with three deliveries.
> Position of fire - the store room under the poop deck, oil and paint burning rapidly,
> got fire under control or would have been serious.

May 29th 1933
> Musk rat killed at Old Dock, satisfied dock company as to identity.

June 9th 1933 Friday.
> Ministry of Health called to Old Dock to check out rat menace, also checked
> Marshfield pools and various places on canal.

June 12th
> Another musk rat reported at old dock. Ministry men hunting musk rats on the canal.

December 27th 1936
> SS "Argentina" aground. Paid men £1 a tide to assist in rigging up a grab.

TRAFFIC ENTERTAINMENT AND THE CINEMA

Road traffic was on the increase after the First World War. Lorries and cars were replacing carts and carriages. Roads were numbered outwards from London, from the A1 across country to be our own A38 - the longest country lane in the country; a narrow twisting road with high hedges and overhanging trees, it stretches from the Midlands to the South coast. Villages like Cambridge, Newport and Stone and Falfield were cut in two by the ever increasing fast-moving traffic. People more used to the slow moving carts found it hard to adjust; one took one's life at great risk crossing this road. In the twenties and thirties road improvements were made. Roads were made wider, dangerous bends were straightened, the old turnpike houses were demolished and white road markings and hazard signs were painted on the roads.

More road traffic moved from Sharpness Dock which was never built to accommodate the use of road haulage and had no road to support it. The road from the A38 was a mere country lane, a winding lane overhung with massive elms and oak, with boughs thicker than a man's body, which formed an archway over the road.

"Barnets Corner" (note narrow lane to Newtown)

The Berkeley Vale

No worse a place was there than Baylane - between Wanswell and Newtown.

Dark and eerie in daytime and a place to be avoided at night, with ponds at the edge of the lane without any fencing, so many people walked into them and some were drowned.

In the early thirties the large trees were grubbed out, the roots and stumps were dumped into the ponds and these were filled in. Bends were taken out, the roads widened, and tops of hills were taken off. A pavement was made from Berkeley to Sharpness and the road under the railway arch at Berkeley Station was lowered to give more headroom, but this still restricted traffic to the dock. Transport had either to travel through Newtown and up Station Road (Oldminster Road) or through the old coach road from Brookend. From the coach road junction with Station Road, the road to the Station and down over the viaduct and the high bridge was Railway property and its main purpose was the movement of railway goods.

Severn Mills Limited, the manufacturers of "Sharpex" Cattle, Pig and Poultry food, was in full production supplying farms throughout the county with much of its animal feed - most of it travelling by road transport. Severn Port exported grain to flour mills via lorries. One fleet of lorries caused a stir as they chugged along the new roads with black smoke billowing from a large black funnel protruding through the cab roof, a fire box between the front wheels, the embers glowing red as they puffed their way from Sharpness to Draycott Mill at Cam loaded high with bags of wheat, the words "Workman Bros" written in gold lettering across the front of the cab advertising these steam wagons of Cam Flour Mill. Frequent stops were made at farmyard pools to take on water for the thirsty boilers.

ENTERTAINMENT

Until the coming of the cinema the people of the Vale had to make their own entertainment. Football was always strong in the Vale, with Sharpness and Berkeley having two of the top teams in the district. The rivalry between those two clubs was so intense that often violence not only on the playing field but among supporters of both teams would break out and would even spill over into the pubs at night. After a local derby match brothers or cousins in opposite teams would not speak for weeks. Cracked heads and split lips even occurred on the dockside weeks after a match.

In the 1930's the Union Church at Newtown had its own football team. Their home ground was up the old lane on the way to Berkeley (by the sub electric station). Brookend had a successful team and their pitch was up Lip Lane at Damesdown. Halmore also had a team, a hard team that took a lot of beating (Halmore Hornets). Their headquarters was the "Fox and Goose" inn.

All these teams played on the local farmers' fields and it was not unknown for the groundsman to spend the morning before a match removing cow pats. George Conway the local cobbler at Sharpness made the leather footballs for most of the local teams.

Purton ladies' hockey team was also prominent on the field. Both Berkeley and Sharpness could boast of having tennis courts and the Pier View Hotel was one of the few places to have a bowling green complete with floodlights and electric generator. The Railway and Severn Bridge Hotel had a dance-hall and held regular dances there.

Most villages had a cricket team; one popular venue was Purton. Cricket as played out on the foreshore in front of the Berkeley Arms inn where refreshment could be taken in the form of the local brew - a strong cider, a lethal dose to the unwary! An exciting hit for six would put the ball out into the Severn or through the bar window. Wally Hammond, Billy Neale and many of the Gloucestershire cricket team of the thirties practised against these local teams. At Sharpness in the winter when the docks were idle and the timber sheds empty of timber, the dockers could earn beer money by bowling on the concrete floor to Wally and his friends at the rate of 6 balls a penny.

Purton could lay claim to a race course. The Purton Derby was raced on a straight mile from The Royal Drift to near the Berkeley Arms inn. The short foreshore grass was ideal for such a venue. One well known owner and trainer was Denny Allen of Sanigar. His jockey Ern Denning had many successes for this stable and was always a safe each way bet. At one meeting there was heavy betting on one particular horse with a certain bookie. Now country folk may be slow but they are not daft.

Mr Oliver Hughes and Mr Curly Spiers were detailed to watch this bookie and to thump him if he did not pay up. Suddenly the bookie was missing, he was spotted running up the road towards the Berkeley Hunt inn with Oliver and Curly in hot pursuit. The swing bridge was opened so the bookie dived in the canal and swam for the far bank quickly followed by his pursuers. They caught up with him as he ran up Pick's Hill and grabbed his money bag, gave him a good hiding, turned him upside down, shook all the money out of his pockets and sent him on his way penniless!

Greyhound racing was also a popular sport in the Vale. Flapper tracks they were called; one such track was at Wanswell near Sissons. Portable generators lit up the track and the "hare" was operated by a cable connected to a drum driven by the back axle on a jacked up lorry.

For one week in the middle of Summer the roads and lanes in the Berkeley Vale were blocked with decorated lorries, floats and cars. It was Berkeley Hospital Carnival Week. The lorries toured from village to village collecting money to support the running of the Hospital and brought colour and gaiety to the quiet villages and hamlets. The final night was Saturday in the market place at Berkeley where all the decorated floats and tableaux were lined up for judging. Much time, a lot of thought, energy and money were put into their making;

wonders were worked with wood, canvas and coloured paper. After the judging the good folk of Berkeley would let their hair down and the market square was filled with dancing and singing. There was no traffic moving through Berkeley that night. The people of the Vale were proud of their hospital and did everything possible for its up-keep. Dances, whist drives, football matches, product shows and sporting events all brought coppers to the coffers of the administrators.

Berkeley Show on August Bank Holiday Monday (the first Monday in August) drew large crowds to the show ground. People from as far away as Gloucester and Bristol came; trains off-loaded hundreds of passengers from the Forest of Dean with the Foresters walking from Berkeley Station to the Show Ground, calling in at the pubs on route. Held on what is now called the old showground, the parade of giant shires was always an attraction. There was a display in the main ring, sometimes an army horse-drawn team, a marching band and of course horse jumping. The beer tent was always crowded for this was the one day in the year when one could drink from ten in the morning until ten at night (and some did!). As the day wore on fights often broke out between rival gangs from different villages and often spilled over into the public houses at night.

Berkeley Horticultural Show was held on the last Saturday of August and was a much more leisurely and domesticated affair. The venue was the Berkeley Football Field at Station Road. The competition between the rival gardeners for the best vegetable and flowers was very keen. The marquees were full of beautiful flowers of garden, green-house and hedgerow. The vegetable tent full of garden produce was the envy of the not too successful gardener whose parsnips and carrots never reached more than four or five inches, let alone the magical 12 inches or more. The ladies were not to be outdone, with a wonderful display of cakes, needlework, knitting and wine-making. The fair in the evening with its steam-driven roundabouts, the wonderful sound of the steam organ, high swings, side shows, coconut shies, ginger snap stalls, cockle stall, fish and chips and the dazzling display of coloured electric lights gave a fairy like atmosphere to liven up the lives of both young and old for a few hours.

CINEMA

The first show was held in the yard at the back of The Mariners Arms in Berkeley in the year 1919. Held under canvas, to give ventilation the canvas sides would not reach the ground by about a foot which made the legs and feet cold in chilly weather. But people flocked to see this new flickering silent picture show. The first film shown was called "Rebecca" which was made at Chepstow using the Castle and grounds for the film setting. The next cinema in Berkeley was a wooden shed again ventilated by canvas vents at floor level, but now they could be rolled down in inclement weather. The site was where the Health Centre now stands. After a new brick cinema was built in High Street the old one was converted into a garage cum workshop by Mr Tommy Brooks, a local inventor. The new cinema was down an alleyway behind Number 32 High Street and was owned and operated by Mr Allan Mason. Films with names like 'The Clutching Hand" or the "Black Ace" would run as a serial week after week until one forgot what the beginning was about.

By the year 1938 a new modern cinema was built for Mr Mason in Marybrook Street. Shirley Temple starred in that first film shown, called "Heidi". In the 1920's about the same time as the wooden cinema was operating in Berkeley a cinema was also held at the church rooms in Newtown. The films drew a full house and people walked from outlying districts in all winds and weather to follow serials of Tarzan and the Apes or to watch Pearl White, Buster Keaton or the Keystone Cops. It ran under the auspices of the church and Parson Clark would take the money at the door (2 pence each)and he would in general keep the boys in order. Mr Tom Hicks operated the projector from a room above the entrance door.

Mr Matt Francis worked the gas engine to generate the electricity from a shed behind the outside gent's toilets. Lily Hoare or Lottie Lightfoot played the piano accompanied by Mr Skidmore on the violin. As these were silent films these performers had to adapt to the mood of the film, a no mean feat, where without rehearsal they had to watch the film and change the music to suit the film part, from a waltz for a love scene to cowboy music for a western. Two films were shown with a break in between. During the break the boys sitting in the front row would troop outside to the toilet and on returning to their seats they would bring in their friends who could not afford the admission fee. Instead of 20 boys to a row there would be 30 all squeezed together. The Vicar knew what was happening but turned a blind eye. (not until St. Andrew's Church moved to Newtown was the projector removed from its concrete base).

One of the treats for the children of the Berkeley schools in the thirties came towards the end of the summer term when both juniors and seniors were invited to the Castle for tea with the Countess of Berkeley. Track sports for both schools were played on the lawn under the shadows of the large scotch pines. A conjurer and Punch and Judy show were offered as light entertainment and school plays and folk dancing that had been rehearsed for weeks before now took place beneath those red sandstone Castle walls. Tea was taken in the marquee where cakes, buns, jellies and lemonade were consumed in record time and then to close the afternoon as a special thank you to the Countess all the children sang her favourite hymn "Jerusalem".

Sharpness was in a fortunate position by being built near water. It had many good swimmers among its inhabitants and when the old dock closed in 1926 a swimming club was formed and it took over the old levelling lock as a swimming pool. Competitions in racing, high diving and water polo became regular features on a summer's afternoon and evening. The high-light of these galas was the mile race. Starting at the old dock the course was to the Severn Railway swing bridge (over the canal) and back with supporters lining the canal tow path cheering on their favourite. The old donkey stables once used to house the tow horses and donkeys were now the changing rooms. School children were taught to swim in this old lock but as the water was too deep (15ft to 20ft) a band of canvas was passed around the chest and attached to a rope on the end of a pole, the child would jump into the water and was supported by the rope and the pole, the instructor walking along the edge of the pool while the learner thrashed about in safety some six foot out in the pool.

Marshfield, better known as the timber pond, was the site of another swimming pool. Water lilies, bulrushes and pond weeds that could endanger a swimmer were kept cut back to the edge of the swimming area; a couple of changing huts and a diving board were all that was needed for this natural pool. With the depth of water varying from 3 feet to 9 feet it was comparatively safe for children to learn to swim and many took advantage of the excellent coaching; available. The dreaded "Means Test" whereby a Government snooper could check the homes of the unemployed and make the householder sell anything that was not necessary to the bare living standard (e.g. piano, wireless set, gramophone, carpets etc.) before he could claim extra benefits was now becoming rare; the depression was on the decline.

The new leader of Germany started to rant and rave, people in Europe lived in fear; Germany re-armed at an incredible pace. The red swastika of the Nazis and the black cross of the Luftwaffe were seen over the Berkeley Vale on a quiet Sunday afternoon in the mid thirties, as an airship - the Graf Zeppelin-flew slowly down the Vale passing over Purton, Brookend, Wanswell, Berkeley and on down the Bristol Channel. People stood in silence as the graceful ship sailed by. A few ex-servicemen shook their fists in the air and to the children going to Sunday School it was very exciting and they shouted and waved,

little realising it was the shape of things to come.

Ship building and industry in general improved and the trade at Sharpness Docks in grain and timber rose. Timber was needed to build the new aircraft hangars that mushroomed in the Cotswolds and the Severn Valley. The Power Petrol Company already had a depot on the east bank of the tidal basin and a sizeable trade in carrying petrol developed. Off loaded into five large storage tanks enclosed in a high concrete compound, fuel was transported in road tankers to Walsall in the Midlands. The green petrol tankers were a familiar sight on the roads in the Vale. This trade was enlarged upon with petrol barges travelling from Avonmouth to Gloucester and on up the Severn to Worcester and Stourport.

A new grain silo was built in 1936 out of the ruins of a brick warehouse that was gutted by fire on bonfire night 1934. With a capacity for storing 10,000 tons of grain this new silo vastly improved the grain trade. Unrest on the Continent of Europe erupted into the Spanish Civil War and was brought close to the people of Sharpness on a Spring day in 1939 when they heard the firing of rifles on a Spanish ship in the dock as crew members fought crew members for the control of the ship. Franco supporters were trying to shoot the loyal crew and armed police were rushed to the dock quay where they too came under fire from the ship. Eventually the Spanish Consul from Bristol arrived and with an armed police escort boarded the ship and restored order.

Saturday February 4th 1939 brought home to all who used the River Severn the risk that was involved in navigating its waters. For on that Saturday night six men lost their lives in the River:- Reginald Stokes of Gloucester, Granville Knight of Saul, Charles Phillips of Purton, Joubert Matthews of Pitbrook, George Butler of Epney and Walter Caperner of Clifton, Bristol. All were crew members of three barges travelling from Avonmouth to Gloucester. The "Severn Traveller", "Severn Carrier" and the "Severn

Pioneer", all owned by The Severn and Canal Carrying Company Ltd of Birmingham, were loaded with petrol and fuel oil.

The "Traveller" was towing the other two barges and while swinging around at the pier-head prior to entering the dock tragedy overtook them. It seems the tankers were put out of control by the state of the tide, for it was a Severn Bore tide which swept them towards the pillars of the Severn Railway Bridge. The skipper of the "Traveller" Albert Tonks noticed the tow rope was slack and realised it had parted from the "Carrier". He rounded up the other two barges in an effort to take off the crews, two of the barges hit the bridge and all three capsized.

Mr Tonks of Gloucester and Mr Fred Vincent of Olveston were flung into the water, but as the "Traveller" righted itself they managed to climb back on board. The members of the other crews were swept away and disappeared in the dark waters of the Severn. The two men, Tonks and Vincent, drifted on up the River in the doomed "Traveller". Their cries for help were heard by Mr Lionel Keedwell of the Berkeley Arms Inn at Purton who rowed out in his boat to try and save them but had to turn back to the shore or he too would have been lost in that rush of water. Mr Keedwell's father had already raised the alarm and five local men from Purton rowed out to the barge and took off the two men when the "Traveller" ran aground.

Meanwhile, at Sharpness a hastily gathered crew of tug-men boarded the tug "Resolute" and put out to assist the tankers. The first tanker they found was the "Pioneer" being carried by the ebbing tide towards Bull Rock (Berkeley Pill). Captain Oliver Powell and Mr C. Turl jumped on board and in the darkness searched for the crew but found no one aboard. In the cold light of the early morning the next day the "Carrier" was found overturned some distance out in the River at a point midway between the Bridge and Sharpness Point.

Upturned Carrier towed into Sharpness Docks

WORLD WAR II - 1939 September 3rd

We all knew that war was imminent in those last few days of August but we prayed for a miracle to happen and that war could be averted. It came as a great shock to me on Friday 1st of September to glance skywards and see a German aircraft flying over Sharpness.

On that same Friday at about 10.30am the visibility was poor with a low cloud base of probably 150 feet when through a break in the clouds I saw a plane, or was it a plane? For it had an oval shaped fuselage, grey in colour with plenty of cockpit window space and it was hovering (like a dragonfly) with blades revolving about the fuselage. (With hindsight I know now it was a helicopter or the forerunner of one). But what amazed me more than this weird uncanny flying machine was the marking on the fuselage just behind the cockpit - the black cross of Germany and towards the tail the red swastika of the Nazis. I heard no engine noise because the noise of the working at Severn Mill drowned it out. It was in full view for at least 30 seconds over the then entrance stores before veering away to disappear in clouds over the railway lines towards Newtown. I would have dismissed this as an apparition or a figment of my imagination if Mr Era Barrett of Wanswell had not shouted to me and pointed skyward. "There's a bloody jerry up there" he shouted. Mr Barrett was checking numbers on railway trucks in Severn Mill's siding,

Captured enemy documents at the end of the war revealed that German aircraft were active in the Bristol Channel and Severn Estuary before the start of World War II (August 29 - September 1st). Survey Map - Flugplate Yate 10-284 showed photographs of both Parnell's and Newman's of Yate with the airfield clearly indicated, also the railway tracks from Gloucester to Thornbury and Yate. The Severn Bridge and Sharpness were also clearly marked.

On the 3rd of September at 11am we heard on the radio that "We are now at war with Germany" to quote the Prime Minister's words. People were calm but apprehensive as to what the future held. They listened intently to the radio and they also listened out for the drone of the Dorniers, Junkers and Heinkels of Göering's Luftwaffe but these were otherwise occupied over Poland. 285 aircraft were lost over the skies of Poland with only 413 aircrew killed. After this action the Luftwaffe combat units pulled pack to the rear bases in Germany to rest and refit. This was a time of waiting and preparing for the battles yet to come, the period known as the 'Phoney War'.

Petrol was rationed on September 16th and was known as "Pool Petrol" at one shilling and sixpence (7p) a gallon. Gas and electricity for domestic consumers were limited to 75% of the corresponding quarter of the year ending in June. Coal was rationed to two tons a year and heavy fines of £100 or 3 months in jail were brought in for failing to observe the blackout. On that first Sunday of the war people looked skywards at the first sound of an aircraft; everyone expected the sky to be filled with planes both German and British but things were very quiet in the Vale. The first touch of war came in the evening with the testing of the blackout. Windows were blacked out, cars and cycles used dim headlights and the night was dark and still.

For the farmers it was a busy time with good autumn weather, and the harvest of wheat, barley and oats was safely gathered in. The potato crop was a good one and was stored away in frost-proof sheds or even under the stairs, for this precious crop, if all else failed, could sustain the family through the months ahead. Fruit of the orchard and hedgerow was bottled or made into jam or wine while the sugar was still available.

Autumn gold turned to winter grey and from Christmas day the temperature began to drop and by January the 21st it fell to 2° below Zero 30 degrees of frost. This weather lasted until February the 18th - the coldest winter since 1895. But not all was lost to the gloom of war and winter.

The winter sun glistened on the icebound trees and the laughter of children and grown ups could be heard coming from Wanswell Court where the moat was frozen over and was put to good use as an ice rink. Dozens of children made slides on the ice or if they possessed skates ice hockey was played. The farmer provided mugs of hot cider laced with ginger for the watchers (a collection was taken for Berkeley Hospital) but for the over-heated hockey players a jar of ice-cold cider left on the draw-bridge was very welcome. Conditions were very bad for travellers, branches of overhanging trees snapped with the weight of the ice and crashed into the roadways impassable due to the icy conditions.

On the war front things were quiet but not still. A.R.P. First Aid and Rescue crews practised and fire fighting services were formed and manned day and night. April the 9th saw an end to the Phoney War.

Without warning Germany struck out at the unsuspecting Denmark and Norway and by May 10th they attacked Holland and Belgium, and the allies began to retreat.

The British turned towards Dunkirk where by the morning of June 4th 338,226 men had been snatched to safety.

Once the Dunkirk evacuations were over the main body of the Luftwaffe turned its attention to Britain and by July 17th could put up 2,600 aircraft.

ENEMY ACTION IN AND AROUND THE VALE

The Home Guard was formed although at that time it was known as the L.D.V. - Local Defence Volunteers. They trained with broom handles for rifles, had practically no weapons and only a few farmers had shot guns and bottles filled with petrol. Older men who could remember the Somme and even the Boer War trained alongside young men not yet old enough to know the horrors of war.

July 1st 1940 was the day they received their first alert. Road blocks were set up - barbed wire on wooden frames was dragged across the roads. All roads in the Vale were manned and every traveller was checked for identity. Parachutists had been seen to land on Stinchcombe Hill; extensive searches were made but no evidence of enemy landings or actions were reported. Later it was found that a freak whirlwind had whipped up the haycocks into the air and at that time with the invasion of England foremost in people's minds it was easy for the imagination to run wild!

Folk in the Dursley and North Nibley districts did not need any imagination when at 10.15pm on the 4th of August four high explosive bombs of 100lbs each were dropped in fields at Waterly Bottom. No damage was reported - could these bombs have been dropped in the wrong valley? Could they have been intended for Lister's works just the other side of Stinchcombe Hill?

Bombs had already fallen at Gloucester, Quedgeley and Beveston when on August 3rd the first bombs to fall in the Vale landed on the telephone exchange at Falfield. On August 11th at 11.45pm six high explosive bombs were dropped at Pitbrook, Wanswell, near by, a few days to the last enemy action by a foreign power which took place in the Vale - in the year 903-1,037 years ago (the battle of Wan swell Green). The bombs damaged a farmhouse at Haines and a few houses in Pitbrook. A horse and a cow received shrapnel wounds.

On August 28th six high explosive bombs were dropped at Floodgate Farm, Hamfields, Berkeley. Also on that same night two bombs were dropped behind the "Star" inn at Heathfield killing one cow (the first casualty in the Vale!). The next night (August 29th) bombs fell at Hawley Farm and Kitenest west of Wotton-Under-Edge. 22 small bombs fell but no damage was reported. Seven bombs had fallen in or near Wotton on the 8th of August and again on the 25th.

Four HE bombs fell at Moreton near Thornbury on the 17th of August. Frampton-on-Severn was on the receiving end on August 24th when two bombs fell but one failed to explode. In the month of August 1940 forty-eight bombs fell in the Berkeley Vale. September the 15th was a bright and sunny Sunday with many vapour trails showing in the clear sky as Spitfires and Hurricanes circled high over Gloucestershire to gain height and wait for their call to dive into the Battle of Britain. On September the 25th there was a heavy raid on Filton. In which 80 enemy planes took part. 70 people were killed. On 27th of September another attempt to raid Filton took place. This was fought off by Spitfires and Hurricanes and over 20 enemy aircraft were claimed as destroyed.

Sirens were sounded at Sharpness on the night of October the 22nd and bombs were heard to fall near the Severn Railway Bridge. It was later reported that one bomb had failed to explode and the other was a near miss. The next night (23rd October 1940) the sirens sounded again and bombs dropped soon after again near Pitbrook. Four bombs fell in fields near Oldlands Farm and across to Houses Grove behind the village of Brookend. It was very fortunate that the one near the Halmore to Wanswell road failed to explode for it was a 1,000lbs bomb and a courting couple were walking by at that very moment. The road was closed while the bomb, nearly 12ft down in soft clay, was defused and the explosive substance steamed out.

A week later on October 29th bombs were dropped in a field near Berkeley - one was an HE bomb that failed to explode and there were a number of incendiary bombs that burnt out harmless in the fields. Two HE bombs were reported to have fallen at Rockhampton on the night of November 21st. On November 24th a heavy raid took place on Bristol. German planes circled around overhead waiting for their turn to go in and bomb the centre, Oldmarket, Park Street and Canon's Marsh. 70 people lost their lives that night.

December 3rd and 7th brought further raids on Bristol and Parnell's of Yate. Most nights the alert sounded at dusk and the all clear about 8am the following day. One bomb fell at Shepperdine on December 3rd. Raiders were busy in the Severn Estuary and on Christmas Eve two high explosive bombs fell on the Severn House and at Frampton-on-Severn one calf was injured and one rabbit and one partridge were reported killed. 1941 saw no letup in air-raids on the country but things were quiet in the Berkeley Vale.

On January 18th two HE bombs were dropped between North Nibley and Wotton but no damage was reported. The next four weeks were quiet due to unfavourable flying weather.

Most of the bombs dropped in and around the Vale were from planes trying to escape the searchlights. In sets of three they threw a cone of light into the night sky and held on to a plane until the night fighters could deal with it. To evade the lights they would jettison their load of bombs and make for the home base. Another theory put forward by country folk was that "Old So and So" was out poaching for rabbits that night and flashed his lamp about so much that the Germans thought it was a signal to drop their bombs.

On February 27th 1941 poachers could not be blamed, for it was the first of two daylight raids on Parnell's of Yate. One enemy aircraft was seen flying low over Charfield Station and was soon following the railway track to Yate where it dropped six bombs of which only three exploded. There were nearly 4,000 workers in the factory at the time - 53 were killed, 10 of them unidentified, and 40 were seriously injured.

March the 7th started as a dull misty morning; as the mist cleared it left a low cloud base. Just before midday on that Friday the alert sounded at Sharpness but work was to carry on as usual as long as there was a yellow flag flying from the top of Severn Ports Silo. Only when the army gunners changed it to a red flag was the workforce to take to the shelters.

I was working on the top floor of Severn Mills (some eight stories high) when the lights flashed on and off three times which was a signal to those people unable to see the flag that danger was imminent and to take cover. I ran out onto the flat roof of the mill and scanned the sky for signs of enemy planes (foolish, but one did foolish things when young!).

There was low cloud but visibility down river was good. The noise of the mill's machinery ground to a halt and all was quiet; the Severn Estuary looked still and peaceful. There was no sound of ack-ack guns firing down channel, only an R.A.F. training bomber, an Anson flying leisurely into view just above the Nass cliffs on the Lydney side of the River. Then I saw something else, another plane, a lot larger than the first, flying just behind and slightly lower, the brown and green camouflage blending in with the backcloth of the red brown and green of the cliffs. But what stood out was the markings - the black cross with its outline of white and the black swastika on the fin.

It was a German bomber; the Anson could not see the enemy plane for it was flying under the Anson's tail, as the Germans were fully aware - a blind spot. The army gunners manning the two machine guns at the lock entrance could not open fire for fear of hitting the R.A.F. plane. I lost sight of both planes as they disappeared behind the rise of land that is Sharpness Point and at that precise moment Mr Sid Embery, the mill foreman, arrived on the roof to take up his duty as fire watcher. I received a good ticking off and was told to report to his office afterwards but to first get to the shelter. The lift had stopped with the rest of the mill's machinery so I ran down the stairs, but not to the shelter. The adrenaline was running too fast to sit out the only bit of action I might see in the war.

I reached the dockside in time to see a Heinkel HE III of the Luftwaffe roar down the dock at about shipmast height. Fortunately there were only two ships at berth at that time. A few days before the dock was full; a convoy of ships had been diverted from Southampton because of the heavy bombing there, but now all had sailed. If the port had been full of ships the bomber might have been tempted to bomb the lock gates and with the tide out had the gates been hit it would have had disastrous results. The flux of water gushing out into the river would have swept away the piers, the entrance walls and the lock gates. The dock walls would probably have collapsed and brought down the brick warehouses. The canal at Gloucester docks drained of water would have left all shipping stranded on their sides in the mud. Maybe the continuing firing of the guns at the locks deterred the bomber from making that approach.

A small Dutch Coaster was waiting near the locks for the tide. The crew were ashore at the Pier View Hotel for a last drink prior to sailing. The only member aboard was the cook preparing lunch He came on deck to throw a bucket of slops overboard just as the plane flew down the dock. Dropping his bucket he raced to the gun mounted at the stern and started to fire. When the bomber was nearly overhead and well within his sights the bren gun jammed. In his rage and frustration he wrenched the gun from its mountings and threw it overboard and he was still dancing about and shouting abuse as the disappearing plane flew on out over the River Severn. Perhaps if he had kept his cool and cleared the blockage he might have had a second chance when the Heinkel turned around and made another run at the dock. This time coming in between the Severn Road houses and the south pier it was so low behind the row of shops near the lock that the gun crews were unable to aim their Lewis guns because when they fired the bullets only hit the brick warehouse and sheds. The plane was low enough for me to see the pilot and what I thought was the bomb aimed in the nose cone. One could quite clearly see the rivets in the blue-grey under-belly as it flashed by dead over head. The other ship in the dock at that time was the SS "Roxby" a 6,000 tonner, berthed under the steam cranes.

The gun crew on top of the silo were unable to fire their Lewis gun as the plane was flying lower than the roof of the silo and the gunner could not get enough downward angle. When he did manage to fire the bullets flew out and hit the houses at Brookend and Wanswell. The plane veered to the right and passed over Newtown and Wanswell, circled Berkeley Railway Station, then flew on to Berkeley Road Station where it followed the railway track to Yate and unloaded 12 bombs on Parnell's factory killing two people and seriously injuring six others.

The gun crews on the Vindicatrix opened fire on the Heinkel. There were two Lewis guns aboard - one for'ard and the other aft. As with all gun sites at Sharpness they were manned by the Staffordshire Regiment and as the plane rose to fly over the Severn Bridge bits were seen to fly off the tail plane. The gunners on the "Vindi" had scored a hit; however no real damage was sustained for the Heinkel lost none of its power or control and returned fire. A comic situation arose, for caught in the crossfire were two men, one a passenger and the other a signalman-cum-ticket collector. Both were standing on the platform at Severn Bridge Halt waiting for the train to Sharpness. As bullets flew over their heads from the British guns they took cover behind a wooden

building but when the enemy returned the fire they had to run back around to the front again. This exchange of fire continued for several minutes while the plane circled around the Bridge and Purton. Bullets were ricocheting off the steelwork and stone parapet. The two men were exhausted with running around the shed and fell in a heap on the platform. Their ordeal ended when the plane flew down the canal to the dock having completed his reconnaissance.

That episode was told by Mr Childs (for he was that passenger!) on his arrival at Mrs Greatrix's house in Wanswell. After numerous cups of tea he was able to relate his experience to her (Mr Childs, as older members of the public would remember, was a travelling salesman and with his bicycle and his suitcase packed with items of clothing would cycle from Lydney to the bridge, cross over on the train, and then cycle around the Sharpness district selling shirts and socks etc.)

The Heinkel HE 111 was one of the most important bombers in the Luftwaffe during the first half of the war. Two Junkers Jumo 211 engines each of which developed 1,340 horse - power. Armaments - up to 4,400 pounds of bombs was a normal load. One 20mm cannon and five 7.9mm machine guns. Maximum speed 258mph at 16,400ft. Range 760 miles with a normal bomb load. Wing span 74ft, length 54ft.

On March 7th 1941 a Heinkel HE 111 believed to be the one that had bombed Parnell's at Yate. Was shot down in flames by a fighter aircraft near Devizes.

March 1st 1941 - One HE bomb fell at Falfield. A fortnight later on the night of the 14th a night Beaufighter shot down a Heinkel III with a full bomb load at Milbury Heath, Falfield, killing the crew of four. The same night bombs were dropped near the Stone - Berkeley road (B4509), two HE bombs and one UXB (unexploded bomb) which closed the road for some considerable time.

March 17th - Bristol had one of its heaviest raids of the war, when between 500 and 800 people were killed.

April 7th - Bombs fell at Wisloe crossroads, Slimbridge. There were no reports of casualties.

April 13th - Three HE bombs fell missing the Severn Bridge. One sheep was reported killed.

April 12th - Again Bristol had a heavy raid.

May 3rd - 14 enemy bombers were reported to have been shot down by night fighters over the Bristol Channel and the West Country in the last two months. Later reports put the "bag" at 33. Two were shot down by "Ack Ack" guns. One HE bomb was dropped on Wotton on the 31st of May smashing windows, and two soldiers were cut by flying glass.

July 14th - Bombs were heard to drop in the Sharpness area. Later confirmed to have dropped near Lydney.

The following November on the 25th a sea mine dropped at Oldbury Naite killing two people and injuring several others. The intention had been to drop the mine in the shipping lane.

April 4th 1942 - Brockworth bombed - 19 killed and 147 injured.

April 25th - Raid on Bath.

April 26th - Again Bath was bombed, 400 killed and 1,200 injured - many were buried in a common grave.

After the Bath raids the bombing in the West diminished until March 27th 1944 when one HE bomb and ten parachute mines were jettisoned at Hill; all exploded on impact causing a massive crater. The plane, a Junkers 88 A4 of KG 6 Squadron, was shot down by a Mosquito night fighter and crashed at Clapton under the wall of the Deer Park, setting fire to a hayrick; the crew of four bailed out. The Home Guard and the Police were put on alert and as the airmen drifted over the Park towards Stone and Newport the Newport attachment was called out by the Newport Police. One airman landed in the churchyard at Stone Church, another landed in a tree and was injured by the fall, both were rounded up by the Home Guard. The other two landed in fields near Woodford and were taken away by the police. All were taken to Newport Police Station where one of them was found to be still in possession of his fire arm. It seems the Home Guard was more intent on cutting up the parachutes for the wives to make frilly underwear than searching the prisoners! The German who broke his leg in the fall was the pilot - Uffz (Sergeant) Tulsckel, the others were Uffz Wirth, Objster (Corporal) Wiedener and Gefr (Leading Airman) Bauch. Tulsckel was taken to Berkeley Hospital where Dr. Bryans set his broken leg and he was put in a side ward to recover. It was of no great credit to the people of Berkeley that they besieged the Hospital shouting abuse at the injured airman. Feelings were running high, the war had dragged on for four long years and perhaps some of the people had lost loved ones and were giving vent to their feelings. Anyway the Home Guard had to mount a guard on the ward until the prisoner could be moved elsewhere. Gefr Bauch kept asking in broken English about his friend. What could be made out from the conversation was that there were two Junkers 88 on the raid and his pal was in the other plane. But no one could enlighten him, nothing was seen or heard of any other plane. (That was until the Severn Railway Bridge was being demolished in 1967 and a massive floating crane was brought over from Germany with its salvage crew. Divers were sent down into the deep navigating channel to locate one of the bridge spans using powerful underwater search lights. In the murky water the shape of a plane's fuselage came into view clearly showing German markings. The engines and wings were missing. The young divers described the shape of it to the older members and it was established that it was a Junkers 88. Two old wrecks of barges were also sighted. How well the Severn holds its secrets!).

On examination of the wrecked plane under the Park wall, target maps were discovered with the destination Sharpness Dock ringed in red ink and the target time set for 23.58 hours. The crew were only a matter of a minutes flying time away from their target.

At that time Sharpness Dock was full of shipping. Bombs, shells, boxes of ammunition and thousands of tins (jerry cans) of petrol were stacked around the dock all waiting for D.Day. If the Germans had reached Sharpness and dropped their load of 10 land mines and the other Junkers had followed in with a load of incendiary bombs there would not have been much of Sharpness and the surrounding countryside left - so all thanks to a Mosquito's crew who probably never realised that their action saved the port of Sharpness.

Special Police Sergeant John Hancock of Berkeley (Undertaker) received the award of The Gloucestershire Special Constabulary Commendation for capturing two of the Germans. The Home Guard received a ticking off for pinching the parachutes!

PLANES LOST IN ACTION OR ON ACTIVE SERVICE IN AND AROUND THE VALE DURING THE WAR

October 21st 1939 - Gloster Gladiator of 263 Sqn crashed in the Severn near the Severn Bridge. The crew, Sgt. Watson and Sgt. Parker, were rescued by fishermen in a boat. The plane sank in the quicksand's.

June 19th 1940 - Bristol Blenheim crashed in the Severn on Lydney sand and was lost in the sand.

September 24th 1940 - Airspeed Oxford (a training plane from South Cerney) hit electric power lines and crashed at Frampton-on-Severn killing flying instructor and pupil.

February 12th 1941 - A Wellington bomber returning from a raid on Bremen made a forced landing in the Severn at Frampton, its engines shot up.

September 3rd 1941 - A Hurricane fighter crashed into a tree at Oldbury.

September 10th 1941 - A Hurricane crashed at Owlpen, Uley - pilot landed in a tree.

October 6th 1941 - A Hurricane dived into the ground at the Newgrounds, Slimbridge.

October 22nd 1941 - A Hurricane dived into the Severn attempting to fly under a span of the Severn Bridge.

February 10th 1942 - A Miles Master (a training plane) crashed at Berkeley killing Sgt. Arm, Pilot.

May 14th 1942 - Spitfire flew under a span of Severn Bridge and hit water. The pilot was saved but the plane sank and was never found.

July 15th 1942 - Spitfire crashed at Rockhampton.

September 13th 1942 - Spitfire crashed at Frampton.

January 26th 1943 - Spitfire crashed in the Severn near the Severn Bridge. Sgt. Caldwell's body was never recovered.

March 7th 1943 - Spitfire hit high tension cables at Slimbridge, pilot killed.

July 23rd 1943 - Whitley bomber dived into the Severn killing all four of the crew.

January 1st 1944 - Beaufighter crashed at The Patch, Slimbridge. The pilot D.C-Greville was killed.

The Berkeley Vale

May 14th 1944 saw the last of the bombing in or near to Berkeley Vale; bombs fell at Rangeworth but there were no reports of casualties. Not directly involved with enemy action in the Vale but as a point of interest was the bombing of Gloucester by a V1 flying bomb in August 1944. There is said to have been a Luftwaffe report but I must state that I found no record of this incident in the records office at the Shire Hall, Gloucester. Vengeltunsg Wafle I - the V1 or as we knew it the "Doodle Bug", was a small pilotless aircraft with a wing span of 17ft and a length or nearly 25ft. Made of pressed steel the machine weighed a little over two tons of which 1,870 pounds of high explosives made up the war head. The power unit was a single Argus pulse jet engine, developing 740 pounds of thrust and with an operating life of about half an hour; speeds of 400mph could be reached.

The Heinkel HE 111 was modified to carry a single flying bomb between the starboard engine and the fuselage. The weight and drag penalty of the externally carried missile imposed a severe performance limit on the already out-dated Heinkel. According to Luftwaffe statistics, the bomber made its approach flight by night, flying low down over the sea at 300ft - below the cover of radar. Passing nearby Portsmouth, Salisbury, Warminster and on to Bath it rose from 300ft to 2,000ft and fired the missile, made a quick turn and dashed back to base leaving the VI to fly on up and over the Cotswolds at Hawkesbury, Upton and Nailsworth to Gloucester.

In the County of Gloucestershire between 1939 and 1944 the casualties of bombing were 237 killed - 166 men, 50 women and 6 children and 15 unidentified. 696 were injured. There were 4,000 high explosive and 20,000 incendiary bombs, 10 mines and 1 sea mine, and 2,400 houses were damaged.

Thornbury Rural District Council reported in June 1945 a summary of enemy action between 1939-1945. 557 air raid warnings. 383 in 1940,

121 in 1941, 34 in 1942, 13 in 1943 and 6 in 1944. The number of bombs dropped in Thornbury Rural District (which then included Berkeley and Sharpness) was 556 plus 15 in the River Severn. High explosive bombs which did not explode were 83, about 1,538 incendiary bombs, 30 oil bombs, 2 phosphorus bombs, 10 mines and 1 sea mine. Casualties - killed 7 males, 2 females. 8 males and 6 females were injured. There were two crashed enemy aircraft, killing 4 and injuring 1. Live stock killed - 27. Houses damaged - 584, 8 totally destroyed. The highest number of HE bombs dropped in one raid was 95 on August 22nd/23rd 1941.

SS "Kai", an Estonian ship laden with timber from Canada and bound for Sharpness, was hit by a German sea mine off Lundy Island. She limped into Sharpness with most of her cargo intact. It was incredible that Sharpness was never bombed. The crews of German ships visiting the port in post war years stated that the Luftwaffe Bomber Command (the "Kampfgeschwader") knew the importance the river and canal played in the transport of millions of gallons of fuel by barge and small tankers to Worcester and Stourport to serve the bomber airfields of the Midlands. Many crew members were ex-Luftwaffe members, according to Mr Jack Evans, a life long servant of the dock who had access to the ships and struck up many friendships with captains and crews.

Every war had its heroes and its casualties. The First World War had the soldiers of Flanders (one of whom I have already named). Thousands were nameless. The Second World War was different; everyone involved from the smallest child to the most senior citizen could relate to some incident of that war. One event that caught the imagination of the public was No. 617 Squadron of the Royal Air Force, known as the "Dam Busters" and led by Wing Commander Guy Gibson. At the age of 25 he was one of the top pilots in the R.A.F. A tough guy (excuse the pun!) he was firm but very fair to his men - ground crew as well as air crew. (I met Guy Gibson on two occasions, once in the line of duty -I serviced his aircraft; the other socially when he accompanied Winston Churchill to Canada in August 1943).

Guy Gibson's first task was to hand pick 20 pilots and their crews. This story is about one of those pilots - Flight Sergeant Townsend D.F.M. Born in Brookend on 12th of January 1921 (his mother was "Miss" Townsend - a school teacher at Newtown Junior School who had the arduous task in the thirties of teaching me and several hundreds of children the rudiments of maths and English, in my case not very successfully). Bill Townsend joined the army in 1941 and was transferred to the R.A.F. on May 14th 1941. He was made a Sergeant Pilot on 24th of January 1942 and a Flight Sergeant on 1st of April 1942. He flew 26 operations and received the D.F.M. on May 14th 1943. Among his many trips was one on the first thousand-bomber raid of the war. On one occasion he flew his Lancaster Bomber back on three engines. He was a man well suited to the needs of Guy Gibson.

Bill Townsend took delivery of his new latest type Lancaster ED 886 , O for Orange, on April 23rd 1943 and was soon flying at zero feet (60ft) and practising dropping a new type of bomb that resembled the front wheel of a steam roller - that was the way the air crews described it. Everyone thought it was the Tirpitz they were going to bomb or the U Boat pens.

The great day came and the aircrew knew the target was the Rühr. The first group consisted of nine aircraft led by Gibson; Young, Hopgood, Mallby, Astell, Martin, Knight, Shannon and Maudsley were the other pilots to the Möhne and Eder dams. The second group, led by Squadron Leader McCarthy with Byers, Rice, Munro and Barlow, was to bomb the Sorpe dam. The third (reserve) group was led by Flight Sergeant Townsend and included Anderson, Brown, Burpee and Ottley. They were to fly the Southern route and if one and two groups breached all three dams they would be recalled.

Number 2 group was the first to leave Scampton in Lincolnshire for the Sorpe dam. The first plane

took off at 9.28pm on the 16th of May 1943. The others followed at two minute intervals. Number 1 group led by W C Gibson took off at 9.39pm. Number 3 group led by Bill Townsend took off at 00.14am and was over the enemy coast at 1.3lam.

The first crew to be shot down was Sergeant Byers' of 2 group at 10.57pm, who was hit by AA fire while flying at 300ft over Den Helder in Northern Holland. The second plane to crash was Flight Lieutenant Astell's of Number 1 group. They hit a high voltage cable at Marbeck in Germany. The third to be lost was Flight Lieutenant Barlow also of the 2nd group. They also hit a cable and crashed at Emmerich, Germany. The fourth loss was Flight Lieutenant Hopgood D.F.C. who was hit in the head, his wireless operator and rear gunner were also wounded and the front gunner was killed. As they crossed over Holland they regained control and flew on to drop their bomb on Möhne dam. At the same time they were hit by gun fire; the bomb bounced over the dam, exploded and destroyed the power station. Flames poured from M for Mother and the Lancaster crashed at Ostonnen. F.O. Burcher and P.O. Fraser both parachuted to safety.

Pilot Officer Rice of Number 2 group flying over the Zuider Zee hit the water, ripping out the underbelly of the Lancaster and the bomb with it. He returned safely to base. The fifth to crash was Pilot Officer Burpee of 3 group. This plane hit some trees at 1.53am and the bomb blew the Lancaster to pieces. Number six to go down was also in Number 3 group. Pilot Officer Ottley D.F.C was shot down by Ack Ack fire near Hamm in Germany. Flight Sergeant Tees the rear gunner, although badly burnt, bailed out and landed safely. The seventh plane lost was Squadron Leader Maudsley of Number 1 group who was shot down after hitting the Eder dam. The eighth and last plane to be lost was that of Squadron Leader Young of Number 1 group. After attacking Möhne dam he was on the return flight when they were hit by AA fire near Amsterdam.

Meanwhile Bill Townsend flew on towards his target - the Ennepe dam. It was now getting light and it took three runs at the dam before he was satisfied as to the approach. Early morning mist hampered his attempts and as he dropped his bomb it bounced once and exploded throwing a column of earth and water high in the air. (Later a Spitfire reconnaissance plane reported that the Ennepe dam had been breached by Flight Sergeant Townsend).

No other Lancaster of his group arrived at the dam so he turned his aircraft and flew back over the Möhne dam and observed a sheet of water about 4 miles wide rushing down the Rhür. There was no time to linger, the sun was rising so at zero level and a speed of 240mph he hedge-hopped over Germany and Holland. German fighters were up in force but none spotted him. Reaching the Dutch coast near Vlieland the coast defences opened fire but they were not hit. Bill Townsend, crew and aircraft O for Orange landed back at Scampton at 6.15am.

For his part in the Dambuster raid Bill was awarded the Conspicuous Gallantry Medal (C.G.M.) and was made a Pilot Officer on the day he breached the dam.

On 15th of July Bill Townsend was again in action, flying a mission to bomb an electric power plant near Milan in Northern Italy. Taking off at 10pm they reached their target at 3.24am. Bill dropped his bombs from about 800ft missing the power plant but blowing up an armoured train. The squadron then flew on to Blida in North Africa. While serving in India on March 16th 1945 he reached the rank of Flight Lieutenant. Bill was demobbed on May 3rd 1946.

At a reunion in 1988 to celebrate the 45th anniversary there were only 17 survivors out of the original 133, and 4 of them were members of Bill's crew. On that Dambusters raid 53 men lost their lives and just 3 were taken prisoners. There were others less fortunate than Bill Townsend. Two from the same village, lads still in their teens,

all flew on missions over Germany. "Jeff" Phillips of Brookend, just past his 18th birthday, "Rolly" Meadows also of Brookend, and Ken Higgs of Halmore all paid the supreme sacrifice. Incidentally all were class mates of mine at Newtown School.

In that war 42 men lost their lives in the Berkeley Parishes, they were; F Barge - 43 Rec. Corp; A L Brisland - Glosters; G W Butcher - Glosters; A J Cole - RN; G M Crossman - Royal Gloster Hussars; V F Deacon - RN; T A Everett - Royal Armoured Corps; A J Fryer - Royal Berks; K G Higgs - RAF; V Hill - RAF; E Hoare - RAF; E J King - Royal Artillery; I Kingscote - Somerset Light Infantry; F Knott - RN; F Lewis - MN; R Meadows - RAF; J Neale - Glosters; F Newick - Grenadier Guards; F Newman - RE; W Newman - Glosters; D Nicholls - RAF; A Organ - RAOC; E Organ - MN; E Palmer - RN; G Phillips - RAF; L Pratt - Royal Artillery; B Price - RAF; W Ruther - MN; T Scott - MN; M Simmons - RN; R Skidmore - Scots Guards; A Small - Glosters; G Smallwood - Glosters; D Smith - RAF; R Storky - RAF; R Taylor - RAF; W Watkins - MN; A Williams - RN; and J Workman - Royal Artillery.

RATIONS

By August 1942 the sugar ration was down to 8ozs a week and the fat ration down to 8ozs of which only 2ozs could be taken in butter. The meat ration was one shilling's worth and 2 pence worth of corned beef. Bread was not rationed until after the war.

Points Rationing allowed the housewife to choose where to shop without being tied to the one grocer that she was registered with for her basic rations. Sweets went on personal points in July 1942. Whale meat was on offer off the rations, as was rabbit and tripe. Dried egg took the place of eggs and many a housewife worked wonders with that pale yellow powder. Tea was rationed to 2ozs a week in July 1940. Free orange juice for children helped to ease the tea rations as the children preferred it to tea.

Bacon was replaced by mutton - mutton was cured similarly to bacon but it never managed to get that bacon smell or taste. Pig clubs were formed whereby neighbours would invest in a pig, ration it for pig balanced meal and help out with potato peelings and household scraps - for this they forfeited their bacon rations. People could save up their points, 16 points for one whole month, and blow the lot on a tin of salmon or cautiously spend them on tins of spam, pilchards or baked beans. Beer was never rationed but was often diluted. Local pubs worked a roster so that they would open at different hours or even days. Farmhouse cider was readily available. The common potato again came into its own - suddenly it was not just fattening anymore or just a filler - potatoes were used in beer making, fillings for cakes, pies and sandwiches.

"Dig for Victory" was the slogan of town and country folk alike. The numbers of acres under cultivation in 1939 was 12 million which rose to 18 million in 1945. Swamps were reclaimed and golf courses were dug up and planted and Stinchcombe Hill grew linseed for oil. Front lawns from the humble cottage to the mansion were tilled and prepared for crops of potatoes, cabbages and root crops. Even after a hard day's work the householder still found time to dig and plant, in between his duty in the Home Guard, ARP or Fire Service. Most farms had a new workforce - Land Girls of the Women's Land Army. These were girls from all walks of life; some had never even seen a cow let alone milked one. Women were doing men's jobs for a very poor rate of pay - one pound and eight shillings a week. They lived locally in hostels in Berkeley, Wicks Elm. A large house at the bottom of High Street was taken over. Some lived on the farms while others rented tied cottages.

There is a lovely little story I would like to relate of a docker, an army reservist, recalled to his unit in the month of August prior to the start of the war. He finished work on the dock, had a last drink with his workmates, shook hands all round, packed his kit, kissed his wife and little girl goodbye and was off to war. One morning in early September the dock workers were greeted by a soldier with rifle and fixed bayonet and the shout of "Halt, who goes there?" at the dock entrance. There stood their old workmate of a few weeks earlier demanding to see their identity cards and passes. He guarded that entrance gate all through the war and one week after being demobbed he was back the other side of the gate ready to start work as a docker again.

The Merchant Navy training ship "Vindicatrix" ("Vindi" to everyone locally) arrived on June 17th 1939 before the outbreak of war. The school of cadets was evacuated from Gravesend, Kent. It berthed in the Old Dock and it lay there until 1967. Built on the Clyde in 1893 and named "Arranmore" she sailed the Seven Seas until she was sold to the Germans in 1910 and was renamed "Waltnaute". She became a rest ship for U Boat crews at Heligoland at the beginning of World War I and served the German Navy all through that conflict. In 1918 she was returned to the Merchant Navy and was used by the Shipping Federation as a store ship for supplies. At the outbreak of war she arrived in Sharpness as a training ship. In 27 years at Sharpness the National Sea School passed out some 75,000 seamen and stewards and many lost their lives in service to their country during the war years.

During the years between 1939 and 1942 improvements were made to the dock at Sharpness. From the time the dock was opened the west side of the dock towards the low bridge was known as the "Green Bank". It was a grassy bank rolling down to shallow water, but money ran out before the quay wall could be completed. Now in wartime money was found to finish the job. The dockside was dredged to a reasonable depth, steel piles were driven down into the red sandstone rock and back filled with earth, then topped with concrete. Railway and crane tracks were laid. The first of the two new electric cranes were ready for testing on Wednesday 11th of December 1940 and was driven by Mr George Williams.

The Berkeley Vale

By December 27th 1940 Vickers Armstrong's men were busy repairing the old dock. The dock company's men cut down the beautiful large trees in the Pleasure Ground and used them to shore up the dilapidated lock gates while repairs were made. The Old Dock had to be modernised and made operational as a stand-by for shipping to use if the main entrance to the dock was put out of action by enemy bombers. Fortunately it was never put to use.

On September 5th 1940 a proposal was made to make a new road into the dock. Until then all road traffic used the viaduct over the railway lines and the high and low bridges. Work started on May 13th 1941 with the felling of the large elm trees south of the dock. Trentams, the contractors, had the road ready for use by September 11th 1941. Mr Harry Phillips of Brookend made and hung the new wooden gates at the new entrance and the road was opened. Called the "Burma Road" by some wit, the name stuck.

By the year 1942 a new sound could be heard coming from the grandstand on the Sharpness Football field. Not the sound that had rung from the rafters for over twenty years - the Sharpness Footballers song, "Sharpness boys for ever", but new songs and tunes; tunes like "The Chattanooga Choo Choo", "Paper Doll", "Pennsylvania 65000" and "American Patrol"; the Yanks had arrived at Sharpness. Stationed in the field by the side of the football pitch and billeted under canvas they made use of the football stand as a bandstand. With their jaws working overtime the local children listened to jazz played by a coloured American band.

250 coloured soldiers with white officers were used to help the dockers with the unloading of the war supplies. They were welcomed into the local community and people felt that they were not alone anymore. Friends and allies had come to help them fight their battles. The children certainly welcomed the Yanks with part cupboard love and part curiosity. The games of baseball and American football were introduced to them but were not met with much enthusiasm. It was only the lure of gum, cookies, candy and tins of fruit that persuaded the children to take part.

The same thing was happening at Berkeley, with the Americans camping in the Show Ground under the Castle walls. Children would even take their own cup and plate down to the camp at meal times and sit down with the troops for dinner or supper; no one was ever turned away. The local people did a roaring trade, dusting off the old bicycle that lay rusting in the shed; a new chain, a spot of oil, a coat of paint and the bicycle was sold to the Yanks for three or four times the price that it had cost in the early thirties, and cycles were often brought back for repairs. Twisted wheels or handlebars were commonplace, for the Americans were not used to riding on the left side of the road, or was it the twisting country lanes, after sampling the local brew of cider?

Sharpness Dock prior to the D Day Landing was at its busiest. For months the dock was packed with ships of all shapes and sizes, some painted battle-ship grey, others camouflaged with strips of black, grey and blue, most armed with machine guns for protection against air attacks and the larger ships had fitted to their stern end a 4" anti-submarine gun. There were Free French, Dutch, Norwegian, Danish and American as well as British ships. There was the loading and unloading of mysterious miscellaneous crates, but some cargoes were no secret, shells, bombs and ammunition, and the dock reeked of petrol as the dockers handled jerry cans from ship to shore. One leaking can, a spark or a naked flame and Sharpness would have disintegrated, but fortunately no serious accidents occurred.

One of the biggest ships to dock during the war was an American (nameless) with a cargo of bombs. While she was unloading, an incident occurred. Mr Cyril Savage was driving the No. 6 crane, slinging a 500lb bomb from the ship's hold to the shore with one sling attached around the fin and the other around the nose cone, when the sling on the nose cone slipped off and the bomb hung in mid-air before dropping onto the concrete dockside. Within seconds the dock was clear of dockers. One eye witness said he never saw dockers move so fast before or since! The bomb was not fused and there was no danger of an explosion but then no one was going to hang around to find out. The mark that the bomb left in the railway line and concrete is still there to this day.

Another amusing incident, although it was not so at the time, involved a Greek ship unloading crates of flares; someone in the hold lit up a pipe and discharged the still flaming match which set fire to a small pile of rubbish. The alarm was raised, the crew including the Captain abandoned ship and did not stop running until they reached the shelter of the trees in the Plantation. The docker guilty of the offence was suspended from duty until the ship sailed.

Suddenly, as if over night, all the ships disappeared. The dock was quiet and empty of even the smallest ship. The date was June 5th 1944. The greatest Armada of ships the world had ever known was sailing from ports all around Britain to the South coast. D Day had started.

Entertainment in those dark war years was somewhat different from the First World War. People were better informed and entertained, for they had the radio, with the BBC putting out endless programmes of music. There were at least twenty dance bands a week on the air and many programmes like "I.T.M.A.", "Band Wagon" and Jack Warner's "Mind my bike". The public houses were full and women now had taken their place alongside the men in the forces, at the work bench, in the fields and at the pub bar - a thing unheard of before the war. With troops stationed at Sharpness, Searchlight Units at Berkeley and Purton and the walking wounded at Berkeley Hospital, the public houses had an influx of new faces and new talents for singing or playing the piano. With high wages and nothing in the shops to spend their money on, people flocked to the pubs to make their own entertainment to sing and dance for a few hours and forget the troubled outside world.

Gilbert Hill of Berrycroft, Berkeley, ran a boy's club and a youths' football team and spent much of his time and money in pursuit of his aims. Many a budding footballer owes much to Gilbert's patience and understanding. I and many others thought he should have received some recognition in his life time for his contribution to the youth of Berkeley and district; others received awards for far less effort. With the men of the Vale away at war, local football clubs closed down but Gilbert managed to run a team of boys, while Bert Denning ran a ladies' team. Gilbert, rather shy of the ladies, stayed in the background but was ready to lend a hand if required.

The ladies played football on a Saturday afternoon and gave pleasure and entertainment to many football fans. A collection for war charities was taken at these matches.

When the cease-fire came to end hostilities in Europe the people celebrated victory -some quietly in their own homes bringing out the bottle, kept safe throughout the year, to be consumed by family and friends and to toast absent friends. Others held street parties, lit bonfires and brought out from pub and farm barrels of beer and cider. The women folk managed somehow with the rations available to bake a cake or make sandwiches. There was dancing to a late hour or until the drink or the legs gave out!

The sacrifices of the war years seemed worthwhile and people looked forward to a bright new future. The war had moved away to distant lands and a few months later with the dropping of the atom bombs on Japan the war was over.

With the death of Randal Earl of Berkeley in 1942 the Earldom of Berkeley became extinct and with it, helped by the war years, went the last of the old way of life. No longer did a man step from the pavement and touch his forelock when the Earl walked down the street, nor his wife curtsy to the Countess as she drove by in her carriage.

The shadow of the Castle over Berkeley after 800 years was shortening and the final chain of serfdom was broken. But not until the war ended did the break-up of the Berkeley Estate occur.

Large estates and combines of estates moved in to buy the large parcels of land that the Berkeley Estate was forced to sell to pay death duties and other taxes.

THE CHANGING VALE

At the end of hostilities with Japan a new era was promised. Not the old promise of "A land fit for heroes to live in"- the Politicians could not use that old chestnut again but to a certain extent that promise was kept. The nation's health was the concern of everyone. New housing estate were built to house the ex-servicemen and their families.

The old collapsing sewers at Berkeley (some were only hollowed out tree trunks that ran down to discharge in the Pill) were renewed and extended to all the houses in Berkeley and a new sewer and filter beds were built at Oakhunger. Newtown had its old sewer replaced but the raw sewage still ran out into the Severn behind the South Pier. At the same time there was the arrival of the water mains, a new development by the Gloucester Water Company, until then only a few houses in Berkeley had a supply of piped water. Supplied from the Holywells at Wanswell, a supply of water ran to a deep well at the Castle where it was pumped to a tank in the Castle roof and from there fed to some of the houses of the Berkeley Estate. Berkeley Hospital and the Berkeley Arms Hotel had large tanks in their roof-space to store the water, for the water pressure was at its greatest at night and the tanks filled up for daytime use. Others had to rely on wells and pumps.

Berkeley always had a good supply of sweet water, for 30ft down through the red sandstone, lying in a dish of clay, is a table of water. Other towns and villages were less fortunate and villagers had to carry water long distances from well or pump. All this changed with the coming of the water mains. Houses could now be built without the need for a local water supply. The post-war housing boom was in full swing. New housing estates were built at Stone, Newport, Slimbridge, Berkeley, Newtown and Sharpness to house the increasing population. With Government grants, pre-war properties were modernised and were both private and council owned. New gas mains were taken to outlying villages and new sewers brought comfort and eased the labour of the country housewife.

Farmers took advantage of agricultural grants, new modern cow sheds and milking parlours were built and new draining methods made more land available. Cattle troughs took over from the cow and duck ponds. But all was not for the better; woods and coverts the likes of Tintock, Bushy Groves and Redwood were stripped of their large and beautiful broad leaf trees. Alterations to the Vale countryside had begun. Meadows, wetlands and hedgerows were vanishing at an alarming rate and most of the old hay meadows disappeared. Gone were the clover fields, the fields of moon daisies, cowslips and buttercups and in their place were fields of coarse rye grass planted to satisfy the hunger of large herds of beautiful fat sleek-coated milking cows in the peak of condition - a hundred or more to produce milk to enlarge the milk lake or raise the butter mountain even higher.

With the rabbit population killed off by myxomatosis there were no small animals to keep the vegetation cropped short near the hedgerows which encouraged the 20 or so varieties of wild flowers, herbs and plants to grow there. Weed killer and fertilisers not only killed off these plants but also the small rodents, reptiles, insects and rare birds. Ponds and pools gave way to cattle troughs and were filled in and we lost many of our frogs, toads and newts. We also lost the bulrushes, marsh flowers and wild irises and the moor hen lost its natural habitat; as did the beautiful dragonfly.

The Berkeley Vale

With the grubbing out of the oaks, chestnuts, beech and elm from the woodlands we lost a haven for many birds. Replaced by endless rows of conifers, easy and quick to grow, the turn around on profit would be 20 to 30 years. The old Earls of long ago planted oak and elms and not even their grandchildren reaped the profits, only the beauty of watching the trees grow into beautiful woods, but then the beauty was for their eyes only. Today we can walk through row upon row of conifers without the fear of being ejected by a gamekeeper for now there is no game to keep. Nothing to see but dark dank endless rows of evergreens where no thrush or blackbird worth a song would be found. The foxgloves, primroses, the waving carpet of tall bluebells and the wood anemones among others are now protected by law. What more beautiful sight is there than a dell full of bluebells, the frail wood anemones bordering the cart tracks through the woods, or the sun's rays of Spring shining down through the leafy boughs of the great oaks to fall on a cluster of pale primroses; or the call of the pheasant to its mate hidden in the thick bracken; or the echoing sound of the woodpecker as it labours to enlarge a hole in a tree? What are we leaving for our children and grandchildren? Is this the price we must pay for progress?

The Vale landscape altered dramatically in the early 1970's; this time it was due to nature not man. Not since the cutting back of the forest and the introduction of strip cultivation had the country changed so much. At first it was just an odd elm tree here and there and then suddenly the Dutch Elm Disease was rampageous. All the elms, from the majestic giants to the slender sapling in the hedgerows, died from that beetle attack leaving grey skeletons silhouetted against the sky line, later to be cut down and burnt, thus opening up the Vale-first the church steeples were prominent and then as more elms fell to the woodman's axe, other landmarks came into view. Villages that seemed miles away were now only a few fields away.

One landmark, weather permitting, could always be seen standing high on a knoll - the guardian of the Vale, the monument to the memory of William Tyndale, a son of the Vale and truly a man of God who paid the supreme sacrifice, the most horrible of all deaths, burning at the stake. Through the years many a soldier returning home from the holocaust of war gazed towards the Cotswold Hills at North Nibley and seeing that monument knew he was home and safe.

THE POST WAR SEVERN

In March 1945 the SS "John", loaded with coal on the way down the Severn, became stranded on the rocks known as the Gruggy on the west side of the "Shoots". The vessel was submerged at high water with only her mast and funnel showing. The owners A J Smith Ltd. of Bristol gave notice in April that the vessel was a total loss and notified its abandonment to their underwriters. The SS "John" became a menace to shipping. Tug Masters from Sharpness refused to take dumb barges down river on ebb tides when the river was foggy, for fear of hitting this obstruction. The Admiralty was going to remove the wreck by means of explosives but as the "John' was near to the Severn Tunnel no such action was taken.

Fortunately the action of the tide and wind destroyed the wreck sufficiently to prevent it being a danger to shipping.

On the 2nd of April 1947 the SS "Stancliffe" bound for Sharpness with a cargo of about 3,000 tons of aspen logs went aground in the estuary of the Severn off the North Pier at the entrance to Sharpness Dock. The pilot had been down channel several days waiting for a ship that did not arrive and when the "Stancliffe" arrived at Walton Bay the pilot brought her up to Sharpness. But unknown to the pilot (he was not informed of a change in the River,) a sand bank had built up off the North Pier and the "Stancliffe" went aground

SS Stancliffe

on it. After several attempts to refloat the vessel the crew abandoned ship and the owners, the Stanhope Steamship Company Ltd., gave notice of abandonment to their underwriters. The wreck caused an obstruction to navigation and impeded the entrance to the dock for it was lying in the navigational fairway. This presented an immediate and serious problem, for the waters were under the jurisdiction of the Trustees and the legal position appeared to be that any expense incurred by the Trustees in the removal of the wreck could not be recovered from the owners or the underwriters after the vessel had been abandoned, unless it was proved that the wreck was caused by the negligence of the owners or their servants or agents.

The Trustees asked the Canal Company for financial aid and practical assistance; the Ministry of War Transport agreed to give the guarantees

required and work started immediately. A part of the cargo had already been recovered but there was a problem - while the cargo was discharging from the forepart, the vessel split in two about amidships. There were still 1,605 tons remaining in the ship. Steps were taken to repair this damage and to remove the vessel to a safe place. Work was undertaken by I.P.Langford of Sharpness and Messrs Metcalfe Salvage Experts of Falmouth, at a cost of £20,000. This operation was successful and the vessel was beached above the North Pier and the remaining cargo was then recovered. The cost of the recovered cargo was met by its owners - The Board of Trade, and £5,869 was received by the Trustees. The "Stancliffe" was eventually sold for £20,000.

On February 1st 1950 the motor schooner "William Ashburner" ran into thick fog and went aground on Chapel Rock. The pilot and crew

SS Ramses

were able to walk shore. Notification was received that the vessel had been abandoned. The "William Ashburner" floated off at high tide and was sighted near Newport, returning up river on the next tide; she ran aground near Slimeroad and was temporarily moored. She later came into the possession of the Chepstow Yachting Club. Later she sank in the mouth of the River Wye where her hulk can still be seen at low tide.

Motor Barge "Safety" went aground near Hill Flats in December 1950. She was owned by Thomas Silvey Ltd. of Bristol and fortunately no damage or expenses occurred as the "Safety" was successfully refloated in January 1951 and sailed on to Bristol.

On March 23rd 1951, a Good Friday, the Egyptian grain ship "Ramses II" grounded on a sand bank between Sharpness and Lydney, loaded with 7,000 tons of Russian maize destined for Sharpness. All efforts to refoat the vessel failed and steps were taken to remove the cargo. From the date of grounding to September 28th 6,000 tons were successfully salvaged. During these operations the "Ramses II" broke her back and the underwriters paid a total sum to the owners. The Trustees were thus once again faced with the serious problem of a wreck that was a real danger to shipping. The Trustees could only rely on the sale of the wreck for scrap. Port Clearance Facilities who had been responsible for the salvage of cargo were asked if they would remove the cargo and they agreed. This firm did intermittent work until March 1952 when they transferred their interest to the Produce Marketing Company who in turn assigned the removal of the wreck to The Wansford Syndicate. Work continued at a very slow rate and many difficulties occurred over the next few years. The most troublesome was the lighting of the wreck. In 1958 the arrangement with Wansford Syndicate was terminated although the wreck was still unsafe.

It was not until 1960 that completion was achieved by members of the maintenance staff of British Waterways. And so after nine years this major problem was resolved.

An incident occurred on the 4th of April 1952 when the MV "Darleydale" scraped over Haywards Rocks and sustained damage amounting to £550 (no great amount by today's standards) and J Harker Ltd. the owners of the craft entered a claim against the Trustees for the recovery of this sum, it being alleged that the cause of the damage was the buoy not being on station. Hayworth Buoy had broken away from its mooring on March 25th 1952 and was remoored after repairs on the 8th of April 1952. It is recorded that the Harbour Master at Sharpness verbally informed all users of the River of this matter.

This claim was resisted by the Trustees and a writ was issued by the owners to recover the cost:

1. The provisions of the Harbour Order are permissive and not obligatory.

2. The vessel must have been considerably out of its normal course as the Hayward Rock is about 350ft from the centre of the channel. The buoy is a marker buoy only and unlighted at night and not to be used as a leading light for the purpose of steering a course.

3. Between 25th of March 1952 and the 4th of April 1952 84 loaded vessels sailed through the channel inwards and 102 vessels in ballast outwards- total of 186 craft in 10 days including 3 large ships all having navigated the channel without incident.

4. The Master of the "Darleydale" had taken his vessel through on 5 occasions when the buoy was not on station.

5. The buoys placed in the Severn Estuary are placed there by the Trustees as an aid to navigation which implies that their presence does not necessarily mean that vessels can navigate without due care and attention and that precautions in navigation must be the same as if the buoys were not there.

The Berkeley Vale

In September 1954 it was reported that the Plaintiff's Solicitors had by agreement taken out of court settlement of their claim - the deposited sum of £200 and the payment of costs amounting to £274. This action was therefore concluded at a total cost to the Trustees of £474.

That report shows how busy the Severn Estuary was in the 1950's. 186 crafts in 10 days, or nearly 500 vessels a month, and it must be to the credit of both pilots and crew members that incidents were kept so low.

On the 20th of September 1958 Lighter No. 9 in tow and loaded with logs on passage to Lydney dock foundered off Berkeley Pill. The owners F.A. Ashmead and Son Ltd. were held liable. This craft was observed a week later drifting in the flood tide towards Sharpness, where it became wrecked off the Entrance Piers in the middle of the channel. The Harbour Authority took steps to remove this obstruction to shipping.

On November 4th 1960 the barge "Shinfield" loaded with logs, whilst in tow with the tug "Robert A", came adrift in the river and eventually sank in deep water.

On the evening tide of October 25th 1960 several tankers left Avonmouth for Sharpness laden with petroleum spirit and fuel oil, unaware or the pending conditions in the Severn Estuary. On reaching the neighbourhood of Berkeley Pill a dense fog developed rapidly and the whole area became hazardous for shipping. The "Westdale" of 229 tons and the "Arkendale" of 321 tons, both owned by John Harkers Ltd. were close at hand and both vessels eventually found themselves past the entrance of Sharpness Dock and on collision course. Both took evasive action but a collision occurred from which neither vessel could separate. Both craft swung to a south-easterly heading and out of the fog loomed the piers of the Severn Railway Bridge. The "Westdale" struck the pier and heeled over to port and caught fire. The fire spread to the "Arkendale" and both

vessels became a total loss. The Bridge carried a gas main that served 6,000 homes in the Forest of Dean and when No. 17 Pier was hit the gas main broke and the escaping gas added fuel to the fire, helping to take out two spans of the Bridge and damaging Piers 16 and 18. Cries of help were heard by people on both sides of the River. The cargo of spirit and oil spread over the water and soon the Severn was ablaze from bank to bank. From a distance of one mile firemen and engines stood by helpless, unable to reach the stricken vessels.

Three men, one of them injured, were pulled from the muddy river by volunteers who risked their lives to go out in small boats and search for survivors. James Dew (42) of Burnham on Sea, George Thompson (35) of Gloucester and Jack Cooper (43) of Cinderford were saved and taken to Lydney and District Hospital where they were discharged the next day. It was feared that the rest of the crews were swept away down river on the ebbing tide. Herbert Dudfield (46) of Corse, Alex Bullock (40) of Gloucester, Percy Simonds (35) of Gloucester, Robert Nibbet (25) of Hardwicke and Malcolm Hart (17) of Gloucester all lost their lives on that foggy night. Among the rescued men were Mr Dew - Skipper of the "Westdale", Mr Thompson - Skipper of the "Arkendale" and Mr Cooper - his Chief Engineer. Mr Cooper was pulled to safety near Lydney Dock after being in the water for three hours.

Seven minutes before the explosion the last train of the day had passed over the Bridge. The signalman on the Bridge at that time was Mr S.Griffey of Sharpness.

The following morning a section of the track was taken out in the cutting at Sharpness and a large railway sleeper firmly roped to the track above Sharpness Station as a further safety measure. Captain Berbridge the Harbour Master at Sharpness, had to make a decision on whether to allow the remaining craft in the river to dock or turn them back to Avonmouth. With the fear of fire reaching to the entrance of the dock and with many tankers loaded with spirits he decided to close the port to all shipping.

Tankers holding station in the fog and racing tide waiting to enter between the piers at the dock entrance had now to rev their engines to maximum power and hope to God there would be no engine failure. Inch by inch they edged their way away from the piers, any engine failure or a mistake by the skippers and tankers could have collided and the swiftness of the tide would carry them into the inferno raging a mile up river. Thanks to the skill of all crew members any further disaster was averted. All hands with the exception of the engineers were stationed to look out and shouts were exchanged across the fogbound river to find the positions of other crafts. Meanwhile below deck in the engine room the engineers were trying to coax the last ounce of energy from the already overworked engines. Buckets of petrol drawn from the cargo pump were held under the air intakes of the diesel engines, the petrol vapour sucked into the engines giving a boost to the output, and the revs jumped from 500rpm to 650. With engines running flat out, the governors were wedged open with anything that was at hand - broom handles, hammer handles or spanners. The crews drove their craft back down river to Avonmouth. The exhaust manifolds were literally glowing red hot and it was a miracle that not one engine seized up. They all anchored safely and a rush was made to the shore to phone home to wife and loved ones to say that they were all safe.

A Court of Enquiry convened by the Minister of Transport was held and the findings of the incident were as follows:-

"No fault in navigation by either Masters, but the general increase over the past few years of traffic using the harbour at Sharpness, including craft carrying inflammable cargoes had created great hazards, more particularly in bad weather.

In the opinion of the Court, more consideration should be given by all concerned to two general matters:- Better communications between Sharpness and various positions down river and secondly better communication between Sharpness and craft in the vicinity of the Harbour.

"Subsequently as a result of this Report:-

1 Improvement of the present arrangement to notify Captains of deteriorating weather conditions in the neighbourhood of Sharpness.

2. Provision of VHF Radio Telephone set at Sharpness to keep in close contact with craft in the vicinity of Sharpness and whilst on passage up the estuary.

3. Provision of Radar equipment on the vessels navigating the Severn.

4. Sound signal near Sharpness Old Dock for use in time of fog mechanisation of existing fog; signal in Shepperdine.

5. Erection of tide gauges at certain points in the estuary.

6. Facilities for life saving in the area. It was agreed however that in view of the nature of the estuary and tidal conditions this would not be feasible.

7. A new survey of the river to be carried out."

All the enquiries, surveys and safety measures taken did not stop a further disaster in the river four month later. For on 16th of February 1961 on the p.m. tide the MV BP "Explorer" capsized and the crew of five lost their lives.

The "Explorer" laden with 437 tons of motor spirits proceeded up channel without event until she reached the leading lights at Inward Rocks. She was seen by a reliable witness to have made the turn necessary to take her through the Counts

The Berkeley Vale

Channel (Shepperdine) and appeared to be following a normal course for such a vessel in the tidal conditions then prevailing. Shortly afterwards however the same witness looking again in the same direction where he had last seen the "Explorer's" lights could see nothing of her. The vessel was not seen again until about 8.20pm on the same evening when she was observed from Lydney floating in an upturned condition in the strong current. The bodies of the crew were found at various times and places. They were H Middleton, Captain - 193 Longford, Gloucester; A Hook, Engineer - 108 Beaufort Road, Gloucester; K Foster, Mate - 131 Matson Avenue, Gloucester; A Griffey, Engine Room - 6 Baylands, Newtown, Berkeley; and M Holder, Deckhand - 29 Deans Way, Gloucester.

At 8am on the following day the "Explorer" was upside down under the first span of the Severn Railway Bridge. "Just like a large black shiny whale" was the comment of an eye witness standing on the bridge. With the rising tide she drifted on up the river, turned round with the turning tide and passed through the gap where the disaster of the previous October had happened. Later she lay aground on Lydney Sands a mile below Sharpness. The late Mr Jimmy Tonks, skipper of the "Kendale", said he saw the "Explorer" some 500 yards astern near the inward Rocks at about 8.20pm. It was a clear night and there were no navigational problems.

A Court of Enquiry was ordered and was held on the 7th and 8th of November 1961. An annexe to the Report read:-

"The Court having carefully inquired into the circumstances of the above shipping casualty finds that the cause of the casualty was the vessel touching the ground in such a manner and at such speed as to produce an immediate reduction in positive stability and make her vulnerable to tidal forces. The casualty at present under investigation has no significant feature in common with the other recent casualty arising out of a collision between two tanker barges off

Sharpness and it would be wholly wrong for the public to entertain any idea that the navigation on the Severn is unacceptably hazardous. The River Severn is a river on which navigation requires good judgement and common sense based upon experience and none but experienced persons ought to attempt to navigate it".

The MV "Explorer" was towed to port, overhauled and refitted and went back into service under the new name of BP MV "Driver". After two or three trips she ran aground on the Nass near Newport and was a total loss - truly a jinxed ship.

It was the beginning of the end of an era for the small tanker craft; soon the only two commercial vessels to use the inland waterways were the "Chasley" and the "Tirrel", both grain barges trading between Avonmouth and Tewkesbury. A new fleet of tankers took over the crews of the smaller craft. Bowker and King traded the Bristol Channel, the Severn and the canal as far as Gloucester (Monks Meadow) and Quedgeley. With the closing of the petroleum depot at Quedgeley the fleet of 1,000 tonners - "Bisley", "Berkeley" "Bude", "Borman", "Blakenly" and the "Budleigh" disappeared from the waterways and now only an occasional tanker trades to Gloucester. The Sharpness-Gloucester canal is now used mostly for pleasure craft and also as a reservoir to supply Bristol with water.

But there were still casualties in the River Severn. In the 1980's five people lost their lives within a mile of Sharpness. A family of three - husband, wife and small child were drowned on the sands off Lydney Harbour. The child was never found. A local lad from Sharpness was swept away by the swift current off the Old Dock.

The river has no respect for young or old, experienced or inexperienced, for it took the life of a 70 year old man who was a fisherman with a lifelong experience of salmon fishing in the Severn.

His body was never recovered.

THE WEATHER IN THE VALE

The winter of 1947 was one of the coldest in living memory. Between January 1st and March 9th there were 53 frosts with the temperature dropping at times to below zero - 33 degrees F of frost; This was followed by heavy snow falls after March 13th.

In the Severn large ice floes were a danger to shipping and blocks of ice could be heard grinding and banging together as the flood tide pushed them over the sand banks and when the tide ebbed it left them piled up on the mud and sand to await the next tide, when procedure started all over again. Sharpness Dock and canal were frozen over and at times were impassable. Even the steam tugs found that as fast as they cut through the ice, it formed back again behind them. The snow made travelling difficult, railway points froze making the movement of coal impossible and coal merchants ran out of stock. Most homes relied on coal for heating and cooking and some were forced to chop down trees and even break up furniture to keep warm.

Electricity supplies were cut off sometimes because the heavy snow brought down the overhead cables or the power stations had closed for lack of coal. The heavy snow was followed by heavy rain and, helped by the melting snow the Vale flooded. Berkeley was completely cut off and buses to Berkeley stopped at Mobley. The floods across Longbridge were too deep even for lorries and buses. Boats that were normally used on the Pill were brought into operation ferrying people in and out of Berkeley. The roads to Sharpness were flooded at Berkeley Station archway as were the roads at Haynes and Pitbrook, Wanswell.

The only way to reach Sharpness was by train or to walk along the railway track as all low lying land was under water.

The worst winter of the century, and the longest, started on December 29th 1962 with deep drifts of snow whipped up by the gale force winds. As fast as the roads were cleared the driving winds blew the snow back again. Roads were closed throughout the Vale and by dawn the next day 30°F of frost was registered. Water pipes froze and even some water mains which were at a depth of 2ft under the ground.

Farmers had problems supplying water to their cattle. Diesel froze in the pipelines of both tractor and lorry. The horse and cart, if a farmer still had one, came into its own. Hot manure from the cow shed was piled high around the boarded-over cattle troughs leaving just one end free for one cow at a time to drink, so keeping the water flowing.

The Dock and the canal were again frozen over. Children had the time of their lives tobogganing even on the slightest slope and skating was in constant progress on the timber pond. And so it was from December until the late spring sunshine of May.

Severe as that winter of 1962-63 was, there was no comparison with winters of long ago. In the winter of 1564-65 the Severn was frozen over and large ice flows closed the river to the wooden ships of the day.

A savage winter occurred in the year 1607-08. Snow fell in the last week of November to the depth of 2ft and stayed until the end of February. The lanes and byways in the Vale were closed to all but men on horse back and even they could only make short journeys. Many people who attempted to travel perished in deep snow drifts.

From 1670 to 1689 the winters were long and severe. Cottagers brought their livestock into their dwellings to share the heat from the hearth. From 1716 to 1796 there were very cold winters with the temperatures well below freezing for most of the time.

In 1815 snow lay around Berkeley from January until the end of April and in 1881 on January 11th work was abandoned at Sharpness docks as bitter gale force winds brought heavy snow and the workforce employed at the docks found the lanes and roads impassable. This was followed by intense frosts causing the docks and canal to freeze over.

When the dockers eventually reach the dockside work was still impossible; not only were the blocks, tackle and ropes frozen but the hatch covers and even the cargo in the holds of the sailing vessels was frozen too.

1890-91 saw another severe winter and on the 15th of December the first of the frosts that lasted throughout January until February the 7th showed temperatures dropped to zero, 32° of frost. Berkeley Castle set up soup kitchens throughout the Vale to help feed the labourers forced out of work by the Arctic conditions.

The last of the very cold winters ended in 1895 after nearly 300 years of a mini ice age, the weather abated and the winters became milder.

In 1907 on April 27th snow fell to the depth of 6 inches. By mid January 1912 deep snow closed all roads and it was particularly deep in the Dursley, Nibley and Wotton districts.

On Christmas morning 1927 people awoke to a white Christmas. The rain during the night had turned into a heavy snow fall and after Boxing day 3 to 4 foot snow drifts were reported.

In February 1929 the Sharpness canal was frozen. Mr Bertie Goodman of Sharpness, a man of diminutive stature - he was less than 4ft tall-skated from Sharpness High Bridge to Gloucester but he had to leave the canal at every swing bridge as the ice under the bridges was too

thin to bear his weight. He was carried piggy-back around the bridges by the bridgeman at each bridge. Mr Goodman was also known to have dived off the top of the span of the High Bridge into the canal (in summer time of course!)

A well known character with a vast knowledge of the Severn he was the last tiller man on the old pilot sailing cutters.

The first winter of the Second World War in 1940 was the coldest since the mini Arctic weather of 1895. From Christmas day 1939 until February 18th 1940 there was frost on 49 days, the temperature dropping to 2°F.

December 13th 1981 showed a hard frost followed by a snow blizzard in the Severn Estuary and within one hour 3 inches of snow fell.

Summers - 1890 was a very dry summer and 1925 was an even drier one. 1901 and 1921 were very wet. In May and June of 1940 the temperature was in the 70's but July was very wet and nearly 5 inches of rain fell. August was one of the driest months on record and the drought lasted until October 7th.

In 1947 the summer compensated for the bad winter with temperatures between 70 and 80°F and October was the driest month since 1887. In 1955 May was wet as was June but July, August and Septerber made up for the wet start with sunshine up to 14 hours a day. 1959 saw another good summer with temperatures of between 75 and 90° and September was the driest and warmest month for 59 years.

The summer of 1968 was one worth remembering. Thunder and lightning filled the night sky on July 10th followed by heavy rain that did not abate until well into the next day. With a tide in the Severn of 28ft and flood water rushing down the Little Avon, the Show Ground near the Castle was soon under 2 feet of water. All roads into Berkeley were closed and the retaining wall of the moat between the Castle and the kennels collapsed under the weight af water that rushed across the road on its way to the Severn. Lamp standards were snapped off as if they were twigs of a tree and bales of hay bobbed up and down in the fast swirling waters. Sheep and lambs, stiff and bloated, were swept by. The banks of the Little Avon and the Pill disappeared under the torrent and there was just one wide expanse of water with a few cows and steers standing belly deep in water on submerged hillocks.

Sharpness canal rose 2ft overnight and was closed to all shipping. Ten days later the floods had subsided enough for the banks of rhines and ditches to reappear but these were quickly blocked by rotting hay and polluted with effluent from broken drains and overflowing cesspits.

This was the last serious flooding at Berkeley; the Little Avon was dug out deeper and the earth piled on the banlts to make steep sloping sides to retain flood water. The Mill stream down to and under the Sea Mills was filled in and a new water course cut across fields to flow into the Pill which was also dug out to a greater depth.

Across the mouth of the Pill steel piles were driven in to form a barrier against the Severn tide. Sluice gates were fitted into this steel barrier to allow the fresh water of the Little Avon and the brooks that surrounded Berkeley access to the Severn thus making the Pill into a fresh water river - an extension of the Little Avon.

Berkeley had now lost its Pill and its status as a sea port. For 2,000 years it had been navigated up until 1926 by Barques of 40 ton and 120 ton Schooners, which negotiated the twisting bends to bring their commerce to Berkeley; now trout and other fresh water fish inhabit this stretch of water.

In 1975 temperatures rose to 82/84° which meant a hot, dry summer. But if 1975 was hot 1976 was even hotter, it was the hottest summer for 200 years and perhaps for more than a thousand years.

When rain fell in September a drought ended that had lasted all through the summer months. Heaths and woodlands were in danger of fire. The Fire Service was on call for 24 hours a day and some firemen were on the point of exhaustion because no sooner had one fire been extinguished than another one started. Trees on the Cotswold slopes were drying out and dying and the foundations of houses were cracking due to the drying out of the sub-soil. The temperature was well into the 90's on five consecutive days. The work force, where possible, started work early in the morning and finished at midday to miss the heat.

The first week in June saw the temperature well into the 80's and the night of July 11th was hot and sultry. Bedroom windows were thrown open and bedclothes abandoned until 2am when a loud clap of thunder awoke people from an uneasy sleep. Followed by gale force winds and lashings of rain, the thunder and lightning lasted until late in the afternoon of the following day. 3 inches of rain fell in one hour in parts of the Vale and it was the longest thunderstorm in living memory.

SHARPNESS DOCKS - POST WAR

The war period of intense activity ended with the end of hostilities in Europe. Sharpness Dock trade declined and the port reverted back to a small timber and grain dock again, with Britain having to pay for its imports and the export trade not yet geared to peace time. Aid from U.S.A. diminished and the dollar was being used to rebuild Germany and Europe. Timber trade was poor as the forests of Europe and Russia had not yet recovered from the ravages of war. The building trade, the main users of the imported timber, was not yet geared to a peace time building programme. Dockers were out of work for long periods and the dock and canal were near to closing. Only the revenue of the petroleum traffic passing through the port and travelling on the canal kept the dock open. Gradually trade improved although it never reached the heights of pre-World War 1.

The loss of the Severn Railway Bridge in October 1960 ended a link with the Forest of Dean after 90 years and by 1969 all that was left was a pile of stones on the west bank, a few broken pillars showing at low water and the round base of the swing bridge on the canal tow path. It seems that with the loss of the bridge the decline of Sharpness started. First the fleet of small river tankers left our waterways to be replaced by a fleet of larger tankers carrying 1,000 tons or more of petroleum and black oil to Quedgeley and Monks Meadow at Gloucester, but with the closing of the

Dismantling Severn Bridge 1967

Sharpness Station

Quedgeley depot these ships disappeared also. Severn Mills closed its doors and the buildings were demolished to make way for Cooper's Metals, a scrap yard exporting scrap metal. Severn Mills, a provender mill, provided a large variety of cattle food under the name of "Sharpex" between the wars and carried a workforce of 60 to 70.

Sharpness lost its Railway Station in 1967 and with it its passenger service, whereby one could board a train at Sharpness (or Berkeley) and travel to any part of the British Isles and guarantee to arrive on time.

The Gas Works on the canal bank was dismantled and the manager's house pulled down.

The people of Sharpness and district waved a sad farewell to the "Vindi" as she was towed from her berth to the breakers' yard at Newport. Farewells were also said to the Officers and staff who had manned her for the last 27 years.

The bus service dwindled to one bus a day and, to some villages, only once a week.

The Sharpness Hotel closed its doors as a public house and later too did The Railway and Severn Bridge Hotel.

The Dock that once employed 200 men was reduced. Many men, some in their seventies, were retired while younger men took over the handling of cargoes. With new methods and modern lifting gear the way of manhandling in the old-fashioned way was finished.

New roads were built around the Dock to take the ever increasing weight of the lorries. A new by-pass road was promised to help bring new life to the docks. Eventually it was built but the expected industry (at the time of writing) never materialised. True, they built a new factory but it cost the public their playing field; to date; its doors have remained shut.

Sharpness Football Club also lost its' ground and facilities and seems unable to obtain another ground.

The small community of Dinmore Road was rehoused and the old houses demolished to make way for a lorry park.

New development has been promised for the future. Let us hope it is for the benefit of the local people. Their forefathers built the docks and strove hard in both work and play to maintain a standard rated highly in the County.

It is our **INHERITANCE** and that of future generations yet unborn.

Appendix A

Diary of George Smith 1821 - 1823

August 1st 1821
Paid John Ford for straw £1-15 shillings.
Went down the Berkeley Pill to vet the widening and shoaring, at the same time made a complaint to Mr W Powell the surveyor respecting the manner in which the opposite bank was done, cost at 2 shilings and six pence a perch.

August 4th
Paid Richard Winter for preserving pheasants nest - 7 shillings. In the morning went up the Newground to Frampton Pill and seized of the following livestock on John Nicholls land, 2 milch cows, 4 yearling beasts and 4 weaning calves.

August 5th
A Sunday. Two men came to me about Job Davies stealing a horse.

August 6th
Paid W Allen for hauling stone and bark -£1-6 shillings.

August 7th
Went with C Jenner to examine the turnpike house at Mobley.

August 10th Paid Farmer Watts mowers six shillings. Went to Aust and Rudgeway, suspect Job Davies. Paid Jo Brown on account for shoaring Berkeley Pill - £2.0.0. Paid Richard Roberts for geese killed by the foxes eight shillings. Paid E Kennett in full for repairs to Sea Wall and putting up bridge at Newgrounds - £4.

August 14th
Paid John Mansell in part of years wages as earthstopper - £10.

August 20th
Paid Richard Weatherstone £27 for covered mares.

August 22nd
Met John Purnell at Sharpness Point to arrange about a new Boat House there.

August 25th
Paid Betty Howard 4 weeks wages - 8 shillings.Paid self in part of salary - £30.0.0.

September 1st
Went with Cook and Adams to show them over Haynis Farm Wanswell offered it at £175 a year rent.

September 2nd
Went to Micklewood to look out some Oak timber for post at Boat House. Colonel Berkeley began hunting.

September 4th
Tho'd Watts discharged from his situation as Porter and Tho'd Browning engaged in his place at £8 -18 shillings a year.

September 5th
Went to Luggs Farm to look out rough timber for Matford bridge.

September 19th Paid J Baker Whipper in, his wages £6 -2 shillings

September 22nd
Paid E Kennett for throwing the mud away from the Boat House - 18 shillings. Paid E Kennett for cutting down timber at Luggs Farm - 12 shillings. Paid E Munday for masonry -£8. Paid Col. Berkeley - £50. Paid John Dowell sailors wages - £8 - 6 shillings.

September 24th
Paid John Hall for night watching - £2-18 shillings. Paid J Brown and G Chair for throwing mud from the new Boat House at Sharpness Point - £1.0.0. Paid W Humphrey for sawing at new Boat House -£1.0.0.

October 3rd
Paid William Long for a dead horse - £1.0.0. Went to Damery to tell G Nelmes that he must quit the cottage and Colonel Berkeley's service.

October 5th
Paid W Long for labourers wages £50. Paid Richard Pick for cutting down timber in Micklewood for Boat House - 10 shillings.

October 6th
Paid Tho'd. Nelmes 10 shillings for taking Job Davies.

October 15th
Paid 16 shillings to W Birch for gathering fruit in the gardens for 7- days.

November 3rd
Paid W Millard for thatching at World Ends Farm - £15-7 shillings and 8 pence.

November 17th
Paid J Mackintoch 5 shilings for beer for the gardener.

November 19th
Paid John Clearwater £3-3 shillings for taking poachers.

November 22nd
Paid W Humphrey for sawing at Boat House -£13.14s.6d.

November 23rd
Paid D Ford for foxes - f4.4s.0d.

November 27th
Paid J Cullomore for poultry killed by the foxes £1.0.0.

November 29th
Paid Turnpike Toll for Berkeley Gate - £1.3s.2d.

December 1st
Paid W Hunt for repairs to boats - £16.15.2.

December 3rd
Paid self in part of salary - £50.

December 8th
Went in the evening to Flowers Cottage at Woodford, Let it to them at £3 a year.

December 15th
Paid T Clark, the park keeper half a years wages- £28.7.6. Paid J Dowell and other boatmen- £1.13.0.

December 17th
Went to Wotton, paid Dan Millard for hedging - £4.0.0.

December 19th
Paid W Philpots for Baskets - £2.2.0.

December 21st
Paid Stephen Jenner for medicine for the house-hold - £17.3.0.

December 25th
Received of David White half a years rent - £26.

December 26th
Received of Geo. Hall in full a half years rent £10. Paid J Woodman for poultry killed by foxes - 14 shillings.

December 28th
Went to Gloucester to pay taxes, Coach hire and expence - 16 shillings.

December 29th
Paid Henry Light 13 weeks wages for Turnpike -£6.4.2. Paid Wm. Perkins for thatching roof of the ice house - £1.2.6. Paid R Payne and W Rupell for going to the Tump at Frampton with the boats - 10 shillings.

December 31st
Let Oakhunger Farm to J Barber. Daniel Derrett at £90 agreed to build a small house at Tiley.

January 1st 1822
Paid John King a years wages - £64.10.11. Went to Gloucester and saw the Inspector of Taxes who agreed to a declaration of 24 horses, 4 ponies and 4 greyhounds but objected to the number or other dogs.

January 3rd
Went to Alvestone to see about Job Davies -prosecution, expences for myself and the constable - 12 shillings.

January 11th
All day engaged with the examination of Job Davies who was again committed to prison.

January 15th Paid W Dimery for Masonery - £2.

February 2nd
Paid W Pictchard £5 for catching rats. Received £20 from Mrs Sharp for part payment of rent.

February 6th
Paid Tho. Richards £112.9.6. for oats and barley.

February 8th
Went to Wick to inspect Job Davies's sale.

February 15th
Went to Slimbridge to seize 12 cows and 5 yearlings for the sum of £105.10.0. for rent due to Col.Berkeley.

February 23rd
Paid E Kennett £10 for banking sea wall at Purton.

March 5th
Paid Sam Hale, Constable of Berkeley - 19 shillings.Paid Robert King, Constable of Berkeley - 10 shillings.

March 8th
Paid Will Pick £15 to buy him a horse.

March 18th
Paid Dan'il Varey - 8 shillings for conveying two poachers to jail.

March 25th
Paid James Allen for Porkers - £4.10.4. Paid John Saniger for a Porker - £1.11.0.

March 29th
Paib Tho'd. Gough for a fox - £1.11.6.

April 1st
Paid John Savage for Turnpike - £1.

April 3rd
Received of B Mills £65 for 24 elm trees.

April 8th
Paid Ham Turnpike toll - 10 shillings and 8 pence.

April 9th
John Dowell for hauling freight up Berkeley Pill - £4.

April 27th
Paid wages of 8 keepers for a week - £7.4s.0d.

May 3rd
Paid W Wood for foxes - £5.5.0.

May 7th
Received from Colonel Berkeley £1,000.Went to Cheltenham to pay Col. Berkeley's Bills:-
    Paid Simon Turk for saddle £40. 0. 7
    John Gunton for confections £100. 1. 0.

Jo Shipton for Hats	£15.17. 0.
Tho'd Jordan for meat	£10.14. 4.
Elz. Roberts for Stationery	£9.14. 8.
James Wilday for Poultry	£45.15. 4.
John Henry for shoeing horses	£11.13. 6.
Wilson - Hairdresser	£9.19. 0.
Will. Long - bread	£14. 3. 0.
Richard Humphrey- Livery Stables	£240. 4. 8.
Will. Gyde - grocery	£167. 6. 4.
Tho'd William - coats	£32.13. 0.
Will. Balliniger - cream	£3.18. 3.
James Ackett - Hay and Corn	£348. 4. 2.
John Yates - Earthenware	£5. 0. 0.
James Neyler - Tavern bills	£50. 0. 0.
Will. Perry - milk	£4.12. 7.
James Wilday - Poultry	£45. 8. 8.
Edw. Young - Fish	£10. 0. 0.

Paid expences and coach to Cheltenham - £1.8.0.
Received of various tenants for rent due at Lady Day - £9,526.9.0.

May 14th
Paid John Ford for sage cheese - £6.10.0.
Paid W Hoplin for 2 fox cubs - £1.1.0.

May 18th
Paid W Appley 5 shillings and four pence for stone digging.

May 20th Paid John Davies £10 for a horse.

June 3rd Paid Robert Cox £54.12.0. for 39 sheep.

June 5th
Paid Tyler and Young £3.13.6. for fox cubs.

June 10th
Received of Richard Denning for quarrying stone 31 loads at £1.11.0. a load.

June 25th
Tolls at Berkeley Gate - 10 shillings and four pence.

June 29th
Paid John Dowell for freight up the Pill - one load of stone - £5.0.0.
July 1st Col. Berkeley went back to Cheltenham.

July 4thPaid Dan Poole for foxes - £4.16.6.

July 6th
Went to Breadstone Farm to inspect upstairs.

July 11th
Ordered Tho'd. Workman to bring ant eggs for Pheasants next Monday which will be the 15th.

July 12th
Paid W Wills Mower - 2 shillings. Paid W Foxwell and G Ponting 6 shillings for mowing. Col. Berkeley went to London.

July 20th
Paid W Reynolds to discharge servants, wages -£200.7.3. Paid John Mayo for pump repairs - £2.

July 23rd
In the afternoon went to Neale's at Wanswell to demand rent.

July 25th
Paid self a months travelling expence - £13.8.0. At home all day in the Castle.

July 30th
Went to Simoned Hall with farmer Neale to inspect the coming crop.

August 1st
At the Castle all morning, went to inspect theBrown Mill in the afternoon.

August 10th
Paid Jos Brown and I Phillips - 12 shillings for sinking a well.

August 15th
Started to inspect all farms with W Long, 7 farms at Alkington.

August 16th
Inspected 7 more farms at Alkington.

August 19th
Went over 13 farms at Hinton with W Long. Paid Richard Wilkins - 2 shillings for preserving pheasant nests.

August 21st
Went over all the farms in Slimbridge, Cowley, Cam and Stinchcombe.

August 23rd
Went over Nibley and Wotton farms with W Long.

August 30th
Paid Susan Fryer for washing - £15.17.0.

August 31st
Paid W Long salary - £30.0.0.

September 1st
Went to Newgrounds with Col. Berkeley and W Long and met W Cowley there, inspected the farm. Colonel Berkeley ordered a notice to quit to be served on Cowley.

September 2nd
In the morning to Mickelwood with W Pick, ordered a few dead Oaks to be cut of Oldlands Groves, for repairs of fences there, and to Micklewood farm-house to inspect the state of the building.

September 3rd
Received rent of Berkeley School - 10 shillings.

September 4th
Went to Slimbridge to serve farmer Cowley with notice to quit.

September 6th
Went to Clapton, offered to reduce Mary Pullen's rent to £45, she is to give notice.

September 7th
Paid John Maddey for tuneing the organ - £2.2.0.

September 8th
Col. Berkeley went to Cheltenham.

September 9th
Hounds and part of the horses went to Cheltenham.
Paid Robert Neale for earthstopping - £5.5.0.
Paid Robert Neale for Bark stripping - £2.6.6.
Received of W Cowley part rent due on Lady Day - £100.

September 21st
Paid Robert Preace meat bill - £50.

September 24th
Paid William Burton - 6 pence for a weasel.

October 3rd
Co. Berkeley went hunting. Paid Jos Hall -£116.14.7. for groceries. Paid John Luxton for ironmongery - £29.18.6. Paid John Cooper for mops and buckets - £20.15.0.

October 7th
Paid J Phillips for well sinking - £19.7.0.

October 9th
Paid John Dowell - sailors wages - £7.14.3.

October 19th
Paid W Haviland for going with boats to get Withey sets - £3.3.0.

October 23rd
Paid Dinner bill at Wotton for-court - £5.8.2.
Paid Betty Howard 4 weeks pay - 8 shillings.

November 4th
Received of various tenants rent due at Lady Day- £9,084.9.6.

November 6th
Paid Tho'd. Manning for nails - £61.1.8.

November 7th
Went to Cowley and seized stock of T Longney.
November 8th
Received of T Longney in full rent for Lady Day - £10.

November 9th
Paid John Dowell - £21.15.0. for freight of stone to repair sea wall. Paid John Dowell sailors wages - £3.

November 11th
Paid Isasic Palmer for painting fire engine -

November 12th
Paid half years rent on my house - £11.

November 13th
Paid Tho'd. Clark for vermin and Turnpiker -£4.8.7.

December 1st
Col. Berkeley, the hounds and horses came down from Cheltenham.

December 11th
Paid vet for attending my horse - £1.15.0.

December 19th
Paid W Long for labours wages - £29.14.9. In the afternoon went to W Cowley's farm at Slimbridge, who declined taking the Newgrounds on Colonel Berkeleys terms. Colonel Berkeley went to Cheltenham in the evening.

December 21st
I went to Tockington and ordered 8 vermin traps of Stevens the Blacksmith at £1.5.0. each.

December 24th
Paid W Longman for pitching stone at Pedington -5 shillings.

January 2nd 1823
Paid Ic. Nelmes for a martin cat - 10 shillings and six pence. Went to Purton understanding that the

Canal Company had trespassed upon the land there in W Jones's occupation - Found two men excavating, ordered then to quit the premises. Afterwards saw their employers - Mackinzie and Mc-Crew who after many threats withdrew the men. Afterwards went to Dursley to see Bloxsome the solicitor on the subject and brought an answer back from him.

January 3rd
Went again to Purton in the morning to see if the Canal Company had continued to excavate. Afternoon went again with men to pull down canal huts. Paid the men 1 shilling and sixpence for beer.

January 7th
In the afternoon went again to the Severn bank to pull down canal huts, where all was pulled down but one. Paid men for beer - 8 shillings.

January 24th
Paid J Sheppard - £2.2.0. for a fox.

January 29th
Went to Gossington to demand rent of White, afterwards to W Cowley, issued notice to quit. Received of W Cowley in full rent to Michamas - £50. Paid W Cowley £25 expence of fixing new fences at Newgrounds.

February 22nd
Went over to Breadstone to check workmen onto Hurst Farm to order painters' work, and to Priors Wood Farm for the same, and to demand the rent, looked at some trees by the roadside at Purton on land in Robert Hoptons occupation and directed what topping to be done. W Oldland took Hinton Farm at £250 per Ann.

February 26th
Cot. Berkeley went to Cheltenham.

March 6th
Paid Jacol Pick for hire of carriage and pair - £4.10.2. Took account of Powell's vermin - 22

cats, 2 owls, 2 jays, 10 weasels, 1 fitcher and 7 crows.

March 8th
Paid John Powell for Barley in the straw - £30.

March 10th
Went coursing for hare with Mr Strange.

March 11th
Went up the line of the canal with Mr Fletcher the company's Engineer and W Long.

March 15th
Paid Tho'd. Rufield - Constable for taking Herbert to prison - 14 shillings.

March 16thSunday. Went to Cheltenham met Col. Berkeley on the subject of the canal. Paid my expences to and from Cheltenham - £1.1.0.

March 17th
Paid William Gough for a fox - £2.10.0.

March 25th
Paid Ceo. Ponting for fat heifer - £13.0.0.

March 26th
Paid John Hickes for musical attend to the household and Col. Berkeley - £7.2.4.

April 1st
Went over Hinton Farm with W Oldland and measured the line of the canal from Purton to Sharpness Point. Paid to canal men for measuring the canal - 4 shillings.

April 19th
Went to Leatherbottle to inspect the Turnpike road.
Paid Betty Howard - 8 shillings for 4 weeks pay. Paid W Long for labourers wages - £40. Paid John Purnell for carpenter work - £8. Paid Gee. Davies for paintwork - £5.

April 22nd
Paid for earthstoppers dinner - £40.8.8.
April 23rd
Paid W R Pearce for Malt and Hops - £192.6s.4p.

April 25th
Paid Cath Sharp for fish - £16.19.7.

May 6th
Paid James Gay for foxes - £3.12.0.

May 8th
Paid Sarah Workman for fowls killed by the hounds at Gossington - 6 shillings.

May 12th
Paid William Jordan for meat - £44.7.8.

May 23rd
Paid Toll on Mobley Gate - £1.0.4.

May 24th
Paid John Powell half a years wages - £34.10.0. Received of John Powell half a years rent - £10.0.6.

May 26th
Paid Poor's Rate on the Castle in Berkeley Bough £19.13.9

May 27th
Paid a man for walking a bull from Cheltenham - 14 shillings.

May 29th
Paid R Saunder for a boat - £1.9.0. Paid J Copens for fish - £74.4.3.

May 31st
Paid earthstoppers and game keepers - £78.13.0. Paid Ed. Munday for mason work - £20.0.0.

June 2nd
Paid Constable for taking poachers to prison -£1.16.0.

June 5th
Paid William Gough for 3 fox-cubs - £1.11.6.
June 7th
Received of Robert Pearce in part deposit of Bark - £130 - £60 paid.

June 12th
Paid Dan Marltlove 5 shillings for banking sides of Avon at Browns Mill.

June 19th
Paid John Manns for hens to hatch Pheasant eggs - £3.8.6.

June 20th
Paid Tho'd. Gough £1.11.6. for foxes.

June 23rd
Paid W Day for coach hire - £112.0.0. Received from W Day half years rent - £25.0.0.

June 26th
Paid John Weeks for painters work at keeper's cottage in Michelwood - £1.13.9.

June 27th
New whipper in came by the name of Wilson.

July 5th
Paid Robert Pearce for salt - £16.1.6. Paid Col. Berkeley's hotel bill - f72.10.4. Paid postage on Col. Berkeley's hotel bill - £2.8.2.

July 7th
Paid William Hunt for wine - £14.17.9.

July 8th
Paid Turner for Oats and Oat Meal - £136.2.0.

July 9th
Went to Weymouth to inspect estate, returned on July 13th.

July 25th
Received of William Smith £6 for a cow.

July 27th
Sunday. Colonel Berkeley came to the Castle but no housekeepers needed.

July 30th
Paid Emanual Nelmes - a mower - 6 shillings.

August 11th
Paid mowers on Oakley Farm - £1.1.0. Paid mowers on Gabb's Farm - 1 shilling. Went to Wanswell about moving the pound.

August 27th
Paid a man 1 shilling for taking a letter to Bristol.

August 31st
Housekeeping begane at the Castle. Col. Berkeley came down in the evening.

September 1st
A bad sovereign which I took last aldit and paid to Mr Alpass was returned to me this day.

September 5th
Paid £5 to Mrs Hobbs for poultry killed by foxes. Paid Jess Rupill for a heifer and 8 sheep killed by a greyhound - £17.3.7. Received of Jess Rupill in full for rent - £53.

September 6th
Paid N Neale for bricks - £114.10.3. Paid George Davilge for Page work - £5.0.0. Paid John Cornock 3 weeks board and wages - £2.2.0.

September 8th
Advanced Col. Berkeley £30 which is to be returned.

September 18th
Paid Col. Berkeley £20 which he is to pay back.

September 20th
Went up the line of the canal with Mr Fletcher to look at the propose line for the streams of water to be deviated.

September 22nd
Paid Cot. Berkeley £30 which he is to pay back.
September 25th
Went to Wotton fair.

October 4th
Paid self 1 years saddle money - £7.10.0.

October 6th
Inspected Middle Mill at Woodford, went on to Browns Mill to order a wall at the mill head.

October 9th
Paid John Dowell - sailors wages - £5.3.6.

October 20th
Paid Robert Stevens - servants wages - £10.15.6. on quiting the service.

October 21st
Paid John King half a years wages - £33.12.2. Received of John King years rent - £6.0.6.

October 25th
Paid wages due on the quarter for servants - £231.15.2.

November 4th
Received of Woodward for firewood out of Mickelwood - £6. Paid Ed Munday for masonary - £20.

November 8th
Paid Sam Bendall for Bark hauling - £7.17.6. Paid C Cook for the hire of boat to stop the sheep from drowning - £1.11.0.

November 13th
Paid Will Page part of money due on contract for building two houses in Berkeley - £100.

November 17th
Went over Nibley woods to inspect hedging done by Millard.

November 18th
Paid John Fryer for fish bill - £8.16.5.
Paid John Payne coachman wages - £23.0.9.

November 25th
Paid John Dowell for shipping stone to sea wall - £16.3.4.

December 8th
Paid Martin Spillman for cooper work - £8.4.4.

December 13th
Paid Tho'd. Skuse for preserving foxes on Colonel Kingscot Manor - £2.2.0. Paid William Perkins for thatching at Bevington - £1.3.6.

December 16th
Met Mr Fletcher to inspect the injury done by the water overflowing from the canal at the Newgrounds. Mr Fletcher admitted the injury and that the canal company to pay for it.

December 25th
Paid Pardise - a boy, for bringing in a lost hound - 2 shillings and 3 shillings and six pence for calf skin, of calf eaten by the hound.

December 30th
Went with W Long to Slimbridge to view the place where the water from the canal came over at old brook and where W Cowley himself had cut away the bank to make a sheep wash.

December 31st
Horses and Hounds went to Cheltenham. Paid Ann Ruther servant wages - £3.5.5. Paid Jos Rowe servant wages - £9.18.9. Paid Tho's Gates servant wages - £13.2.6. Paid self Quarter salary -£63.10.0.

Appendix B

Tradesmen

1830 Charles Edmonds - Saddler, Newport.
1859 James Phipps - Boot and Shoe Maker,
Church Lane Berkeley.
1859 James Eley - Saddle and Harness Maker.
1859 Samuel King - Boot and Shoe Maker.
1867 George Long - Shoe Maker, Mobley.
1867 Harriet Smith - Boot and Shoe Maker,
Market Place.
1874 Arthur Rodway - Saddler, Clapton.
1879 Edwards Groves - Saddler,
Canonbury Street.

Blacksmiths, Farriers and Ironmongers:

1859 John Hurcombe - Blacksmith.
Thomas King   - Blacksmith.
Jasper Goole   - Blacksmith,
Canonbury Street.
Benjamin Wyatt - Blacksmith, Hinton.
Daniel Wyatt   - Blacksmith, Halmore.
E. Woodward - Blacksmith, Newport.
1867 William Trotman - Shoeing Smith,
Marybrook Street.
1874 P. Clark - Ironmonger.
J. Gabb - Farrier, Woodford.
Thomas King - Blacksmith,
Canonbury Street.
John Smith - Blacksmith, Breadstone.
Edward Wyatt - Blacksmith, Purton.
1885 Thomas Knight -Shoeing Smith,
Marybrook Street.
Alfred Mallett - Blacksmith, Halmore.
1889 William Bennet - Blacksmith,
Salter Street.
1902 Charles Allen - Smith, Halmore.
George Hobbs - Shoeing Smith,
Berrycroft.

Wheelwrights -Berkeley and District:

1865 J. Ayliff - Salter Street.
J. Bick - Marybrook.
Henry Dyer - Newport.
1875 Henry Andrews -Stone.
Absalom Cornock - Newport.
John Howard -Lower Stone.
James Thomas - Marybrook.
1885   Thomas James - Berrycroft.
William Organ - Newport.

Plasterers. Plumbers and Carpenters:

1859 William Cope - Plasterer, Salter Street.
H. Phillips - Plumber and Glazier,
High Street.
1867 George Code - Plasterer, High Street.
Gastbell Phillips - Plumber, Glazier
and Painter, High Street.
1875 Joseph Stabbin - Plumber, Glazier
and Painter, High Street.
Thomas Wilkins - Plasterer, Salter Street.
1889 William Boulton - Plumber, Lynch Road.
1902   T Harris and Sons -Plumbers, Salter Street.
1865   Charles Aycliffe - Carpenter, Salter Street.
1875 Henry Andrews - Carpenter, Stone.
1879 James Thomas - Carpenter and Undertaker,
Marybrook Street.

Huntsmen, Gamekeepers and Decoymen:

1867 Thomas Estop - Head Gamekeeeper,
Halmore.
Charles Hamblin -Huntsman, High Street.
John Hancock -Gamekeeper, Mobley.
William Hazell - Gamekeeper,
Michaelwood.
Elias Mills - Head Gamekeeper, Icefield.

1875   William Backhouse -Huntsman,
High Street.
William Nicholls - Decoyman,
Decoy Pools, Purton.
James Pullen - Gamekeeper, Coldelm,
Alkington.
1885   Henry Grant - Huntman, High Street.
1889   William Rawle - Head Huntsman,
High Street.

Butcher of Berkeley and Sharpness:

1859 John Allen - Salter Street, Berkeley.
Stephen Alpass - Market Place,
Berkeley.
Henry Burchell - Upper Stone.
George James - Stock Lane, Berkeley.
William Smith - High Street, Berkeley.

1866   Thomas King - Bacon Merchant, Stone.
Henry Peglar -Butcher and Shopkeeper,
Purton.
John Shipp - Bacon Curer, Stone.
Samuel Summers -Butchers
and Shopkeeper, Newport.

1875   William Bendall - Shopkeeper,
Breadstone.
George Hodder - Butcher, Grocer, Purton
(Berkeley Hunt)
James Hodder - Butcher, Grocer,
Sharpness New Dock.
Martin Neale -Butcher, Bacon Curer,
High Street, Berkeley.
William Smith - Grocer and Butcher,
Sharpness Point.
Samuel Summers - Butchers, Haines,
Wanswell.

Coffee Houses in Berkeley:

1885 Alfred Merret - Salter Street.
1889 Edward Lovelock - Coffee Tavern,
High Street.

1889 Edward Lovelock - Coffee Tavern,
High Street.
1902 Hannon Blakemore - Refreshment Rooms,
Marybrook.
John Jacobs - Refreshment Rooms,
Salter Street.
1906 Mrs Mary Pick - Coffee Tavern,
High Street.
1858 James King - Candlemaker, Market Place,
Berkeley.

Hairdressers:

1869 Joseph Sturge - Market Place, Berkeley.
1879 Edward Aldridge.
1889 Walter Long - High Street, Berkeley.
1902 John Fisher - Canonbury Street, Berkeley.
William Fisher - Sharpness Docks.

Chemist Shops in Berkeley:

1830   Stephen Jenner - Druggist.
1859   Pope and Co - High Street.
H Pullen - High Street.
Hester Warner - High Street.
1865   Edward Collinson Bell - High Street.
1867   Henry and Broad - Druggist and Chemist,
High Street.
1875   Robert Mitchell - High Street.
1885   Albert Cowen - Chemist and Druggist,
High Street.
1889   William Stepen Parker - Horse and
Cattle Medicine, High Street.
1902   George Warner - High Street.

Surgeons in Berkeley:

1858 Francis Hands - Surgeon, Salter Street.
John Cox Hicks - Surgeon, Stock Lane.
Charles Leek - Surgeon.
1867 Hands and Bridge.
1875 Issac Thomas Bridgeman
(Cottage Hospital attendant)
1885 Walter Robert Alwdry - Surgeon Medical
Officer and Public Vaccinator to Berkeley
Districy, Thornbury Unions, High Street

also Medical Officer at Cottage Hospital (later the Berkeley Hospital).

1902 Mrs Flood - Matron of Hospital.

1906 Miss Ship - Matron.
Arthur John Awdry - Surgeon, High Street.

Police

1865 James Harris - Police Constable, Purton.
Charles Mason - Police Sergeant, Canonbury Street.

1875 Thomas Taylor - Police Sergeant, Canonbury Street.

Charles Hawkins - In Charge, Purton.
James Eshelby - Constable, Wick.

1889 Edward Cooke - Sergeant, Berkeley.

Brewers:

1865 Fear and Son - Coopers, Maltster, Canonbury Brewery.
Pearce Thomas Taylor - Maltster, ales, Malt House, Hinton.
Thomas Woolwright - Maltster, Salter Street, Berkeley.

1874 Benjamin Fear - Brewer, Canonbury Street, Berkeley.

Appendix C

LANDLORDS

My gratitude to Mr John Langford of Newtown for his knowledge of names of the Landlords of local inns and public houses.

"The Monkey House"

(so named by the local inhabitants) was also known as "The Three Salmons", "Bunch of Grapes" and "The Hook Street Inn". Situated in Hook Street it was the first inn travellers met on the road (Old Lane) from Sharpness, also visited by tide bound sailors on the Berkeley Pill or by sailors waiting to load bricks from the brickworks.

Landlords

1865 Miss Mary Alpass.
1875 John Alpass.
1894 James Herbert Gazzard.
1906 Cornelius Lord.
1923 Sydney Cooper.
The inn closed about 1927-28

"Brewers Arms"

(Three Tuns, Three Tubs) : situated in Lynch Lane near to Brickworks also had a wharf, and was later used as a coal wharf by Mr "Jumbo" Lewis;

Landlords

1865 Joseph Stratford.
1885 George Nicholls.
1906 Oliver Nicholls.
1923 Miss M Nicholls.

1927 Mrs Eva Coveneney
1931 Mr William "Jumbo" Lewis.
195? Mrs Mary Lewis.
It closed in the 1960's.

"Boars Head", Lynch Lane.

Landlords

1842 Charles Dowell (Boatman on the Pill).
1867 George Bennett (Baker).
1879 Elizabeth Bennett.
1885 William Bennett.
1889 Mrs Emma Mills.
1897 William Browning.
1910 George Else.
1914 John Northncott.
1935 Bob Fryer.
1945 Albert Palmer.
1954 Marcel Knowles.

"Mariners Arms"

- was situated at the top of Stock Lane. It is said to be the site of the "Ivy Bush Inn" mentioned by Smyth in 1600 (I disagree with that arguement (R. T. Denning). In the reign of Edward II (1307) Robert Avery held the wharf on the Pill at Stock Lane. His Mansion or Manor House was on top of the land overlooking his stock of goods (hence its name - Stock Lane). The Mansion House was known as Avery Mansion; later this property came to the female side of the family the Thorpe family of Sanigar and Wanswell Court in 1639 and stayed in the family for many years:

The Berkeley Vale

Landlords

1844 William Gabb.
1852 William Parslow.
1859 Elias Hale.
1870 Isaac Godfree.
1875 Charlie Groves.
1879 Egbert Jenkins.
1885 Henry Bruton.
1902 John Martin.
1906 George Jones.
1910 George Hodges.
1914 Tom Haynes.
1923 Harry Green.
1927 Albert Green.
1931 John Foster.
1935 Mrs Lucy Foster.

POST WAR
S Barrett.
A Daley.

"Ship Inn"

Pill Wharf, Stock Lane, in 1820 was held by John Dowell who was Pill Master (In today's terms Harbour Master). He was also a ship owner - whether he was an inn keeper as well is not known.

Landlords

1842 Rachel Minett.
1859 John Dowell
(Coal Merchant and Brickmaker).
1870 Benjamin Jones.
1874 William Denning.
1885 John Horseman (Coal Dealer).
1889 Samuel Rice.
1897 Charles Nind Workman.
1902 Catherine Stone.
1906 James Nelmes.
Closed - now a private residence.

"Berkeley Hunt"
Salter Street
(Next door to the Union Chapel).

Landlords

1874 Elias Hale.
1885 Mrs Hannah Hale.
1902 Francis William Beecham.
1923 Albert Davies.
Closed about 1936.

"Black Horse",
Salter Street.
(The opposite of Salter Street to the Berkeley Hunt).

Landlords

1859 - 1889 Robert Reynolds.
1906 John Launder.
Closed with the closing down of the Cheese Market in 1910.
Demolished in the 1960's.

"George Inn"
(George and Dragon).

Landlords:

1844 Henry Cook.
1859 Henry Poole.
1867 Hester Poole.
1870 Maurice Wallace.
1874 Mrs Martha Spence.
1875 Henry Mills.
1889 Elias Baker.
1897 William Knight.
1914 Percy Stump.
1935 Alfred Brisland.
Post War: Harold Brisland.
Closed 1990.

"Lamb Inn"

Market Place, Lamb Court. (Up an alleyway by the side of the George Inn - now Aldridge's Shop). In the 1400's this site was connected with the selling of sheep.

Landlords:

1859 James Allen.
1866 Henry Birch.
1875 John Baker.
1897 Henry Cook.
1902 George Jones.
1906 William Bird.
Closed about 1910. Now demolished.

"Berkeley Arms Hotel"

Posting House, Cononbury Street. Owned by the Berkeley Estate.

Landlords:

1865 John Cary.
1870 Benjamin Harris.
1874 William Denningham.
1879 Pearce Thomas Taylor.
1885 Edward Gregory.
1894 Edward Brown.
1902 Nimrod Long.
1906 Lewis Hunt.
1910 George St. John.
1927 Berkeley Arms Trust House Limited.
Post War: F Browning.

"White Hart Hotel"

High Street. (White Hart Inn - a coaching inn which brewed its own beer - 1885). In 1540 it was the Excise Offices for Berkeley.

Landlords:

1830 John Lait.
1844 Elizabeth Lait.
1859 Webster Swan.
1870 Eli Rodger.
1874 John Pickard.
1885 Edmund Pickard
(Commercial Hotel, Posthouse and Brewery).
1889 Henry Knight.

Post War: Smith
Now closed as a Public House.

"The Swan",

High Street.

Landlords:

1844 Hugh Baker.
1859 John Cope.
1889 Ellen Cope.
1902 William Heaven.
1906 Jesse Feris.
1914 Ernest Bevan.
1923 Alec Hayes.
1927 Francis Cole.
Post War: Percy Roddick.
Closed in 1968.

"White Lion"

High Street.

Landlords:

1844 - 1853 Webster Swan.
1859 - 1889 Thomas Pick.
1902 Charles Thomas Roberts.
1906 Henry Clutterbuck.
1931 Robert Atkin.
1936 Reginald White.
1989 Albert Saunders.
1941 Frank Irwin.
1954 Jack Heavens.
Closed in 1961.

The Berkeley Vale

"The Bear Inn"

High Street known as the "Wine Vaults". Built in 1750. The Lord Berkeleys had a trade link with Bordeaux - wool for wine. Fine French wine was shipped by the Berkeley's own ships up the Pill to discharge at the Castle Wharf, High Street, the Lord of the Castle taking his share into the Castle, the captain selling his share to pay for the running of the ship and crew's wages

Landlords:

1852   Alfred William Glover
         (Landlord, Wine and Spirit Merchant).
1874   Mary Ann Glover
         (Wine and Spirit Merchant).
1885   Stephen Barber
         (Wine and Spirit Merchant).
1902 Charles Henry Barber.
1923 - 1935 William Pascall
         (Wine and Spirit Merchant).

Closed in 1935.

"The Bird In Hand",

Mary-Le-Brook Street (Marybrook). It held several names before being called the Bird In Hand:-

1808 - "The Ship".
1834 - "The Kings Head".
1887 - "The Bird In Hand".

Landlords;

1859   Josian Woodman.
1865   Hester Woodman.
1875   George Cook.
1889   John Horseman.
1902   Mary Neskins.
1914   George Blake.
1923   Benjamin Davis.
1931   Fred Cooper.

Post War   Fred Cooper (Son).
            Reg Turl.
            Dick Hewitt.

A Saturday night out for the menfolk was a walk into Berkeley where before 1910 one would have consumed 15 pints of beer if only having one pint in each beerhouse; if one was a glutton for punishment; there was the Plough at Mobley and the Salutation in Ham.

"The Plough" Mobley.

Landlords:

1874 George Long.
1897 Frederick King.
1906 -1923 Absolom Cornock.
1927 Edward Cornock.
1931 -1934 Mrs Rose Cornock.

Closed in 1934.

"The Salutation" Ham.

Landlords:

1858 Edwin Vaisey.
1897 Edwin Vaisey (Son).
1902 James Cope.
1910 Elizabeth Brown.
1931 Edward Hasker.
1939 Jack Minett.
Post War Maurice Brisland.
          D. Smith.

Most of these ale and cider houses were "men only". The womenfolk and children were relegated to the inn's kitchens at the Landlord's discretion. Most of the bars had flagstone floors covered with sawdust, some (if the trade warranted it) had brass spitoons where men could spit out the flow of chewing tobacco, others just used the sawdust floor. The atmosphere was heavy with smoke from the clay pipes that men smoked. Furniture was a bare necessity like a heavy elm table with a heavy form seat each side. Wooded settles were each side of the large open fireplace whereby hung the toasting forks, cider slipper (for warming cider) or a saucepan for boiling snails. These could easily be broken over an opponent's head in the frequent fights that broke out as the evening wore on and as the affects of drink took over. For this same reason there were no pictures on the walls and no ornaments about.

The villages around Berkeley also had their quota of inns for travellers and inhabitants:-

"The Old Bell"

Berkeley Heath. Mentioned in "Pickwick Papers" by Charles Dickens who stayed at the inn on several occasions.

Landlords,

1844 William Parsloe.
1859 William Brown (Cattle Dealer).
1870 John Chard.
1885 John Hooper.
1889 Charles Hooper.
1914 Edward Butcher.
Closed - now a farm.

"The Star Inn"

Heathfield (and shop).

Landlords,

1859 - 1875 John Shipway.

1875 Thomas Wilks.
1889 Mrs Mary Ann Price.
1897 William Eames.
1906 Robert Tarvin.
1914 Thomas Trotman.
1923 Mrs Rose Ruther
    (Husband killed outside inn, hit by bus!)
1927 Ernest Miller.
1931 John Stephenson.
1940 Mrs Stephenson.

Closed - 1964.

"Spread Eagle"

Newport (Newport had nine inns in the village from 1600 to 1750).

Landlords:

1842 Thomas Andrews.
1852 John Hopkins.
1865 William Hill (Haulier).
1889 Henry Cook.
1897 John Webb.
1906 William Gardiner.
1906 Charles Nelmes (Haulier).

Closed - was a farm, now a private house.

"The Crown", Newport.

Landlords:

1842 John Till
1859 David Organ (Farmer).
1870 Mrs Mary Organ.
1874 Epraim Smart.
1875 Job Cook.
1910 William Organ (Wheelwright).
Closed.

"The White Hart" now "The Stagecoach", Newport.

Landlords:

1844 Richard Archard.
1852 Enoch Woodward.
1859 Mary Andrews.
1867 Mrs Mary Wright.
1870 John Stamp.
1874 Robert Allen.
1875 Thomas Oldland (Horsebreaker).
1879 Elias Bragg.
1889 James Barrell.
1902 Esau Meadows.
1906 Denis Allen.
1910 John Morgan.
1914 William Watts.
1923 - 1935 Frederick George Davis.

"Red Lion", Newport.

In 1830 it was a Post Office.

Landlord:

1842 Robert Giles.

Letters from Bristol arrived every evening at 9.30 and were dispatched at 4.30 every afternoon. Letters from Birmingham arrived every morning at 4.30 and were dispatched every evening at 9.30.

"Greyhound" now the "Pickwick Inn", Wick.

Landlords:

1865 John Newth.
1875 Mrs Hester Newth.
1894 James Gough.

1902 John Smith.
1914 Mrs Harriet Smith
1939 John L Smith.
Post War Dusty Miller.

"Fox Inn", Woodford.

Landlords:

1859 J. Ingram.
1867 Walter Locke.
1870 Joseph Davies (Fruiter).
1895 Mrs Catherine Davis.
1902 Tom Thomas.
1906 Joseph Prosser.
1910 George Swain.
1914 W. F. Gwalkin.
1931 Sidney Selwyn.
     Mrs Selwyn.
     Mrs Blick

Closed - 1950?

"Bell & Castle", Newport.

Landlord:

1842 William Nunn.
Closed.

"Crown", Stone - Closed.

Landlords:

1859 Thomas Croome.
1866 Henry Reeves.
1910 - 1923 George Francis Clutterbuck.
Post War J. Applegate.

"New Inn", Stone Green - Closed.

Landlords:

1865 George Andrews
(Carpenter and Wheelwright).
1894 Henry Andrew
(Carpenter and Wheelwright).
1910 - 1936 William Knight Taylor.

"The Crown", Bevington (Ramping Cat).

Landlords:

1875 James Knight.
1894 Mrs Mary Knight.
1902 Sydney Malpass.
1927 Arthur Savoury.
1931 William Marsh.
1935 Samuel Rowles.
    Jack Applegate.
Last Proprietor - Fred Steed.
Closed.

Appendix D

A further list of Landlords

"Berkeley Arms Inn", Purton.
It is situated on the banks of the River Severn.

Landlords:

1858 Daniel Jones (Farmer)
1879 George Hodder
1897 James Hodder (Farmer)
1923 Williams James Cox (Farmer)
1931 Thomas Keedwell
Pre War and Post War Lionel Keedwell
Present Ted Lord

"Berkeley Hunt Inn", Purton.
Situated on the canal bank.

Landlords:

1875 George Hodder (Butcher)
1897 Alfred Hodder
1902 George Nelmes
1930 Lennard Phillips (Butcher)
Post War Tom Tarr
Present Mrs K Musselwhite
          Miss S Nelson

"Pilot Inn", Purton Green

Landlords:

1865 Thomas Woodward (Canal Pilot)
1885 Albert Robertson
1889 Angus Robertson

1902 Mrs Jane Robertson
1923 Mrs Elizabeth Robertson.
1931 Albert Robertson.
Post War Frank Watkins.

Closed in 1965.

"Waifers Arms", Halmore.

Landlords:

1865 George Summers.
1885 - 1906 James Woodward.

Closed - it is now a farmhouse (Jones) - on the dockers' footpath to and from Sharpness.

"Fox and Goose", Halmore.

Landlords:

1865 Richard Griffith Thomas (Shopkeeper).
1875 James Organ (Shopkeeper).
1902 Thomas Edward Cooke.
1914 Albert Wood.
1923 John William Summers.
1927 Bill Workman.
1940 Mrs B Workman.
1952 Garnet Priday.
1965 Frank Watkins.
1987 Stan Cornock.

ILLUSTRATIONS

REFERENCES

Baddeley W 1913, Place names of Gloucestershire.

Rt. Hon: The Earl of Berkeley F.R.S Excavations at Berkeley Castle, 1917 to 1937.

Berkeley Manuscript, 1066 to 1618 (Smyth,).

Berkeley Parish Register 1653 to 1778.

Berkeley Church Magazines 1881 to 1931.

British Waterways, Gloucester.

Burkitt M C 1938, Eastington Gravel Pit.

Clifford E M 1938, The Soldiers Grave, Frocester.

Clifford E M 1961, Bagendon, Excavations 1954.

Dursley Gazette Newspapers.

Ellison A 1980, Excavations at West Hill, Uley.

Fisher Rev J 1856, History of the Town of Berkeley.

Gardener C I 1932, Stroud Valley (recent discoveries).

Hart C 1967 Archaeology in the Dean.

Haywood E 1970, Gloucester, Stroud and Berkeley (Viking raids).

Moore J S 1982, Domesday Book (Gloucestershire).

Pritchard J E 1906, Bristol Archaeological Notes.

Records Office, Gloucester, World War II activity in the Berkeley Vale.

Ryder T A 1951, Mid Gloucestershire through the Ages.

Saville A 1984, Hill Forts.

Sharpness New Dock. 1884 to 1910. Private papers (J Evans)

Smyth John 1600, Lives of the Berkeleys and Ancient Manners.

Smyth John 1618, Berkeley Hundred.

Smith G 1821 to 1823, Diaries. (unpublished)

Smith I F 1968, Late Neolithic Pits at Cam.

Taylor C S 1891, Early Christianity in Gloucestershire.

Taylor C S 1898, The Danes in Gloucestershire.

Walters B. 1991, The Archaeology and History of Ancient Dean
               & The Wye Valley. Thornhill Press.

The Danes in Gloucestershire by the Rev. C S Taylor 1892
    (Battle of Wanswell Green, Minster at Hinton).

Monuments Historica Britannica (Battle of Wanswell).